The Last
Hawaiian
Island
NI'IHAU

NI'IHAU

The Last Hawaiian Island

Ruth M. Tabrah

Press Pacifica

Library of Congress Cataloging-in-Publication Data

Tabrah, Ruth M., 1921–
   Ni'ihau, the last Hawaiian island.

   Includes index.
   1. Niihau (Hawaii)—History. I. Title. II. Title:
Ni'ihau.
DU628.N55T3   1987   996.9'42   87-21429
ISBN 0-916630-60-9
ISBN 0-916630-59-5 (pbk.)

Cover design by Ralph Togashi
Map and book design by Judy Hancock

Typesetting: The Last Word, Kailua, Hawaii

Available from:
Press Pacifica
P.O. Box 47
Kailua, Hawaii 96734

At a pace as ceaseless yet subtle as the waves that reshape its beaches, change has been the nature of existence on Ni'ihau.

Contents

Author's Note

TWENTY YEARS AGO, when he was our State Librarian, James M. Hunt opened to me the treasurehouse of the untapped research resources concerning Niʻihau's rich history. My deep gratitude to him, and to the current staff of the Hawaii & Pacific Room at the main library on King Street in Honolulu for their assistance in person and by phone when I finally got around to letting Jane Wilkins Pultz talk me into writing this book.

Without the enthusiastic kokua of the librarians of the Hawaii Mission Childrens Society and Hawaiian Historical Society Collection, and the convenience of the airy reading room that houses their collections adjacent to the Mission Houses Museum, this book could not have been. I owe an equal debt of thanks to Librarian Richard Thompson and the Director and staff of Hawaii State Archives for tracking so many references and making available so much new material to me.

My *mahalo nui* to Bishop Museum, and the staff of their Photography Collection and Library who generously shared their Niʻihau treasures with me. Kauai Museum, its Director and staff in Lihue were most helpful in giving me access to their collection of old Niʻihau photographs. My special thanks, too, to Bishop Museum's Archaeology Department for giving artist Judy Hancock and myself the thrill of seeing, feeling, and experiencing a rare old *makaloa* mat, a photo of which became the cover design for this book.

I asked no expert opinion of where and when to use glottal stops in the spelling of Hawaiian words, names, and place names used in this book. Until the very recent past, no one used these phonetic clues to the traditional Hawaiian pronunciations. In the case of Ka'u on my home island, Hawaii, it is a phonetic necessity. I feel the same is true for Ni'ihau. In quoting material that did not use this spelling, I have retained the spelling 'Niihau'. Confusing? I hope not too much so!

Ruth Tabrah
Honolulu, June 1987

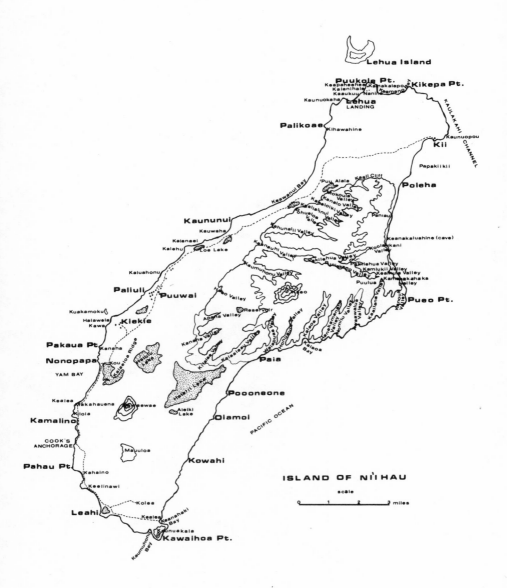

Lehua Island

Puukole Pt.
Keapaheehee Kamakalepoo Kikepa Pt.
Kalinihala
Kaaukuu Nanihaamana
Kaunuokaha Lehua
LANDING

Palikoae Kihawahine

Kaunuopou Kii

KAULAKAHI CHANNEL

Papakiikii

Puu Alala Kaali Cliff Poleha

Mokoula
Valley
Kenalo Valley
Keawanui Bay Keahaloiki Valley
Keelialinui Valley
Paniau
Kaunununui Ohueloa
Valley
Kauwaha Kehunalii Valley
Keanakaluahine (cave)
Kaianaei Keanauhi Valley
Kalehua Loe Lake Koolakani
Valley
Kanjunobo Valley Paelehua Valley
Kaluahonu Kamlukii Valley
Keaumunonu Valley Keawaha Valley
Kakilehua Valley Kamakahaka
Paliuli Valley
Puuwai Niao Valley Reservoir Puulua
Kawa

Pueo Pt.

Kuakamoku
Halawela Kiekie Apana Valley
Kawa
Pakaua Pt Kanaha Kanana Valley
Nonopapa Kou Kiekea Valley
YAM BAY Kalualolea Valley Kalsoa
Bay
Paia

Kealea Poooneone
Kamalino Makahauena Keawewae
Kiloia Aleiki Olamoi
Lake
COOK'S
ANCHORAGE Mauuloa PACIFIC OCEAN

Kowahi
Pahau Pt Kahaino

Keelinawi

Kolea ISLAND OF NI'IHAU

scale
Leahi Kealea Keanahaki 0 1 2 3 miles
Bay
Kaunuhonono Kunakala
Bay Kawaihoa Pt.

(after Bishop Museum map, with notes by Bruce Robinson and Dr. St. John per
Kalani Niau)

The Mystery Island

IN 1934 WHEN Franklin Delano Roosevelt made the first American presidential visit to Hawaii, he spent a pleasant interlude cruising the waters between Kauai and that small, lovely Hawaiian island which is forbidden to all but expressly invited visitors: Ni'ihau.

It seems from private papers found after his death that what FDR had heard about this privately owned island the press called "The Mystery Island" intrigued him. Its silhouette, the tales told him about Ni'ihau, the myths and mystique that seemed to shroud it, hung in his memory. Ten years later, with the war at last going well in both the Pacific and Europe, FDR thought about Ni'ihau as he drafted plans for establishing a United Nations Organization that he dreamed would make possible cooperative rather than combative solutions to the world's problems. Ni'ihau, he mused, might make an ideal headquarters. He made a note of this idea – a note found long after the establishment of the UN headquarters in New York and in Geneva.

I've always wondered what would have happened had Roosevelt lived to pursue his dream about the UN and Ni'ihau. Would the family who for the past 125 years have owned this most westerly of the Hawaiian Islands have agreed to sell or lease it to the UN? Since they were never asked, it is a useless

1

question. Yet the whole story – to me – simply enhances the air of mystery, the fascination of the mystique and myths of what in many ways is the last Hawaiian island: Ni'ihau.

In 1956 when I came to live in that other very remote and Hawaiian place – the Big Island district of North Kohala – I heard about Ni'ihau from a Hawaiian who lived down on the beach at Kawaihae. Eddie was a loner, a gifted, taciturn man in his forties who carved beautiful bowls, cups and fashioned miniature ukuleles out of coconut shells. I often met him when I stopped at Doi's Store for gas and groceries on the way to our beach house at Puako. Like everything else in Kohala then the trip in those days was a leisurely one. No road yet wound along the coast. It was an hour's drive over the mountain road and around the dangerous steep curves down to Kawaihae. The harbor there was not yet built. A palm grove, the old village, and ancient salt ponds were a cool sandy oasis where the sugar loading gantreys, the storage sheds, freight depots, and oil tanks now stand.

From Kawaihae we had another long bumpy drive to Puako over a narrow coral graveled trail that wound past Spencer Park, past the potential flood areas where mauka streams often cascaded hub-deep runoff after heavy rains up in Waimea. The rutted trail, strewed on either side with mufflers and broken axles, wound past Hapuna Beach which was then a long empty stretch of sand and kiawe trees where anyone might pitch a tent and spend a few quiet days. Before I tackled that rough last few miles, I liked to stay at Doi's Store at Kawaihae for awhile listening to Henry and Masaru Doi talk story, and getting to know Hawaiians like Eddie. Eddie liked to hang around their gas station and tell us about the island where he'd been born and raised – Ni'ihau.

"Someday I want to visit that island!" I told him.

"You can't. Never," he said flatly. "Nobody can. If you know the Robinsons – well, maybe. They're the owners. They have the say, yuh? Even me. I left that island. My mother, she's dead now. I got nobody left there so nobody I can ask to visit. Even me, that's my birthplace Ni'ihau but I can't ever go back."

"Even the governor, he can't go there without an invitation," said Henry Doi. "That's why, in the papers, they call it the

the Forbidden Island." He sighed. "Must be some nice place maybe."

"Nice place," sighed Eddie and just thinking about not being able to go to that island made me yearn to have a chance to go there someday.

I somehow thought that the magic of statehood in 1959 would alter a great many things about Hawaii. It did. But it had no effect whatever on Ni'ihau. It did however result in my having the chance to go there, for with statehood came a new set of boards and commissions. Among these was the first elected State Board of Education, and I was on it as one of the Big Island's two representatives. Our *kuleana* – our special domain – was the public schools and public libraries on each of the islands.

As we visited remote rural schools in Hana, Maui; at Kilohana, Molokai; on Lanai; and in upcountry North Kona at Puuanahulu, I began to ask why we couldn't also arrange to visit the school on Ni'ihau. My question was so persistent that I was delegated to approach the Robinson family concerning that possibility. The fortunate and most unexpected result was that in October 1967, I found myself shivering in the pre-dawn chill of half past four in the morning, waiting at Makaweli, Kauai for the five a.m. departure of the World War II vintage landing craft that is the only transport to Ni'ihau. We shared the limited space aboard with barrels of poi, drums of diesel fuel, cartons of freight and ranch supplies (the entire island is Ni'ihau Ranch) and four Ni'ihauans who had been on Kauai for medical care.

Even in the best of weather the Kaulakahi channel is not an easy seventeen-mile passage. The broad-beamed, flat bottomed landing craft smacking and lurching along over the waves is conducive to seasickness. Only a few of the eleven Board members had wanted to risk the uncomfortable trip. Those of us who had were thoroughly miserable all five hours from Makaweli, the Robinson's landing on Kauai, to Kii Landing on Ni'ihau. The one advantage of the landing craft was that at our destination it could skid over the shallow sand bottom so close to shore that we were able to leap out to dry land without difficulty.

Two ranch trucks – venerable, battered, rusty – the only wheeled vehicles on the island, waited to take us the hot, dusty

45-minute drive to Puuwai. This is now the only village on Ni'ihau, the place where I assumed my Kawaihae friend Eddie had been born and knew as a child. I thought of him during that bumpy long ride. As one of two women on the elected Board, I was favored with being invited to ride in the cab of one truck. The men ate dust in the open truck bed. It was not easy to see clearly in the dust clouds our passage spun up into the air, but I kept gazing intently from one side to the other, understanding why Ni'ihau Eddie had chosen to settle on the South Kohala coast since he could not return to his own island. Everything I saw reminded me of the open countryside between Kawaihae and Puako. The same hot dry air at mid-morning. The same red dust churned up by the trucks on the rutted trail that served as a road. The same stands of thorny kiawe trees, their creaking branches dripping with the sweet yellow beans that Kohala people used to gather to feed their chickens and pigs.

At one point we passed a place where a few scraggly looking coconut palms were growing. At another place, for the first time anywhere I saw breadfruit trees planted in a deep, rock-lined pit so that their fruit could easily be picked from ground-level. As with the old trail from Kawaihae to Puako, there was no view of the sea, no sense of being on an island. Bumping along, I had the same sensation as when I drove the old bumpy road to Puako. The entire world, it seems, must be made of dust, kiawe trees and sandy barren soil. The big difference on this Ni'ihau journey was that here and there we glimpsed a few cattle, and at another place a number of sheep. Only as we entered the outskirts of Puuwai did we see the cool bright blue of the ocean beyond a dune-protected shoreline and feel the reassurance that a view of the sea seems to give those of us who feel at home on islands.

The houses of Puuwai reminded me of the still fairly Hawaiian North Kohala communities of Makapala and Niulii. Each Puuwai home had its verandah and was built up on post and block foundations rather high off the ground. Each weathered, dark green stained wooden house had a spacious yard, set off by a low stone wall from its neighbor. In almost every yard, a horse grazed. At the very heart of the village, shaded by huge, magnificently gnarled kiawe trees and boundaried by a low, loose-stone wall, was the Ni'ihau church. On the grounds, a short distance behind the steeple-crowned New England-style wooden church building were the three small wooden buildings that housed the lower, middle, and upper grades of Ni'ihau School.

The entire population of the island – which then numbered about 280 Hawaiians and the ancient Japanese bee-keeper, Shintani, had turned out to greet us. For the first time, I heard nothing but the soft music of the Hawaiian language that is the spoken language of Ni'ihau, and was once spoken exclusively everywhere in these islands. For the first time I saw a village that, with the exception of Shintani, was Hawaiian – with the soft bright eyes, the relaxed dignity, the quiet strength and humour, the subtle sense of privacy and yet, at the same time, the openness of '*E komo mai*', of aloha. It took me some time to realize that, though he was ethnically Japanese, Shintani had become Hawaiian too. There was here an atmosphere that gave the stranger a feeling of having opened an album whose pages walked him into the life of a century ago.

It was with a mix of nostalgia, curiosity, excitement and wonder that I spent the next three hours in Puuwai. By two in the afternoon we were back aboard the landing craft heading to Kauai. Not so choppy a crossing as the morning's had been. Maybe I was getting used to the motion of the vessel. Maybe I was still too immersed in contemplating all I had seen and felt on Ni'ihau to be bothered with seasickness.

I ended this first visit with one firm idea fixed in my head. One day, some day, I must write something about Ni'ihau. When I returned home to Kohala Plantation and our house in Union Mill Skilled Camp B, I recorded all my impressions of this first visit, but I respected the Robinson's request that we not give such accounts to the press.

This period of the late 1960's and on into the 1970's was, politically, one of salvation by conservation which is not something I disagree with at all, but that I am curious to see is applied only where much development cannot occur anyway. The eye of the activists was largely focused on islands like Lanai and Ni'ihau as concrete, steel, and glass high rises rose in monolithic new mountain ranges across the beach at Waikiki, across lovely shorelines like Kaanapali and Kihei on Maui, jutted up the slopes of Makiki and sprawled across downtown Honolulu and along the new freeways. "Saving" open space and the ecologic atmosphere of old Hawaii was the favorite theme of those who, like onetime congressman and lieutenant-governor Tom Gill, were favorites of the headlines and feature stories in Honolulu's two daily papers.

I was dismayed, as were other less frenetic conservationists, when an ecologically planned, population capping development of the island of Lanai was deep-freezed by those who wanted to be able to camp in isolation on beaches like Hulupoe. Yet, I had not been at all opposed when, in 1969 and 1970 Ni'ihau was on the front page week after week as Governor John Burns, worried about the possible oppression of the Hawaiian population there (all of whom worked for Ni'ihau Ranch), proposed the island be acquired as a State Park. Current in the '70's was the idea that Ni'ihau was a paradise that had become a prison. Those who accepted this, I later discovered, were people who had neither experienced the reality of Ni'ihau nor acquainted themselves with the details of its history.

It was this misconception of the realities of Ni'ihau that led to the governor's urging in 1970 that the state of Hawaii buy the island, Burns' proposal was that the government launch condemnation proceedings and plan for Ni'ihau to be a great, island-wide Hawaiian cultural park where everyone might enjoy camping out, and observing the unique Ni'ihauan lifestyle. Caught up in this surge of political do-goodism, and myself then being ignorant of much of Ni'ihau's history, I planned in 1970 to try a *New Yorker* type profile about Ni'ihau, around the general theme question: "Can you save an island people like you save the grizzly bear?"

My enthusiasm resulted in obtaining an interview with Governor Burns, whom I much admired, and who took an hour and a half to tell me about his ideas, dreams, and misgivings concerning the island. I also interviewed Tom Gill, who turned out not to have much to say about Ni'ihau after all. Jim Hunt, then Hawaii State Librarian, thought my idea for a profile on Ni'ihau was so timely that he had his staff thermofax copies of all the material I might need. It turned out to be a stack several inches thick – so much material that I saw at first reading it would be impossible to compress into an article. It also led me to suspect I was using the wrong theme to really tell the story of Ni'ihau.

I put the material away in the folder with my 1967 account of visiting Ni'ihau and went on to other things. I needed to do the research for my biography of Lanai, and the publication of that book in the Liberty House Bicentennial Series led to my being asked to write the Hawaii bicentennial history which was published by W.W. Norton, one of fifty books in their State and Nation series. In 1977, as an elected Board of Education member representing all the Neighbor Islands (including the people of Ni'ihau), I was fortunate enough to again be invited to spend a day visiting Ni'ihau School and once again I opened that old file, then put it away.

Finally in 1984 my friend Jane Pultz, Press Pacifica's publisher, gave me a sharp nudge towards carrying out my long-time intention of writing a biography of Ni'ihau. "Why don't you get busy. We need it!" she urged.

One afternoon at the Hawaii State Archives, quite by impulse I took a look at what they had in their card files under Ni'ihau. Then I did the same at the Hawaiian & Pacific Room of Hawaii State Library on King Street, and at the collections of the Hawaiian Mission Childrens' Society and the Hawaiian Historical Society which are housed in the airy reading room behind the Mission Houses Museum. Such treasures were waiting there to be mined! At home, I pulled out my thick file on Ni'ihau – the journal of my two visits, the wad of thermofaxed research, the clippings I had accumulated over the years, the interview notes from Governor Burns and Tom Gill.

At long last I could view this material with fresh eyes and 'beginner's mind'. As I devoured the logs of early visitors like Captain Cook, as I read Vancouver's fascinating account of two girls from Ni'ihau who were the first Hawaiians to visit Nootka Sound and California, as I went through the records of the Waimea Mission Station's references to its early visitations to Ni'ihau, I began to see the dramatic outlines of Ni'ihau's history – the kind of a story that delights a novelist's heart. The popular attitude of polarization – viewing Ni'ihau as either prison or paradise – receded in importance for me. In a way to which I had been previously blind, I could now see both from the vantage point of personal experience and historical research that Ni'ihau neither was nor is either.

In 1970 I had discerned that there was in the mind of Governor Burns a feeling that Ni'ihauans must be somehow 'set free'. But when I visited there in 1967 and again in 1977 they themselves were not clear about what it was the state was trying to free them from. After all, they told me, they were free to leave their island if they so chose although if they did move away, it was unlikely they would ever be able to move back. Then, in 1970, and still today, to those islanders accustomed to the pace of life and variety of Kauai, Oahu, Maui, Hawaii, and even to those living on the quieter islands of Molokai and Lanai, Ni'ihau sounds too old fashioned, too backward, too much under the domination of its owner-employers. To others the isolation of Ni'ihau sounds fascinating, ideal. The Hawaiian-ness of that island is an environment they envy and admire or – romantically – think they do. For Ni'ihauans, however, Ni'ihau is simply home, their birthplace, the island of their ancestors, the most natural of environments because it is what they love, where they live, all they know.

In his excellent paper on Ni'ihau, U.H. graduate student Edward Stepien remarks that, "Although touched and influenced in small ways by the modern world, the Niihauans remain adamant not to be overrun by it. They are a special breed of people who love the simple things in life, the things that our society has a tendency to gradually erode and ultimately destroy. Their lifestyle is one of contentment and tranquility – one which places a high value on compassion, respect, and love for their fellow man and the *'aina*, rather than on fortune-seeking and its accompanying greed, jealousy, and hatred."

Stepien's is of course the idealized portrait of a society he has never seen. Ni'ihauans, from my personal experience – brief though it has been – strike me as being as human as anyone else. They are not immune from jealousy or hatred. They too know greed. Stepien is correct in his assumption that they are a special breed of people who love the simple things in life, who love their island, and treasure the Hawaiian-ness that is so natural to them and to it. Ni'ihau and its people have a very special history. Geologically, this island was the first of Hawaii's major islands to be spewn up by volcanic activity along the ocean floor. Historically, in Hawaiian legend, it was the first island visited by Pele and the first island where Laka, goddess of hula, taught a *kumu hulu.*

Between 1778, when Captain Cook's shore party spent two nights on Ni'ihau, and 1863 when Eliza Sinclair, ancestor of the Robinson family, bought the island at the urging of King Kamehameha IV, Ni'ihau was an island rich in visitors, many of whom recorded their vivid impressions of what the island and its people were then like. Intermittently, during the last 125 years the isolation of its private ownership has been broken. Territorial Governor Lawrence Judd visited there with a large party, including an inquisitive journalist, in 1929. On December 7, 1941, the landing of a Japanese pilot following the attack on Pearl Harbor catapulted Ni'ihau into headlines across the United States mainland. From 1944 until the early 1950's a small Coast Guard detachment was stationed on the island, although with warnings not to fraternize with the friendly residents.

In October 1967, an editorial in the *Honolulu Star-Bulletin* urged that Niihau be preserved, and things there 'left as they are' – an editorial that endorsed the myth that Ni'ihau was somehow untouched, unspoiled, an island frozen in time. In this book, I hope to dispel this myth for readers, to let them experience the changing nature of Ni'ihau and its people over the years from ancient Hawaiian chiefdom, through Kamehameha's kingdom and its overthrow by a group of American businessmen who ruled as the Republic of Hawaii until their hoped-for annexation by the United States took place in 1898. I hope also to convey that throughout Hawaii's territorial period and now in statehood, in its own unique way, Ni'ihau remains the last 'Hawaiian' island, the one place where private ownership has been exercised as a remarkable kind of stewardship and trust.

How It All Began

FROM KAUAI, SEVENTEEN miles across the Kaulakahi Channel, Ni'ihau is – as an 1870 visitor described it – "a quite uninteresting" long lump on the horizon. No spectacular jagged peaks like the mountains of Kauai, Oahu, or West Maui. No magnificent great shield dome summits like Maui's Haleakala, or the Big Island's Mauna Loa and Mauna Kea, which are two of the world's highest (if measured from their base on the ocean floor). Ni'ihau has no stunning seacliffs threaded with silvery waterfalls as does the north shore of Molokai. No fertile interior plateau, no vast stretches of game country or long miles of empty beaches like Lanai. When you go ashore at either of Ni'ihau's landing places, and take the long dusty ride in one of the ranch trucks to the village of Puuwai, you are struck by the island's very different and very special charm.

Climatically, Ni'ihau is also unlike any of the other islands except, perhaps, the presently uninhabited island of Kahoolawe, which until World War II was also operated as a ranch. Regrettably, since then, Kahoolawe has been used by the armed forces as a bombing target. Both Kahoolawe and Ni'ihau are downwind of larger islands – in Kahoolawe's case Maui, and for Ni'ihau Kauai – so that the clouds have been drained of much of their moisture before they drift down over the two smaller islands.

Like Kahoolawe, Ni'ihau has a scarcity of ground water resources and is prone to intermittent, prolonged periods of drought. In 1864 when King Kamehameha IV succeeded in getting the Sinclair family to take the non-tax paying island off his hands, Ni'ihau had just enjoyed a season of unprecedented high rainfall. Its usually arid plains were lush and green. One quick inspection trip to the island by brothers James and Francis Sinclair and the family made their decision. They offered the King $6000 for Ni'ihau – a handsome sum in the money values of the time. He countered with a demand for $10,000 and this was the purchase price to which the family agreed.

The island that these New Zealand immigrants bought was no isolated, untouched Hawaiian paradise as some may wistfully surmise. By 1864 Ni'ihauans had experienced 86 years of foreign contact, a stream of ship visitors, and hosted numerous visits by both American Protestant and Irish Catholic missionaries. Prior to the initial foreign visit of Captain Cook in 1778, Ni'ihau had a rich treasury of myths, legends, and chants recording the history of over one thousand years of Polynesian settlement.

The chants of the famous priest Kahakuikamoana, as translated by Martha Beckwith Warren, attributed the origin of Ni'ihau and its neighboring islets, Lehua and Kaula, as being like that of triplets born to the same parents. The high priest Pakui, chanting in the reign of Kamehameha I, relates that Papa and Wakea, the progenitors of Hawaii and Maui, separated and took other lovers to conceive Molokai, Lanai, Oahu, and Kahoolawe. They then reunited and Wakea gave birth to Ni'ihau, Lehua and Kaula. Judge Abraham Fornander whose early interest in Polynesian legends and origin is responsible for much of the treasury of Hawaiian lore available to researchers today, translates this chant of Pakui concerning the origin of Ni'ihau as:

"Papa then went back and lived with Wakea,
Papa was restless with child-sickness.
Papa conceived the island of Kauai
And gave birth to Kamaiwaelualanimoku.
Ni'ihau was only the droppings.
Lehua was a border,
And Kaula the closing one."

Still another version, recorded by the Hawaiian scholars sent to every district of every island by Fornander, a Swede who had studied at the University of Upsala before adventuring to Hawaii as a whaler, is given in Fornander's *Hawaiian Antiquities and Folk-Lore* (published by Bishop Museum Press in five volumes, 1916 and 1917):

"Wainalia was the man
And Hanalaa was the woman,
Of them was born Ni'ihau, a land, an island.
A land at the roots, the stem of the land.
There were three children among them
Born in the same day,
Ni'ihau, Kaula, ending with Nihoa.
The mother then conceived no more.
No island appeared afterwards."

In this chant, Lehua is not mentioned. Instead, Nihoa, a barren, rocky, uninhabited island no more than eight-tenths of a mile long and between two-tenths and five-tenths of a mile wide shares Ni'ihau's parentage and same time of birth. Nihoa is by no means a close neighbor. It lies some 120 miles west of Ni'ihau. Small as it is, Nihoa has two fairly high peaks – one 910 feet high and the other 874 feet. The island gives evidence of ceremonial use, occasional residence, and frequent visits by Hawaiians in ancient times – presumably Hawaiians from Ni'ihau and from Kauai. Nihoa is too distant from Ni'ihau to be mentioned in another very special Hawaiian way. Hawaiians believed the souls of the dead left the body and went to a dry plain. Such places were called *ka leina o ka uhane,* the casting off place of the soul. On Ni'ihau this was Kapapakiikii. There was a second such casting off place at Mauloku on Lehua Island.

Creation chants such as those recorded by Warren and Fornander are matched by legends portraying Ni'ihau as the place where the volcano goddess Pele first lived in Hawaii-nei. Volcanologists agree with this ancient interpretation of the order in which the islands and islets of the Hawaiian archipelago were spewed up from a fault line along the floor of the mid-Pacific. In her 1904 booklet, *Hawaii, Its People, Their Legends,* written for the Hawaii Promotion Committee in Honolulu, Emma Metcalf Nakuina tells her version of the legend of the volcano goddess

Pele. According to Nakuina, Pele was the second daughter of Namakaokahai and the god Kane, who lived "above the setting sun", perhaps at Krakatoa. When her elder sister's husband fell in love with her, Pele was sent away from that distant home, outfitted with an expedition and accompanied by her younger sisters – all of whom were named Hiiaka – and by a retinue of "dragons, gnomes, serpents and sharks to serve as her servants and messengers or couriers."

After Pele and her canoes had traveled a long way, they came to a small low island to the northwest, the island which is now called Nihoa. Pele allowed her youngest sister, Hiiaka-i-ka-poli-o-Pele (Hiiaka in Pele's heart) to rest here a while, as this favorite sister complained of exhaustion. Pele began to build a volcano house on Nihoa, but the sea discouraged her and she moved on first to Kaula, then to Ni'ihau and Kauai. Lehua was only a side issue and originally formed part of Ni'ihau.

In his *Hawaiian Legends of Volcanoes*, W. D. Westervelt tells another version of how Pele came to Hawaii. He describes her as having such a wanderlust that her father gave her a sea-going canoe with mat sails. It was large enough to carry a number of people and food for many days. Pele's father, having prepared this canoe for her departure, told her brother, Kamohoalii, the king of dragons, the god of sharks, that she was going to "Bola-Bola, to Kuai-he-lani, to Kane-huna-moku, then to Moku mana-mana; to see a queen, Kaoahi her name and Ni'ihau her island."

This was Pele's desire, and Kane-pu-a-hio-hio, Kane the Whirlwind, Ke-au-miki, the Strong current, and Ke-au-kai, Moving Seas, carried her from one to another of those islands until at last she landed on Ni'ihau. There she was welcomed and entertained until she went on to Kauai.

Many years later, when Pele had moved on from island to island to take up her residence at Kilauea on Hawaii, she changed her form from that of an old hag to a beautiful young girl to go to Kauai and wed Lohiau. She called on the guardian winds of Ni'ihau and Kauai to provide the *olioli mele*, the chant for the hula at the wedding celebration. She called on all the noted winds of the island of Ni'ihau, stating the directions from which the Ni'ihau winds came, the points of land struck when they touched Ni'ihau and their gentleness or wrath, their weakness or power and their helpfulness or destructiveness. As she gave this chant the people outside the house cried out, "The sea grows rough and white. The waves are tossed by strong winds. Clouds are flying. The winds are gathering the clouds and twisting the heavens!"

Then Pele chanted for the return of the winds to Ni'ihau and its small islands and the day was at peace. Pele leaned on her couch of soft mats and rested.

The winds of Ni'ihau are named and called upon in another chant recorded by Abraham Fornander:

"And the wind, for whom is the wind.
For Ku indeed.
Blown is the wind of Laamaomao;
The gentle breeze of Koolauwahine, the wind from below
Kauai – I have known it;
The northwest wind of Kawaenohu,
The north wind of Ni'ihau. . ."

Winds of Ni'ihau are also called upon in the legend of Kuapakaa of Molokai who is on his way to Tahiti, when at his father's urging he calls in a desperate moment on the winds of this island to blow him quickly on his way:

"Arise, look you to the winds of Laamaomao!
Roaring in the mountains,
A sign of the coming of the wind at Kapaa.
The wind is there at Kauai,
The *moae* is of Lehua,
The *mikioi* is of Kawaihoa,
The *naulu* is of Ni'ihau. . ."

In innumerable legends the route a hero must take leads past Ni'ihau. In the legend of Ka-Ehu-Iki-Mamo-O-Puu-Loa, the small blonde shark of Puuloa, Thomas Thrum, a nineteenth century collector of Hawaiian folk-tales (and original compiler and publisher of the *Hawaiian Almanac and Annual* tells how the legend's hero, Kaehuiki was given the eye of the ivory wreath of Kaahupahau, the famous Queen-shark who protected Oahu's waters. This precious gift identified him as a friend of Kaahupahau, a bond that provided him safe transport through the ocean domain of Kuhaimoana, the king-shark of Kauai and Ni'ihau.

In other legends where the hero is a warrior seeking to become ruling chief, invariably –whether the hero is from Hawaii, Maui, Oahu or any of the other islands including Kauai– his yearning when he wins his way to power is to have the soft pliable *makaloa* mats of Ni'ihau to lie down upon. *Makaloa* mats were also woven into the finest sails and these too have a prominent mention in legends of voyages of 'coconut-tree' canoes from Hawaii to Kahiki (Tahiti). Such is the case in the legend of Lono, who left in such a vessel promising to one day return on a floating island bearing coconut trees and many pigs and chickens. The grass from which the sails of Lono's canoe were woven, the grass of the fine mats on which Pele rested, and which high chiefs desired, was a special indigenous plant growing around the two remaining playa lakes on Ni'ihau. Regrettably, this plant no longer exists.

Ni'ihau is famous among *kumu hula* as the first place where the hula goddess Laka taught her art. According to a Molokai legend, Laka was the fifth generation of her line, which originated this style of dance on Molokai. Her first canoe voyage, on leaving her home island, was to Ni'ihau, where she chose an apt pupil and spent several years teaching her to become a *kumu hula*. She carefully instilled in the Ni'ihau young woman the philosophy as well as the technique of the hula so that she in turn could not only teach others but could compose hulas to tell the stories of Ni'ihau. When her pupil had become so skilled, Laka moved on to Kauai to teach a *kumu hula* there and one by one, did the same on each of the other islands in turn. The hula much intrigued the first foreign visitors. During the puritanical sway of the missionaries who arrived in 1820, even on Ni'ihau the art was secretly practised and taught. In 1985, at the sixth Prince Lot Hula Festival held in Honolulu's Moanalua Gardens, one *halau* danced a special Ni'ihau hula that the Ni'ihauans had composed a century ago to commemorate the visit of Kalakaua's consort, Queen Kapiolani.

Like the art of the hula, and the various special Ni'ihau hulas that the people there have composed in both ancient and modern times, the myths and legends of this island have been retold from generation to generation just as were the creation chants. Ni'ihau abounds in lore that stresses the supernatural character of its ancient inhabitants. Two supernatural runners from Ni'ihau are the heroes in the Molokai legend of Manini-holokuanua, a clever thief who stole from everyone, and kept his loot in a cave which opened and closed its powerful rock jaws at his shouted commands. Martha Beckwith Warren translated this legend for the 33rd Annual Report of the Bureau of American Ethnology (reprinted by the Government printing Office in 1918).

It seems that one day, against his grandmother's warning, Maniniholokuaua stole the koa canoe of a famous Oahu runner, Keliimalolo, who could make three circuits of his island in one day. Next, against his grandmother's dire warning that to steal from the two supernatural runners of Ni'ihau would result in his death, Maniniholokuaua stole from them. These two Ni'ihau runners, Kamaakauluohia and Kamaakamikini, were sons of Halaulu. Each of them could easily make ten circuits of Kauai in one day. Their power and speed was such that when he stole from them, they gave chase to Maniniholokuaua and caught up with him just as he reached the entrance of his Molokai cave. Panicking, Maniniholokuaua shouted the open and close commands at the same time. As the cave opened he started to dash inside but just as he did so, the rock jaws of the cave closed, crushing him. The two supernatural runners from Ni'ihau retrieved what he had stolen. The runner from Oahu retrieved his koa canoe. And all the people of Molokai gathered to divide the rest of the loot, praising the two supernatural runners from Ni'ihau.

Perhaps the most famous of all Ni'ihau legends is that of the evil demons who once terrorized the commoners of that island. In *Ghost Gods and Other Legends,* W. D. Westervelt recounts this version. Once long ago, because Ni'ihau was overrun by a band of evil spirits, life for the commoner there was almost unbearable. Ni'ihau people have always journied freely back and forth to Kauai, living on that larger sister island for months and even years at a time when drought on Ni'ihau prevented the cultivation of yams and left no potable water for people to drink. Similarly, Kauai people have always journied freely back and forth to Ni'ihau to enjoy the superior fishing grounds around that island. Thus it is not at all out of the ordinary that it happened to be a Kauai man temporarily living on Ni'ihau who found a way to rid that island of its demons.

Once he conceived how he might do this, he left Ni'ihau in his small canoe, paddling back across the Kaulakahi Channel to Kauai. He had made sure that the demons watched him depart – one man in his small canoe! When he reached Kauai, he hurried to the mountains to find a koa tree suitable for the hull of a large outrigger canoe. Having found a fine tree, he then persuaded a noted canoe builder, a *kahuna kalai'waa* to help him cut and carve the massive trunk with all the proper accompaniment of ritual and chants. As soon as the canoe was finished, and deemed seaworthy, the two men also carved a wooden idol, a *kii*, which they fitted with eyes of opihi shell. They mounted the *kii* in the bow of the koa canoe, fitted the canoe with an outrigger, again with the proper chants and ritual.

When all this had been accomplished, the canoe was launched. The Kauai man who had planned all this paddled his fine new canoe, and his *kii* passenger, back across the channel to Ni'ihau. There, as he had anticipated, the demons waited on a cliff top, ready to harass him. How surprised they were to see this fine big new canoe returning – and even more surprised to see that he had returned with a companion riding in the bow.

As the Kauai man had hoped, the demons mistook the *kii* for a human being. With their evil eyes they watched the Kauai man beach his big canoe and then put it carefully into the *halau*, the canoe shed. When the Kauai man emerged alone from the canoe shed, the demons quickly rushed down to investigate. Seeing the opihi shell eyes of the *kii*, they thought he was awake. For a long time the demons watched and waited. When the *kii's* eyes remained open, and he still was so quiet, they assumed he must sleep with his eyes open and, voraciously, they attacked him.

One demon seized an arm and tried to bite it. 'Auwe!" he cried. *''Paakiki ka poe o Kauai!''* ("Hard are the people of Kauai!")

Meanwhile, the man from Kauai was hiding outside the *halau*, watching and waiting for this chance. As the demons were trying to eat the *kii* in the same way they were accustomed to devouring the commoners of Ni'ihau, the Kauai man set fire to the thatch-covered canoe shed. The flames raced quickly over the dry thatch, trapping the demons inside. They were destroyed, each one of them, along with the wooden *kii* that had been such a successful decoy. And so it was through the cleverness of a Kauai man that for all time afterward Ni'ihau was freed of the evil spirits that had made the commoners' lives almost unbearable.

The First Foreign Visitors

IN HIS 1778 log Captain James Cook, commander of the two British naval vessels that were Ni'ihau's first recorded foreign visitors, wrote the name of this island as his English-oriented ears heard it: 'Oneeheow'.

Ni'ihau was the second Hawaiian island visited by the 'Resolution' and the 'Discovery', and the first Hawaiian island on which these first known foreign visitors to any of the islands spent not only one – but two nights ashore. Cultural curiosity on both sides was intense. Ni'ihauans must have echoed the impressions of their fellow islanders of Kauai who, according to Samuel Kamakau's account, in his *Ruling Chiefs of Hawaii*, regarded the foreigners as strange creatures, possibly gods. To Hawaiian ears, the Englishmen and the few Americans in Cook's crew had a speech like the piping of small birds. To Hawaiian eyes the clothes of the strangers at first appeared to be wrinkled skin. It must have been a great reassurance to find that underneath the three cornered hats, the jerseys and long-tailed coats, the tight breeches and stockings and shoes, these men were no different in physique and sexuality from themselves.

The impression of those on Kauai, the visitor's first stop, was shared by Ni'ihauans. Captain Cook, the British commander, was likely Lono, their great god returning on 'floating islands' bearing white tapa banners (sails) as an ancient legend had foretold.

There had been no indication, as the 'Resolution' and the 'Discovery' sailed from Otaheite towards the North American continent and the hoped-for Northwest passage through it, that any significant island or group of islands existed in these latitudes. Charts showed this area to be open ocean although rumours of islands sighted by Spanish vessels in previous centuries were current among British navigators.

This year of 1778 was the third year of Captain James Cook's voyage to the Pacific Ocean, "undertaken by the command of His Majesty for making Discoveries in the Northern Hemisphere". On January 20, 1778, Cook's two ships coasted slowly along the southeastern and southern shores of Kauai. A few canoes came out from shore. Cook and his men noted that these had stones in their bottoms, which evidently the Kauai men intended to use as weapons if that proved necessary. The stones were thrown overboard when the British ships made friendly gestures and there seemed no need for either defense or aggression on the part of the Hawaiians.

Captain Clerke of the 'Discovery' recorded of this first contact by westerners with Polynesians of these islands that "this is the cheapest market I ever yet saw, a moderate sized Nail will supply my Ship's Company very plentifully with excellent Pork for the Day, and as to the Potatoes and Tarrow, they are attained upon still easier terms such is the people's anxiety for iron."

That first day, Cook sent armed guards along with the watering parties he dispatched ashore. Things went well despite an initial use of arms against one Hawaiian at the beach. Iron had previously been a rare treasure found only in an occasional piece of driftwood. The initial unfortunate incident, which was fortunatly discounted by both Hawaiians and British as minor and to be expected in such a situation, took place when, before he anchored, Cook sent small boats to discover a suitable landing and watering place. Ralph S. Kuykendall, in the first volume (1778-1854, Foundation and Transformation) of his monumental three-volume history, *The Hawaiian Kingdom* writes that: "The leading boat, as soon as it touched shore, was closely surrounded by a crowd of eager natives seeking to pull it on shore. One of the natives made a determined effort to get possession of the boat hook and was shot and killed by the officer in command, Lt. Williamson. The Lieutenant afterward said he had no idea that the natives intended him or his party any injury but that 'it was their great desire for new things they saw, which brought on them so unfortunate a business'".

Clever thievery was much admired in the Hawaiian culture. Those who were not so clever, those who were caught,- like those who were caught breaking a kapu – were speedily put to death by club or garrot. Williamson's 'unfortunate' killing of one of their men did not seem to alarm the Hawaiians who had thus received their first lesson in the efficiency of the visitors' strange new weaponry. It seemed a blurt of killing fire that Kamakau relates the Hawaiians described as like spurts of water gushing from long iron sticks (the muskets of the British). As for the British, this incident was not in the least alarming. People in England also stole, and got their hands chopped off or their lives taken if they were caught doing so. The watering parties sent ashore that same day were pleased to be able to take back nine tons of fresh water to the 'Resolution' alone before they withdrew to their ships at dusk.

The delights of Tahiti were still fresh in the minds of Cook's officers and crew. It was with anticipation they went ashore next day. To the British, with their Puritan western backgrounds, the islands of these Polynesian peoples with their straightforward and open enjoyment of pleasures either hidden or forbidden in England and America were a fair equivalent of paradise.

During the several days his two vessels were anchored in Waimea Bay, Cook himself went ashore on three occasions. Each time, he was aware of the Hawaiians' awe of him for in his log he makes mention of the fact that whenever he came near them, commoners threw themselves prone before him as they did before their *tapu* chiefs.

Finally, having done considerable trading and successful reprovisioning with fresh water at this island he called 'Atooi', Cook weighed anchor to investigate Ni'ihau, which was visible from his Waimea anchorage. In his log he relates that on January 24th, in his command ship 'Resolution', he "steered for Oneeheow, in order to take a nearer view of it and to anchor there if I should find a convenient place." By 11 o'clock that morning the 'Resolution' was about two leagues from the island. However, since his second ship, the 'Discovery', was nowhere to be seen, he decided to "give up the design of visiting Oneeheow for the present and stood back for Atooi (Kauai)". He was fearful "lest some ill consequence attend" having his two ships separated by any great distance.

As was so often to happen in his attempts to travel from one Hawaiian island to another, the wind – or in this case the lack of it – hindered Cook from carrying out his intention to return to Kauai. Light airs and calms set in and continued throughout the rest of that day and all night. Meanwhile, back on Kauai, Captain Clerke remained offshore in the 'Discovery' and was visited by a "handsome young couple" whom he understood to be the King and Queen of the island. Their attendants allowed the royal pair to go only as far as the gangway of the ship where an exchange of gifts between themselves and Captain Clerke took place. Soon afterwards, the 'Discovery' also set off for Ni'ihau and, much to Cook's relief, joined him off the coast of that island. By the next morning, again due to light airs and calms that set in and continued all that day and the next night, the currents "had carried us westward within three leagues of Oneeheow. Being tired with plying so unsuccessfully, I gave up all thoughts of getting back to Atooi and came to the resolution of trying, whether we could procure what we wanted at the other island" (Ni'ihau) "which was within our reach."

And so it was that on January 29, 1778, Ni'ihau entered the historical record of the western world with Cook's painstaking observations of its shoreline, optimum anchorage, appearance, and people. He at once sent 'The Master' ashore in a small boat to sound the coast and look for a landing place where there might be fresh water ashore. By 10 o'clock that morning Master William Bligh and his men returned to report that "he had landed in one place but could find no fresh water; and that there was anchorage all along the coast." In the meantime, Cook had seen a village a little to leeward of his position. Several canoe loads of Ni'ihauans who had come out to see the strange ships informed Cook that fresh water might indeed be got in that village.

The Hawaiian language spoken on 'Atooi' and here on 'Oneeheow' was so similar to Tahitian that Cook and his men had little trouble communicating. Taking advantage of the Ni'ihauans' information, Cook "ran down and came to an anchor (before the village) in 26 fathoms of water about three-fourths of a mile from shore". From that anchorage he logged the Southeast point of the Island as being three miles distant. What he believed to be the other extreme of the Island was, he judged, also about two or three miles distant. He noted "a peaked hill inland, North East a quarter East", and at a location Cook describes as "bore South, 61 degrees West, distant seven leagues," was a clear view of a small island, which the Ni'ihauans called Tahoora (Kaula), and which Cook had "discovered" the preceding evening.

As soon as Cook's ships were anchored, half a dozen canoes came out bringing "some small pigs and a good many yams and mats". Several more canoes came "with no other object than to pay us a formal visit". The men from these canoes crouched on the deck until asked by Cook to get up. The women who accompanied them stayed in the canoes alongside the British ships. These Ni'ihau women and girls, according to Cook's log, behaved "with far less modesty than their country women of Atooi." They sang, beating time upon their bare breasts with their hands in a most suggestive fashion. What other frank gestures they may have offered are not described.

The men did not stay on board long but "before they departed, some of them requested our permission to lay down, on the deck, locks of their hair." One Ni'ihauan, being refused entry in the gun-room port asked whether "if he should come in we would kill and eat him". A second Ni'ihauan on hearing this question, and Cook's question in return as to Ni'ihau's practice of cannibalism "immediately answered that if we were killed on shore, they would certainly eat us." This was said with so little emotion that to Cook, "it was made clear their eating us would be . . . because of our being at enmity with them." Eating of human flesh for the simple desire to eat it was neither expressed by the Ni'ihauan nor so understood by the British.

On January 29th, and again on the 30th, Lt. Gore was sent with three armed small boats to look for the most convenient landing place and search for that most important of the ship's provisioning needs – fresh water. The only source found on the 29th was, according to Gore, "too inconsiderable for our purpose and the road leading to it exceedingly bad". Cook had intended to join the watering party sent ashore on the 30th, again under command of Lt. Gore, and again with an armed marine guard. However, after the first two small boats were launched the surf suddenly came up, changing Cook's plans. By evening the boats returned with several of the party, "a few yams and some salt" – but Lt. Gore and twenty of the men "deterred by the danger of coming off, were left ashore all night, and by this unfortunate circumstance" – laments Cook – "the very thing happened which, as I have already mentioned, I wished so heartily to prevent and vainly imagined I had effectually guarded against."

The violence of the surf did not discourage the Ni'ihauans who came out that evening in their canoes to trade. Cook "distributed a good many pieces of ribbon and some buttons, as bracelets, amongst the women in the canoes." He observed with interest that one of the Ni'ihau men had the figure of a lizard "punctured on his breast" and upon those of other men were the figures of men, "badly imitated". These Ni'ihauans informed Cook that there was no Chief or *Hairee* on their Island, but that it was subject to Teneooneoo" (Kaneoneo), "a Chief of Atooi, which island they said was not governed by a single chief. . ."

That Friday night of January 30th, Cook interpreted the weather signs as foreboding a storm. He moved his ships to a deeper anchorage, further offshore – in 42 fathoms of water. Only a few squalls blew over the ships during the night but the surf wiorsened so that canoes no longer dared come out from shore. As to Gore and the 20 men who had spent the previous night on Ni'ihau, "they had another night to improve their intercourse with the natives."

Not until dawn on Sunday, February 1st were weather and surf conditions such that Cook himself went with the pinnace and launch up to the Southeast point of the Island "to bring the party on board". He took with him on this trip ashore "a ram goat and two ewes, a boar and sow pig of the English breed; and the seeds of melons, pumpkins, and onions, being very desirous of benefiting these poor people by furnishing them with some additional articles of food."

The pinnace and launch were landed "with the greatest ease" under the west side of the point where he found his party waiting, "with some of the natives in company". To one of them, whom Lt. Gore told Cook he had observed as having some command over the others, Cook gave the goats, the pigs, and the seeds. "I should have left these well-intended presents at Atooi had we not been so unexpectedly driven from it." The chance of this visit to Ni'ihau, and Cook's decision not to try to return to Kauai, resulted in Ni'ihau being the first of the Hawaiian Islands to host any foreign animals. It is quite likely that the value placed by the Ni'ihauans on these gifts of livestock much impressed one of Cook's junior officers, George Vancouver, who some fourteen years later would bring his own expedition – and gifts of Hawaii's first cattle and sheep to Owhyhee.

Another gift left by Cook's visit to Ni'ihau was, at first, invisible and indiscernible, and far more of a disaster to Ni'ihauans than the bloody civil war that contention for possession of the goats was to incur. During the two nights Lt. Gore's shore party spent on the island, the British transmitted to Ni'ihauans the venereal disease which Cook was so loathe to spread among these islanders. Kuykendall's conclusion as to the indisputability of this 'gift' is, "The original journals covering the two visits of the expedition contain undebatable proof that Captain Cook's efforts were defeated and leave no doubt that the dreadful disease was propagated among the native people by sailors of the exploring squadron."

On his trip to retrieve the shore party who had spent two nights on this island, Cook busied himself with a walk inland while his men were filling four water casks from "a small stream occasioned by the late rain". He was accompanied by the Ni'ihauan who seemed to be in charge of things, and by two other Ni'ihauans who carried the pigs which had been presented as gifts to 'Lono'. When Cook stopped on a rise of ground to rest and look around, a woman hallooed from the far side of the valley. Hers was evidently the command that a special ceremony should be performed recognizing the taboo status and high rank of the foreign visitor, for this was now done. Cook observed the ritual with much interest.

The account in his journal of this inland excursion is the first recorded description of the appearance of Ni'ihau. "The ground through which I passed was in a state of nature, very strong, and the soil seemed poor. It was, however, covered with shrubs and plants, some of which perfumed the air with a more delicious fragrancy than I had met with at any of the other islands visited by us in this ocean." Upon inquiry of Gore and his party as to what they had seen in their two days and nights on Ni'ihau, they "gave me the same account of those parts of the island which they had traversed. They met with several salt ponds, some of which had a little water remaining, but others had none; and the salt that was left in them was so thin that no great quantity could have been procured. There was no appearance of any running streams and though they found some small wells in which the water was tolerably good, it seemed scarce. The habitations of the natives were thinly scattered about, and it was supposed that there could not be more than 500 people upon the island as the greatest part were seen at the marketing-place of our party, and few found about the houses by those who walked up the country. They had an opportunity of observing the method of living amongst the natives and it appeared to be decent and cleanly."

On Ni'ihau Cook observed that, as he had seen to be the case on Kauai, men and women ate separately. They "baked their hogs in ovens". For lights at night, Gore and his men told Cook, the Ni'ihauans "burnt the oily nuts of the dooedooe" (kukui, or candlenut) as did the people of Otaheite. Cook noted that a particular veneration seemed to be paid here to owls, "which they have very tame."

It was, for him, a most interesting excursion. After the water casks brought ashore had been filled, and after purchasing "from the natives a few roots, a little salt, and some salted fish, I returned on board with all the people, intending to visit the island the next day." Once again, however, chance intervened. During the night the 'Resolution''s anchor dragged and by morning, having drifted a considerable distance offshore, Cook signaled the 'Discovery' to weigh anchor and depart with him.

By noon the two ships were headed north to other islands of this group which Cook records "I named . . . the Sandwich Islands, in honour of the Earl of Sandwich."

As to Ni'ihau, he wrote as they left the island behind them: "We had the opportunity of knowing some particulars about Oneeheow . . It lies seven leagues to the Westward of our anchoring place at Atooi, and is not above fifteen leagues in circuit. This island is mostly low land except for the part facing Atooi which rises directly from the sea to a good height; as does the S.E. point of it which terminates in a round hill."

Of Ni'ihau's small adjacent island of Lehua, which he calls Oreehoua, he wrote, "we know nothing more than it is a small elevated island lying close to the North side of Oneeheow." Kaula island, which he calls Tahoora, he describes as "a small elevated island lying four or five leagues from the South East point of Oneeheow in the direction of South, 69 degrees West. We were told that it abounds with birds, which are its only inhabitants." He recorded the primary anchorage of Ni'ihau thus:

"Oneeheow. Anchoring-place – Latitude 21 degrees, 43 minutes; Longitude 202 degrees, 9 minutes."

Fourteen months later, in March 1779, Cook's two ships again visited 'Oneeheow' but this time the log of the expedition was in charge of Captain James King. Cook had been killed in February in an unfortunate skirmish with Hawaiians protecting the chief whom Cook was trying to take hostage at Kealakekua, on the Kona Coast of the Big island – Owhyhee. In his continuation of Cook's log, Captain King describes Ni'ihau and its neighboring small islands in a manner similar to Cook's earlier descriptions: "Oneeheow lies five leagues to the Westward of Atooi. The Eastern coast is high and rises abruptly from the sea, but the rest of the island consists of low ground; excepting a round bluff head on the South East point. It produces abundance of yams and of the sweet root called *Tee*; but we got from it no other sort of provisions . . Oreehoua and Tahoora are two small islands in the neighborhood of Oneeheow. The former is a single high hummock, joined by a reef of coral rocks to the Northern extremity of Oneeheow. The latter lies to the Southwest and is uninhabited."

The personal appearance and intelligence of the Ni'ihauans is noted in detail by Captain King, who was struck by the Hawaiian custom – which he had seen elsewhere only among the Maori – of tattooing the face. The Maori, King recollected, do this in elegant spiral volutes but the Hawaiians tattoo their faces "in straight lines, crossing each other at right angles. The hands and arms of the women are also very neatly marked and they have a singular custom amongst them, the meaning of which we could never learn, that of *tattowing* the tip of the tongues of the females."

As to intelligence, Captain King wrote: "Their natural capacity seems, in no respect, below the common standard of mankind. Their improvements in agriculture, and the perfection of their manufactures, are certainly adequate to the circumstances of their situation, and the natural advantages they enjoy. The eager curiosity with which they attended the armourer's forge and the many expedients they had invented, even before we left the islands, for working the iron they had procured from us, into such forms as were best adapted to their purposes, were strong proofs of docility and ingenuity."

As to mental illnesses, "we met with two instances of persons disordered in their minds, the one a man at Owhyhee, the other a woman at Oneeheow. It appeared, from the particular attention and respect paid to them that the opinion of their being inspired by the Divinity, which obtains among most of the nations of the East, is also received here."

King was impressed by the physique of the Hawaiians, but he does not describe the Ni'ihauans as being in any way different from other islanders of the group. "The natives of these islands are, in general, above the middle size, and well made; they walk very gracefully, run nimbly, and are capable of bearing great fatigue . . . Their complexion is rather darker than those of Otaheite and they are not altogether as handsome a people. However, many of both sexes had fine, open countenances; and the women in particular, had good eyes and teeth, and a sweetness and sensibility of look, which rendered them very engaging. Their hair is of a brownish-black, and neither uniformly straight, like that of the Indians of America, nor uniformly curling, as amongst the African negroes, but varying in this respect, like the hair of Europeans. One striking peculiarity in the features of every part of this nation, I do not remember to have seen anywhere mentioned, which is, that, even in the handsomest faces there is always a fullness of the nostril without any flatness or spreading of the nose, that distinguishes them from Europeans. It is not improbable that this may be the effect of their usual mode of salutation which is performed by pressing the ends of their noses together . ."

As to the produce of Ni'ihau, probably describing the root which Cook called *tee* (ti) King relates that "At Oneeheow they brought us several large roots of a brown color, shaped like a yam, and from six to ten pounds in weight. The juice, which it yields in abundance, is very sweet and of a pleasant taste, and was found to be an excellent substitute for sugar. The natives are very fond of it, and use it as an article of their common diet; and our people also found it very palatable and wholesome. We could not learn to what species of plant it belonged, having never been able to procure the leaves; but it was supposed, by our botanists, to be the root of some kind of fern."

This second visit to Ni'ihau was once again unplanned. From Kealakekua, the 'Resolution' and 'Discovery' had headed for Kauai and their first anchorage at Waimea, which they thought to make their one last stop in the islands. However, when they dropped anchor there on Monday, March 1, 1779, several canoes immediately came alongside and "we could observe that they did not welcome us with the same cordiality in their manner and satisfaction in their countenances as when we were here before." King soon ascertained the reason from a spokesman in one of the canoes. As Cook had feared, and hoped to prevent, King writes "we had left a disorder amongst their women, of which several persons of both sexes had died. He (the spokesman from 'Atooi') was himself affected with the venereal disease . . . I am afraid it is not to be denied, that we were the authors of this irreparable mischief."

Also, during the fourteen months since their first visit, "wars had arisen in consequence of the goats that Captain Cook had left at Oneeheow, and the slaughter of the poor goats themselves during the struggles for the property of them." Involved in this civil war was a struggle for power. Both Kaneoneo and Keawe were contending for the position of ruling chief of Kauai and Ni'ihau. Each was a grandson of the ruling chief of Oahu, but by a different mother. Their grandfather had given the governance of Kauai to Kaneoneo and that of Ni'ihau to Keawe. However, each wanted governance over both islands. Kauai being in the grip of this conflict, and hostility being expressed because of the venereal disease the ships had inflicted on the people, King remained at Waimea only one week.

"On Monday the 8th at 9 AM we weighed and sailed toward Oneeheow; and at 3 PM anchored in 20 fathoms of water nearly on the same spot as in the year 1778. We moored with the other anchor in 26 fathoms of water. The high bluff, on the South end of the island bore East South East; the North point of the road, North half East; and a bluff head to the South of it, North East by North. During the night we had a strong gale from the Eastward; and, in the morning of the 9th, found the ship had driven a whole cable's length, and brought both anchors almost overhead. We shortened in the best bower cable, but the wind blowing too fresh to unmoor, we were obliged to remain, this and the following two days, with the anchors still ahead."

On the 12th the weather moderated and the Master was sent to the Northwest side of the island to look for a more convenient anchorage. "He returned in the evening, having found, close around the West point of the road where we now lay, which is also the Westernmost point of the island, a fine bay with good anchorage, in 18 fathoms of water, a clear sandy bottom, not a mile from the beach, on which the surf beats but not so as to hinder landing. The direction of the points of the bay were North by East and South by West; and, in that line, the sounding seven, eight, and nine fathoms. On the North side of the bay was a small village, and a quarter mile to the Eastward were four small wells of good water; the road to them level, and fit for rolling casks."

The man who was later to go down in history as commander of the 'Bounty', and whose story was told a century later in the dramatic novels by Charles Nordhoff and James Norman Hall (*Mutiny on the Bounty; Men Against The Sea; Pitcairn Island*), was an enthusiastic explorer on this second trip of Cook's expedition to Ni'ihau. King's record of March 14th, 1779, reads;

"Mr. Bligh went afterward so far to the North as to satisfy himself, that Oreehoua was a separate island from Oneeheow; and that there was a passage between them; which before, we only conjectured to exist." Later that afternoon, "we hoisted in all the boats and made ready for going to sea in the morning".

On March 15, the fourth year of their long voyage to the Pacific Ocean, the two British ships left Oneeheow, setting sail for home with the news of their discovery of this group which they had named the Sandwich Isles.

A Floodtide of Foreigners

SEVEN YEARS LATER, in 1786, the 'King George' and the 'Queen Charlotte' sailed to the Sandwich Islands. Their captains, Nathaniel Portlock and George Dixon, had been with Cook on his 1778-1779 voyages. Both had been in the shore party that spent two nights on Ni'ihau in 1778.

Portlock's memories of Ni'ihau were most affectionate. He writes that on this second trip to the Sandwich Islands he found the political situation of all the islands – including Ni'ihau which he spells 'Oneehow' – much changed. "Taheeterre", who in 1778-9 had been king of Molokai only, was now ruling chief of "Woahoo, Morotoi, and Mowee; Maiha Maiha governed Owhyhee and Ranai; and a chief whose name I understand is Ta'aa is king of Atooi and Oneehow."

It was Wednesday, June 7, 1786, when Portlock attempted to anchor at Waimea Bay on Kauai. Such strong and adverse southerly winds were blowing that, instead, he "stood for Oneehow, under all the sail we could carry. At four o'clock the extremes of Oneehow bore from North North West half West to South West by West about four leagues distant from the nearest land." In his log, Captain Portlock entered a description of Ni'ihau that varied from those of Captains Cook and King only in his comment that "About five leagues to the East ward it has

32

the appearance of a detached island, being joined to the main by a low slip of land, which is not seen more than three leagues distant."

By the time Portlock's 'King George' and her sister ship the 'Queen Charlotte', commanded by Captain Dixon, were ready to find anchorage at Ni'ihau, it was too late in the day to do so safely. The 'King George' "shortened sail, and hauled on a wind to the Southward; intending to spend the night in standing off and on. At eleven o'clock we wore, and made the signal to the Queen Charlotte, but she not observing it continued standing to the Southward." The two ships nearly lost sight of each other but Portlock finally rejoined his colleague and "we again wore at one o'clock and stood to the Northward. This mistake nearly occasioned us to miss Oneehow."

Although a current carried them away from the island, they finally weathered their way back. They spent next morning "stretching along shore, about the distance of one mile, and had regular soundings from twenty to sixteen fathoms of water, over a bottom of fine sand." On June 8, 1786, they anchored in a bay "round the West point, the extremes of the bay bearing from North by South to a bearing from North by South to South East." About the middle of the bay was a fine sandy beach "within a quarter-mile of which a ship may moore in seven or eight fathoms of water over a bottom of fine sand and boats may land with great ease and safety."

As soon as the ships had anchored, canoes came out. Aboard them Portlock, to his great joy, recognized "several whose faces I remembered to have seen when at this island before; particularly an old priest, in whose house a party of us took up our abode when detained all night on shore by a heavy surf, and who treated us in a very friendly manner."

Portlock's ships had come to purchase Ni'ihau's famous yams, which Captains Portlock and Dixon intended to dry and stow according to Cook's recipe for maximum keeping qualities. These vegetables, Portlock records, "I had the pleasure to see brought to us in tolerable plenty." He had also hoped to purchase hogs, but he was diasppointed both by the number available and the small size of those hogs brought to the ship.

"I expected to find no difficulty in getting water, at least sufficient for our daily use; as Mr. Bligh, who was master of the 'Resolution' during our last voyage, and discovered the bay we now lay in, went on shore in order to examine this part of the island and met with two wells of fresh water in the neighborhood of our present situation."

The next morning, June 9th, more yams and some sugar cane were brought out by the canoes. "A chief named Abbenooe, whom I knew when I was at this island before, also paid me a visit, and recognized his old acquaintance the moment he came on board." When this visitor arrived, Portlock at once appointed six of his men to take over trading with the Ni'ihau people. He gave orders that the yams purchased be promptly dried in the sun and stowed away. His business of the day now delegated, Captain Portlock went ashore with Abbenooe "in search of the wells mentioned by Mr. Bligh" during Cook's visit. To his disappointment he found one of the wells "brackish and stinking". The other had good water, "but in no great quantity." An adequate well was situated one half mile to the east of the beach but the path to it was not easy. One must walk around an intervening salt marsh to get to it (and to roll filled casks back from it). In his log, later, Portlock recommended that only if a ship is in distress for water should they try to procure it from the limited supplies of Ni'ihau. He also advised future ship visitors to fit water casks with wooden instead of iron hoops and thus avoid having Hawaiians attempt to steal the casks in order to obtain the iron that was so precious to them.

Portlock felt no qualms about exploring inland with only his friend Abbenooe and a few other Ni'ihauans. Of his excursion with them, following his examination of the three wells, he recorded that "The island appears well-cultivated; its principal produce is yams. There are besides, sweet potatoes, sugar cane and the sweet root which is called *tee* by the natives. A few trees are scattered here and there, but in little order or variety. Some that grow near the well just mentioned were about fifteen feet high and proportionably thick; with spreading branches and a smooth bark; the leaves were round, and they bore a kind of nut somewhat resembling our walnut. Another kind were nine feet high, and had blossoms of a beautiful pink colour. I also noticed another variety, with nuts growing on them like our horse chestnut. These nuts, I understand, the inhabitants use as a substitute for candles and they give a most excellent light."

"Having viewed everything remarkable on this side the island I repaired on board, accompanied by my good friend Abbenooe, and found a brisk trade going on for vegetables. A few hogs also had been purchased, sufficient for daily consumption." Back aboard that afternoon Portlock learned that Oneehow, which belonged to Ta'aao, king of Atoui, (Kauai), was, during the king's absences from Oneehow governed by Abbenooe. Impressed by this, Portlock "made the old man a present of some red baize and two large towes, which he sent immediately to Ta'aao at Atoui." Abbenooe told Portlock that the king would send many gifts to Portlock in return.

"I placed no great reliance on this piece of information," Portlock wrote in his journal, but on the afternoon of the 10th he added. "I was agreeably surprised to receive from Abbenooe's returning messengers a number of fine hogs to be disposed of together with taro and sugar cane."

Desirous of sending the king a thank-you gift for all this, Portlock selected as appropriate for this purpose "a light-horseman's cap" which, however, Abbenooe advised was insufficient. At the old chief's urging, therefore, Portlock added to the gift of the cap "an armed chair which I had in the cabin". This, Abbenooe told him, would "be particularly useful to one of the king's wives who had recently lain in."

A number of Portlock's men were recovering from various illnesses. He sent them ashore each day for a walk and "they found the land air and the exercise beneficial." To do so was in no way a risk for, as Portlock later observed, "the inhabitants of this island are not numerous and they were kept in such excellent order by Abbenooe that our people walked about wherever inclination led them, without the least molestation."

In addition to laying in and drying a supply of yams, and killing and salting the hogs both given to them and purchased by them here at Ni'ihau, Portlock "purchased some salt fish of various kinds, such as snappers, rock cod, and bonetta, all well-cured and very fine." The Ni'ihauans brought calabashes of water to the ship "sufficient for daily use". In addition to such necessities as fish, pork, and vegetables to re-provision his ship's stores, "Curiosities too found their way to market and I purchased two very curious fly flaps, the upper part composed of beautiful variegated feathers, the handles were human bone; inlaid with tortoise shell in the neatest manner, which gave them the appearance of fineered work."

At eight o'clock on the morning of Tuesday June 13, being watered and provisioned with about ten tons of fine yams on the 'King George' and about eight tons on the 'Queen Charlotte', the two ships "weighed and got under sail standing out of the bay which obtained the name Yam Bay, from the great quantity of yams, and we proceeded on with a fresh breeze at North East".

Portlock looked forward to re-visiting Ni'ihau on his return voyage through the islands in February 1787. However, bad weather plagued him on the way to Ni'ihau and cut short his intended stay. He arrived there on Saturday, February 17, 1787 fairly late in the day. "About two o'clock passed the South head of Oneehow, and ran towards Yam Bay; and at 5 anchored with the small bower in 29 fathoms, over fine white sand; the 'Queen Charlotte' anchoring at the same time a little to the Southward." As the two ships dropped anchor, the weather seemed fine and in the hour or two before dusk Portlock went ashore for a brief visit.

He was greeted by Abbenooe who informed him that this year, regrettably, there were few yams to be had since the people had "neglected cultivating the land". Portlock confirmed this during a walk inland where he saw "a great deal of ground lying entirely waste. It appeared to me that a number of the natives that formerly inhabited this island have quitted it to reside at Atoui, as Oneehow is but a poor spot, abounding in scarce anything but yams, potatoes, sugar cane and the sweet root (ti) with a very trifling quantity of wood." This exodus to Kauai was, Portlock surmised, made possible by "the iron which they procured from us formerly" and which "enabled them to purchase possessions in Atoui".

Portlock returned to his ship, intending to visit Ni'ihau again the following day but in the dark hours of the next morning the wind shifted, and a heavy swell set in. Fearing his ship might be driven ashore, Portlock made up his mind to leave.

By 5 AM the situation was such that it was impossible to pull in one of the anchors. Portlock ordered the cables cut, leaving the precious anchor on the sandy bottom of Yam Bay and beating his way – along with the 'Queen Charlotte' out into the still turbulent but safer open waters offshore. Later that same month he and Dixon returned but stayed off Ni'ihau only long enough to retrieve the anchor.

In his own published account of these voyages, especially where Ni'ihau is concerned, Portlock's colleague Captain George Dixon covers much the same material. Dixon makes such additional observations that "nails and such like trifles" were used to purchase yams and hogs and that chief Abbenooe was "a very active intelligent person". On their second voyage when bad weather was everywhere in the island chain, Dixon wrote that on January 20, as the 'King George' and 'Queen Charlotte' were headed for Ni'ihau, his ship lost sight of the 'King George' during a gale. "We were under great apprehensions for Captain Portlock's safety, as his situation we knew must be a very critical one, no harbour at Oneehow affording the least shelter from a southerly or westerly wind. But at one o'clock on the 22nd we saw the 'King George' to our great satisfaction, bearing West by North about three leagues distant."

In the first pages of his book, *A VOYAGE ROUND THE WORLD, but more particularly to the NORTH COAST OF AMERICA, Performed in 1785, 1786, 1787 and 1788 in The King George and Queen Charlotte* (published in London in 1789), Nathaniel Portlock prophesies that the Sandwich Islands will become an important stopping place for those hurrying into the new trading ventures. He points out that it was Cook's suggestion that "a gainful trade might be carried on from America to China for furs". This, he felt, stimulated such pioneer traders as James Hanna's trip from Canton to Nootka Sound in 1785. Nootka was, according to Portlock, "the American mart for peltry". Portlock relates that Hanna's first voyage carrying furs to Canton was made in a sixty ton brig manned by only twenty men. In 1786, the same year in which Portlock and Dixon visited the Sandwich Islands, Hanna made an even more profitable voyage in a larger vessel. Hanna's phenomenal success resulted in "the traders of Bengal" dispatching Lts. Meares and Tipping in two ships on a similar 'peltry' mission. On their way from Nootka Sound across the Pacific to China, Meares and Tipping stopped off at various locations in the Sandwich Islands, including Ni'ihau.

Meares and Tipping were a new kind of ship visitor here. They were more interested in commerce than in culture. Judging from the letter he left to be handed to his friend Captain William Douglas of the 'Iphigenia', Meares was extremely paranoid about the dangers of doing business in these islands. He seems to think that he himself was somewhat immune from the threat he describes to Douglas – at any rate, his log discloses a far different attitude than he reveals in the letter he left at Ni'ihau for the Captain of the 'Iphigenia'.

In his two-volume journal, Meares writes of his two visits to Ni'ihau in much the same general tone as had Portlock. Meares' journal was published by the Legographic Press, London, in 1791 under the cumbersome title *Voyages Made in the Years 1788 and 1789 From China to the NorthWest Coast of America, with an Introductory Narrative of a Voyage Performed in 1786, From Bengal, in the Ship 'Nootka'*.

On his second visit to Ni'ihau, which is the one of primary interest here, Meares anchored at the island he spells 'Oneeheow' about 6 p.m. on the evening of October 25, 1788 "nearly in the same position we had occupied in the preceding year. On arriving off this island we did not experience the operations of any prohibition against us; on the contrary, we were surrounded by a crowd of natives, among whom were many of our old friends, whom we perfectly recollected, so that the ship was very shortly filled with visitors of all ages and both sexes." Prominent among these Ni'ihauans who boarded the 'Felice' was a man whom, Meares relates, "some officers had formerly given the well known and the honorable appellation of 'Friday'.

"If any of the companions of my former voyage should peruse this page, they, I am sure, will recollect with somewhat of a grateful remembrance, the friendly and faithful services of the honest 'Friday'." It was 'Friday' who volunteered to negotiate for yams, which he told Meares were in short supply as this was not the season they could be dug. Since the 'Felice' was out of bread and flour Meares urged 'Friday' to persuade his fellow Ni'ihauans to dig up what they could. By noon of the 27th several tons had been brought aboard and the 'Felice' "prepared to put to sea". 'Friday' remained aboard to the last moment, and was entrusted by Meares with a letter to hold until Captain Douglas of the 'Iphigenia' should arrive at Ni'ihau. The contrast between the contents of this letter, and the generosity and friendship given to Meares by the people of Ni'ihau is a sorry comment on what seems to have been his trader mentality, willing to believe the worst of any strange peoples.

As they had promised, the Ni'ihauans saw to it that when Captain William Douglas dropped anchor at Waimea Bay, Kauai in February 1789 he was given Meares' letter. In it Douglas is advised "to be continually on guard against the designs of the King and of Abinui his minister" (the selfsame trusted Abbenooe whom Portlock and Dixon had described as an active, intelligent, good friend). Kaiana, a Kauai chief whom Meares refers to as Taiana, and whom he had taken along at that chief's request to see the wonderful world of Canton, China, had evidently described to Meares the use of a poison which Meares, in his letter, warned Douglas might be used against him.

Meares wrote that he suspected the ruling chief of Kauai and his Ni'ihau minister Abinui might very well try to poison Douglas and his men with "a poisonous root well known to the Sandwich islanders which when ground to powder, might be easily scattered about the ship, or thrown upon their clothes, without being observed, and whose power is of such deadly nature, that if the smallest quantity of it is inhaled by mouth or nostril the consequence is immediate death."

Meares' letter explains that the reason for such a poison being used would be the desire of the ruling chief for foreign ships, weapons, and goods. Despite his own positive experience, Meares warns Douglas that he believes the chiefs on Kauai and Ni'ihauans like Abinui might well go to such lengths.

It was after receiving this warning letter that Captain Douglas took 'Iphigenia' to Ni'ihau in February 1789. With due caution of course, Douglas intended to trade for hogs and yams. The strong gales that had been Portlock and Dixon's experience this same season prevented the 'Iphigenia' from reaching the island. Trouble of quite a different sort than described in Meares' letter plagued Douglas' ship as it fought the weather off Ni'ihau.

A crew member named Jones was trying to stir his fellows to mutiny. Douglas caught the man doing so and offered him a choice. Either he could stand the usual punishment of lashes given aboard ship or, instead, suffer being put ashore as soon as the 'Iphigenia' returned to Kauai. Jones chose this and when the gale subsided, he was put ashore at Waimea Bay.

To Douglas' dismay this did not end the threat of mutiny. Discontent in the forecastle was still being churned by three of the crew when the 'Iphigenia' sailed for Ni'ihau the following day. Meares, who was later informed of all that transpired, wrote in his journal that "Captain Douglas, being informed of a design agitated by several of the seamen to go off with the jolly-boat (to Ni'ihau) gave orders to the officers to keep a strict watch. Nevertheless, during the night, the quarter-master and two of the sailors had got on shore in some of the canoes that were alongside. They (the three sailors) had formed a plan to get off with the boat and at the same time to set fire to the ship; but being prevented in their diabolical enterprise, they had taken an opportunity to escape to the island. Two of them, however, by the active zeal of honest 'Friday' . . . were shortly brought back to the ship, but the quarter-master, who was the ring-leader in the mischief, could not be brought off on account of the surf and was therefore left behind."

It was in such a way that this spring of 1789 Ni'ihau acquired its first foreign resident. The deserter evidently put little stock in Meares' urging Captain Douglas and his men to "guard carefully against the art and cunning of Kaeo and Abinui for I think them dreadful, mercenary, artful villains. As they attempted to poison the crews of the 'Prince of Wales' and the 'Princess Royal' you will guard against such a diabolical design by inspecting the cocoa nuts, yams, water, etc. making the seller taste each."

What a commentary on Meares' change of heart towards the very people who befriended him on his visit the previous year and whom Captain George Dixon had described as "in their temper and disposition are harmless, inoffensive, and friendly, not subject to passion or easily provoked; in their manners they are lively and cheerful, every ready to render any little service in their power even to strangers, and pursue everything they undertake with unremitting diligence and application . . . It must be confessed that they are guilty of theft, and will not scruple to plunder whenever they have an opportunity . . . yet with all this propensity to thieving, we never met with an instance of dishonesty whenever anything was committed to their charge, no matter how valuable it might be."

From the hindsight of two hundred years, we may surmise that the difference in Meares and Dixon's attitudes towards the Ni'ihauans may well have arisen from the fact that Portlock and Dixon were primarily explorers, not exploiters. Captains Douglas and Meares were traders, and as such tended to be suspicious of those from whom they intended to take as much as possible for a minimal return. Meares was an astute enough business-man to regard Ni'ihau as potentially profitable in its resources, despite the dangers that might be involved. He therefore advised Douglas to remember that "The island of Oneehow furnishes the pearl-oyster. You will endeavor to make Tianna" ((Kaiana) "sensible of the treasures they contain and the importance of them to us, and I have hopes that during your stay you will fully ascertain this point."

Other merchant vessels, like the British 'Jenny' evidently called at Ni'ihau during the next three years, but their visits are not well documented. Then, in March 1792, another of Cook's former junior officers, George Vancouver, visited Ni'ihau as commander of two ships of the British navy on what the thirty-five year old Vancouver described in the title of his published account as a *Voyage of Discovery to the North Pacific ocean and round the World*.

On his 1792 visit, Vancouver had become acquainted with the American merchant vessel, 'Lady Washington' under Captain Kendrick. According to Vancouver's journal, Kendrick had been enthusiastic about the possibilities of both sandal-wood and pearl shell as sources of profit from the islands. As Meares had informed Douglas, Ni'ihau had the latter, and it was there, according to Vancouver, that Kendrick dropped off three of his men to gather pearl shell. This, writes Vancouver in his journal, "appears to have been the effect of a sudden thought, as it was not until his brig was weighing anchor at Onehow that he came to this determination and landed the three men who in consequence of such short notice had no means of equipping themselves and were left almost destitute of apparels."

On his March 1792 visit to Kauai and Ni'ihau, Vancouver records the name of one of these three as 'Rowbottom'. Vancouver took the trouble to replenish their clothing and "such tools and articles of traffic as would best answer their purpose, and some books, pens, ink, and paper, for their amusement, with an assortment of garden seeds and some orange and lemon plants that were in a very flourishing state".

The seeds, and the 'flourishing' orange and lemon plants came from a greenhouse on the deck of the 'Discovery' – Vancouver's command ship. This was a strange object to find on the deck of a man-o-war. It had been built for botanist Archibald Menzies, who also served as ship's surgeon. Menzies was a careful observer, and a distributor of new seeds and plants to the islands as well as ardent collector of exotic native plants to take back for His Majesty's collection in the botanical gardens at Kew. In his journal Menzies logs the 'Discovery' 's arrival at Ni'ihau on March 14, 1792, at 10 o'clock in the morning, noting that they anchored there "under the southeast point (which forms a steep bluff composed of rocks and sand) in 14 fathoms, soft ground, the points bearing N77E, and N 48 W and Kaula S, 58 W offshore about three fourths of a mile and from the bluff point rather more than a mile."

Vancouver wished to procure yams, and according to Menzies "this principal business here was entrusted to Ku, the same chief Mr. Meares named Friday, whose authority over the natives and obliging disposition we, on many occasions, found extremely useful."

Had botanist Menzies been aware of Meares' caution to Douglas regarding the poisonous root that worked with such invisible, deadly stealth, he would undoubtedly have had some scientific curiosity concerning what it might be. However he neither mentions this as a concern in the stop on Ni'ihau, nor does he seem at all worried for his safety on this island. Instead, the following day he and another officer, Mr. Manley, set out on what probably was the first foreign hunting trip to bag any wild fowl they might find on Ni'ihau.

"In the forenoon of the 15th," Menzies writes, he and Mr. Manley, "went on shore to examine the adjacent extremity of the island . . . The coast opposite to the ship being quite rocky, and at this time quite inaccessible by a high sea breaking incessantly against it, we were carried by some of the natives in a canoe to a small sandy cove near the bluff, and there artfully landed by placing the canoe on top of the highest swell, which carried us safe over some sunken piled rocks, by an accelerated motion, to the beach. Here we found a few small huts, seemingly the temporary residence of a party of fishermen, with some little stages to dry their fish on, and about 100 of the natives who, impelled by a curiosity of being near our vessel, had taken shelter in the cover of the rocks round the cove."

When Menzies and Manley asked for fresh water, they were impressed by its scarcity on this end of Ni'ihau, for an ooze of a few drops a minute from one place in the rocks was carefully collected to be given to them in a calabash. "After examining the romantic bluff, which we found composed of dark porous rocks, intermixed with hardened volcanic sand and gravel, we crossed a low narrow neck of land and pursued our journey along the eastern shore for nearly two leagues without seeing anything deserving of notice excepting the desolate and barren appearance of the country we travelled through, covered with loose stones of a black and porous texture and a few stinted (sic) vegetables in a shrivelled state – no trees or bushes – no house or any trace of cultivation were to be seen in the whole tract. The shore was bound by rocky, indented caverns, rugged and bleak in the extreme."

The two intrepid Englishmen then crossed the island "to within a short distance of its western shore". In their judgment, Ni'ihau's "whole width did not appear to be above 6 or 7 miles at any part." On the western shore, they saw "a few villages and some appearance of cultivation". Returning via the interior of the island, they passed some small fields of sweet potatoes "which the natives were obliged to cover over with a layer of grass to preserve the little moisture of the soil from being exhaled by the sun's powerful heat."

In the middle of the island they came across a salt-encrusted patch of low land which they were told overflowed with water in the rainy season. Here and there they met with little rock-shaded natural tanks in the rocks. Either these were dry now, or not potable. "For quenching our thirst we were chiefly indebted to some watermelons we obtained from the natives" – and which, Menzies does not add, were a product which Ni'ihau was now growing from a gift of watermelon seeds given them by Captain Cook in 1778.

During their day ashore Mr. Manley bagged a dozen wild fowl which Menzies identified as "ducks *(anas clypeata)*, curlews *(scolopax tahitiennis)* and cotterels *(Charadrius morinellus)*. The birds shot were a heavy enough burden in the heat but, Menzies remarked, they saw Ni'ihauans struggling at least 10 miles in the heat of the day, carrying yams and vegetables to trade aboard ship for a few nails. To Menzies, it seems that only "the northern and western skirts" of Ni'ihau were inhabited. From this day's excursion he concluded, "I am inclined to think that Captain Cook's estimate of the number of inhabitants on this island on his first visit (about 500) is much nearer the truth" than "the one (4,000) given afterwards" (1779) "by Captain King."

Two Shanghaied Wahines

THE LATITUDE OF Vancouver's anchorage at Ni'ihau was logged by Menzies as being 21 degrees 46 mintues 20 seconds north "and is by far the most eligible situation this island affords, as it is well sheltered from the north and north-east winds, which are generally the strongest among these islands." Menzies had evidently not yet known the southerly gales of a Kona storm! He had no idea how fortunate they were not to experience one during their stay at Ni'ihau. "While we remained here, the weather continued dark and cloudy, but fair; the wind kept steadily between north and nor-north-east, blew at times very fresh, and was felt much colder than we have in general experienced it in the tropics."

In order to encourage Ni'ihauans to continue to cultivate new crops such as watermelons and musk-melons, as they had since Cook's visit and his gift of seeds, Vancouver was careful to pay a good price for these fruits so relished by himself and his men. To encourage further variety in Ni'ihau agriculture, Menzies distributed "a variety of European garden seeds, and particularly of Imperial cabbage seeds which were given me by Mr. Aston, His Majesty's gardener at Kew." (William Aston was then manager of Kew's Royal Botanical Gardens.)

45

On March 16th, 1792, at 5 in the afternoon, Vancouver's two ships weighed anchor and sailed on their way to the Northwest coast of America. After several months of exploration they stopped at the Spanish port of Nootka, on the island which today bears Vancouver's name. Nootka was then a busy trading port much frequented by British and American ships. It was, as Portlock had written, the center for American 'peltry'. It was also a port that both the British and the Americans hoped to take over from the Spanish whose major colonial interests lay much farther to the south.

On October 12th, just one day prior to his leaving Nootka to return to Hawaii, Vancouver "received on board two young women for the purpose of returning them to their native country, the Sandwich islands, which they had quitted in a vessel called the 'Jenny' (originally out of Bristol, England) which had arrived at Nootka on the 7th of October. As that vessel was bound from hence straight to England, Mr. James Baker very earnestly requested that I would permit these two unfortunate girls to take a passage on the Discovery to Onehow, the island of their birth and residence, from which they had been brought, not only very contrary to their wishes and inclinations, but totally without the knowledge or consent of their friends or relations. . ."

A rumour circulating around Nootka during the five days that the 'Jenny' was at anchor reached Vancouver's indignant ears. He claims in his journal that such allegations were often made by "citizens of the United States of America to the prejudice and dishonor of the British subjects trading on the coast of NorthWest America." Vancouver felt that this particular rumour about the two girls from Ni'ihau was as baseless as any he had yet heard, and quite fit into the stories widely circulated by Americans in Nootka that some British subjects "had brought the natives of the Sandwich Islands from thence to the coast of America and had there sold them to the natives of those shores for furs."

The charges made by Americans in the case of the 'Jenny' and the two young women from Ni'ihau are indignantly recorded by Vancouver. "These two young women were particuarly instanced, as having been so brought and disposed of by Mr. Baker, commanding the 'Jenny' of Bristol, and the story was told with such plausibility that I believe it acquired some degree of credit with Sr. Quadra and most of the Spanish officers who heard it. The arrival of the 'Jenny' however, in the port of Nootka, gave a flat contradiction to these scandalous reports, and proved them to be equally malicious and untrue, as the two girls were found still remaining on board the 'Jenny', without having entertained any idea that they were intended to be sold; nor did they mention to have received any ill usage from Mr. Baker, but on the contrary that they had been treated by him with every kindness and attention while under his protection."

At the time of his recording all this in his log, Vancouver had known the captain of the 'Jenny' for only five days. Nonetheless he expresses complete confidence in his fellow countryman, stating: "Although I have not any personal knowledge of Mr. Baker previous to his entering Nootka, yet I should conceive him totally incapable of such an act of barbarity and injustice and if there were the least sincerity in the solicitude he expressed to me for the future happiness and welfare of these young women, it is impossible he could ever have meditated such a design. I do not however mean to vindicate the propriety of Mr. Baker's conduct in bringing these girls from their native country; for I am decidedly of the opinion it was highly improper; and if the young women are to be credited, their seduction and detention on board Mr. Baker's vessel were inexcusable."

What the girls told Vancouver was that "they went on board with several others of their countrywomen, who were permitted to return again to the shore; but that *they* were confined down in the cabin until the vessel had sailed, and was at some distance from Onehow. On the other hand, Mr. Baker states that he put to sea without any knowledge of their being on board his vessel."

The two girls first identified themselves as Taheeopiah and Tymarrow, both of "the island of Onehow". Taheeopiah was about fifteen years old, a girl of *alii* rank. Tymarrow, about 20, was related to her but, Vancouver comments, "was not of equal rank on the island". The change and exchange of names is not an uncommon Polynesian custom but Vancouver was puzzled when "Taheeopiah, for some reason I never could understand, altered her name to that of Raheina a short time after she came on board, and was continued to be so called."

The two girls from Ni'ihau were probably the first Hawaiian *wahines* to visit America's west coast, for on his way to the Sandwich Islands, Vancouver first made a voyage down the California coast. The California stopovers were ones Raheina and Tymarrow greatly enjoyed. This much pleased and intrigued Vancouver who relates that "The sight of horses, cattle, and other animals, with a variety of objects to which they were entire strangers, produced in them the highest entertainment; and without the least hesitation or alarm, they were placed on horseback on their first landing" (at one of the Spanish settlements) "and with a man to lead the animal, they rode without fear and were by that means enabled to partake of all the civilities and diversions which our Spanish friends so obligingly offered and provided."

For this first riding experience of any Ni'ihauan – indeed, the first recorded riding experience of any Hawaiian, the two girls were outfitted in riding habits "as being best calculated for their situation and indeed the best in our power to procure". The adaptability of the girls to European fashion – and custom – was remarkable. Vancouver notes that with the fashions, "which much pleased them", they also seemed to naturally adopt European "delicacy". For example, says Vancouver, in going up and down the ladders that connected the various parts of his ship, Raheina in particular "would take as much care not to expose her ankles (sic), as if she had been educated by the most rigid governess." Raheina was everybody's favorite of the two, and George Vancouver was much impressed by her grace and beauty.

"The elegance of Raheina's figure, the regularity and softness of her features, and the delicacy which she naturally possessed, gave her a superiority over the generality of her sex among the Sandwich Islanders." Indeed, for Vancouver, Raheina epitomized the best and most desirable qualities of her sex even in comparison to females of his own country – high praise indeed of a girl from the smallest and most remote of the inhabited islands of the Hawaiian archipelago.

Whether it was the change of climate or, more probably, their exposure to new diseases for which they had no natural immunity, the two girls fell ill soon after arriving in Monterey.

Vancouver and his ship's surgeon, botanist Archibald Menzies, became fearful the two young Ni'ihauans might not survive to reach their island home for they remained ill during the continuation of the voyage. Vancouver related that "notwithstanding that every means in our power was resorted to for the re-establishment of their health, they did not perfectly recover until after our arrival at Owhyhee."

Since the girls were from "Onehow", Vancouver "had promised to set them on shore on that island". However, on reaching Owhyhee (Hawaii Island)– his first stop in the Sandwich Isles, Vancouver was informed that because of a severe drought the inhabitants of Ni'ihau had "almost entirely abandoned it." On his arrival at "Attowai" (Kauai), Vancouver found this was indeed so and "I came to a determination to leave our female friends at this island." Menzies corroborates this in his journal of the same voyage, saying that in 1793, on their return from the American coast with the two young women of Ni'ihau, Vancouver's ships were disappointed to be told that "a long succession of dry weather had shrivelled and burnt up the greatest part of the produce" of Ni'ihau. No yams were to be had. Indeed, laments Menzies, who had so enjoyed that first stopover and his long excursion with Mr. Manley through Ni'ihau's interior, the general famine on the island was now such that most of its people had moved to Kauai. The two girls did not seem upset by this. Evidently such moves during periods of severe drought were a common experience for people from Ni'ihau.

Menzies states that when the girls, whose health had begun to improve with access to their accustomed diet of poi, heard about the terrible conditions on 'Onehow', they themselves asked to be landed on Kauai. Knowledgable of the force of *tapu* and the retribution that could be exacted on them because, during their long absence, the two girls had broken the most strict prohibition for their sex by "eating at mine and other tables in the company of men", Vancouver extracted a promise from the ruling chiefs of Kauai that the girls "should not be liable to the least injury on that account but that on their landing they should be immediately taken care of and protected."

Menzies' account gives the further detail that Vancouver commended the care of his two female passengers to the chief Inamoo who promised they would be under the protection of the chief of Waimea "in whose district a house and a portion of land should be given to each of them and where all their effects should be protected in safety." In their travels, Raheina and Tymarrow had been given many 'foreign possessions' which, according to Menzies, now made them "the richest at these islands". Vancouver was inclined not to place too much trust in Inamoo's promises and guarantees. Inspecting the lands promised to each girl, the British commander found them so extensive and fertile, and so close to Waimea Bay – where the commerce with foreign vessels usually took place – in short, "so far above our most sanguine expectations, that I was led to suspect the sincerity of the intended donation."

Consequently, Vancouver conceived of a safeguard that he felt would protect the girls' estates, possessions, and their rights to them after his departure. He asked that rather than granting an estate to each girl, the lands be given to him personally as a gift with the understanding "that no person should have any right in it but by my permission, and that I would allow Raheina and Tymarrow to live upon the estates." That apportioned to Raheina, he was pleased to note, was the largest and most desirable, according with her higher rank. The estates of the two girls were adjacent, one to the other, and extended far up into the mountain slopes.

Menzies reports that Vancouver's assurance to the chiefs, and to the girls, that he would return to check on them the following year, was a further persuader to Inamoo to keep his word in the matter of protection of the girls and their property. "Before we came away," says Menzies, "the eldest of the girls (Tymarrow) told us that the chief of the village had made proposals to her to be his wife. This match we endeavored to encourage on both sides." As the 'Discovery' sailed off, Raheina and Tymarrow stood on the beach, waving a fond farewell. They were still dressed in their European fashions – including shoes and stockings but, Raheina had assured Vancouver, they would revert to their native costume as soon as the ship was out of sight.

The wonders that Raheina and Tymarrow could now relate to their countrymen must have seemed as marvelous as the legends told of Kauai and Ni'ihau's mythic past. They of course must have recounted the horseback riding, the very appearance of horses and cattle, and the Spanish entertainments given them. Also, according to Menzies, the two girls were full of stories about their voyage on the 'Jenny' along the Northwest Coast where Mr. Baker's Bristol ship traded for furs with numerous Indian tribes.

The girls told Menzies that "after seeing several such tribes, and observing their manners and customs, they could not reflect on these without expressing their utmost disgust, particularly at their " (the Indians) "uncleanly and filthy modes of living, at their besmearing themselves with grease and dirt, and its consequences – the strong cadaverous stench which constantly attends them." Undoubtedly, also, the girls regaled their Kauai neighbors and Ni'ihau friends and relatives on Kauai with the songs which Menzies says they made up about all that happened on their voyages – compositions "by which they amused themselves" was Menzies' impression, but which a modern anthropologist might view as the girls having concretized their strange experiences into songs and chants as was the long standing custom of Polynesians.

Neither Vancouver nor Menzies makes mention in their accounts of this 1793 visit as to the presence of the several Europeans that had been living on Kauai in 1792. The three men Kendrick put ashore from the 'Lady Washington' as he weighed anchor at Ni'ihau in 1791, and whom Vancouver in 1792 had replenished with clothing and certain amenities probably had by now been picked up along with their collections of pearl from Ni'ihau. Vancouver was much distressed to learn that Captain Kendrick had been killed at Oahu. Kendrick and several of his crew died as the result of the poor aim of a celebratory round of shot from the British vessels 'Jackal' and 'Prince Lee Boo', which were anchored near Kendrick's 'Lady Washington'.

Vancouver does not make any mention in the journal of his 1793 visit to Kauai concerning Inamoo's possession of 'musquets' with which the chief had armed the several Europeans of the island to aid him in putting down an insurrection by those intent on putting young chief Kaumualii in power. Menzies learned of this aborted affair, and the pardon offered one rebel chief who remained in hiding in the mountains. The botanist was much impressed, commenting that "these people on the whole seem to settle their own civil commotions with less acrimony than more civilized nations."

With their mission of safe return of the two girls from Ni'ihau accomplished, and with no reason to stop at deserted 'Onehow', on March 30, 1793 Vancouver's two ships made "slow progress between the islands of Onehow and Atoowai until, clear of Atoowai, we caught the trades and bore up for Lehua to examine its connections with Onehow, or see whether they were separated by a navigable passage" as William Bligh had asserted in 1779. At noon, in lattitude 22.4 North they stood about "two miles to the northward of the north point of Lehua, we then stood close round under the lee of the island, but saw no signs of cultivation or any inhabitants upon it," wrote Menzies. "On the contrary, it appeared to be nothing else but a barren rock of lava, composed of strata, very irregular both in their directions and dimensions and pierced through in several places with hideous caverns". They "stood far enough into the bay on the south side of it to convince ourselves that it was joined to Onehow by a reef of rocks covered with shallow water, and that there was no clear passage for the smallest vessel to go through between them."

It was the spring of 1794 before Vancouver and Menzies again returned to the Sandwich Islands. Politics did concern them this visit. Their journals show alarm at the conniving acts and plots described by Mr. William Brown, commander of the 'Butterworth' of London, in a letter given Kamehameha's trusted European advisor John Young to hold for Vancouver's arrival. According to this letter, "a set of vagabonds residing at Woahoo and at Attowai" (white men) had conspired with a certain minor chief on Kauai who was trying to rebel against Taeo (Kaeo) and Titeeree, the sovereigns of 'Attowai' to capture an American brig, the 'Hancock'. Brown charged that these *haoles* (white skinned foreigners) had so incited the people of Kauai and Ni'ihau against foreign ships visiting them that the situation for vessels calling at these leeward islands had become extremely dangerous.

Brown's view of the situation recalls that of Meares, who five years earlier had given Douglas a similar warning. Vancouver chose to discount Brown's letter for he himself had not personally encountered any hostility from either the chiefs or the white men on Kauai or Ni'ihau.

In the journal of his 1794 voyage, Vancouver remarks that there are eleven white men living on Owhyhee. He was accompanied through the island chain by an apprehensive American ship, the brig 'Washington'. In March the 'Discovery' again reached 'Whymea Bay' on Kauai where Vancouver's ship was visited by "many former friends and acquaintances. Amongst the number were the two young women I had brought from Nootka and settled here; during our late absence they had been treated with great kindness and civility, yet they were both very apprehensive that, on our finally quitting these seas, the attentive behavior they had hitherto experienced would be discontinued. I however embraced the first opportunity of obtaining from all the principal chiefs the most solemn assurances of the contrary."

This was Vancouver's last contact with the two girls, with 'Atoowai', 'Onehow', or any of the Sandwich Islands. He died in 1798, at the relatively young age of 41. That same year his account of his several remarkable voyages, and the careful charts he made of each of the Sandwich Islands and other islands in his travels, was first published in London.

Murder

WILLIAM ROBERT BROUGHTON had been with Vancouver's 1792 expedition to the Sandwich Islands. Four years later, on his return with his own vessel Broughton had every good reason to be extra cautious for during that 1792 visit, three of Vancouver's men had been murdered by Hawaiians on Oahu. Broughton was the officer assigned by Vancouver to take the details of this sad affair home to England on the armed tender 'Chatham'.

Strangely enough Broughton seems to have dismissed this from his mind on his 1796 voyage through the islands with his command ship 'Providence' and tender, on his way to survey the North Pacific, most particularly the coasts of Japan and Korea. Broughton had left England in 1795, crossed the Atlantic to Rio, sailed on down around the Horn and across the Pacific to New Zealand and Australia, then visited Tahiti before arriving in Hawaii on January 1, 1796. There he received the gift of a magnificent feather cloak from Kamehameha I, the Kohala chief who was determined to forge all the islands into one kingdom. Kamehameha had already conquered Maui, Lanai, Molokai and Oahu, consolidated his power on his home island, Hawaii, and was ambitious to conquer Ni'ihau and Kauai.

Broughton's visit coincided with a peak in the Hawaiians' eagerness to acquire foreign weaponry. Kamehameha had used

54

foreign arms, and foreigners who taught Hawaiians how to use them, to effect his conquests. He was hungry for cannon and foreign ships to invade Kauai and Ni'ihau. In turn, the chiefs of these still independent leeward islands were willing to commit murder to gain an extra musket and bayonet to defend themselves from Kamehameha's planned invasion.

Broughton seems quite unaware of the risks that were likely to be involved when, in February 1796, he made his first brief stop at Ni'ihau. His log for February 19th reads: "As the wind this morning came from the North, we steered to the island of Oneehow." On the 19th, ''we passed the SE point of Oneehow in 35 fathoms . . . steered along shore and at length came to in Yam Bay at 2 P.M. in 29 fathoms, coarse, sandy bottom. Some canoes came off next day bartering yams, potatoes, watermelons and pumpkins.''

The drought that in 1793 had moved Ni'ihau's inhabitants to Kauai had ended. Ni'ihauans were again living on their home island and cultivation had been resumed. Broughton's is the first account mentioning the Ni'ihau people raising pumpkins, the seeds of which had been originally distributed by Captain Cook in 1778 and also may well have been among the 'garden seeds' distributed by Archibald Menzies in 1792.

Broughton sent some of his men ashore, and "our boat also in the evening arrived laden with roots. The weather from the South occasioned a great swell in the Bay and prevented us from receiving the supplies we had been promised. However, the boat" (from the 'Providence') "went on shore with the European who had accompanied us from Atooi for the purpose of collecting yams. But nothing being ready we got under way and stood out to sea. The wind increased and we had rain with strong squalls that split the main topsail. After hoisting in the boats and securing the anchor, we stood inshore and bent another main topsail. The European returned on board saying everything was ready but the surf was so great that canoes could not reach us without risque (sic). I therefore gave up the idea of anchoring, as there was no probability of doing so while the wind continued which seemed likely to be the case. The European now left us in his canoe with some recompense for his attentions: this man had been transported to Botany Bay and came thence in an

American brig called the Mercury; he deserted from her at this island and is much courted by Taaua whose cause he has preferred to that of the young chief Tamaerrie (Kaumualii)."

Five months later Broughton again stopped at Ni'ihau on his return from Nootka and the North American coast. He was on his way to accomplish the major mission of his voyage – an attempt to survey the coasts of Japan and Korea. On July 18, 1796, the 'Providence' dropped anchor at Yam Bay in "15 fathoms, sandy bottom, one and one-half miles from the shore". Broughton's intent was to remain only 48 hours for the purpose of procuring yams. He wrote in his journal that "I sent the boat on shore after breakfast with a small tent and three armed marines to protect the articles they might procure . . . " That evening, Broughton himself went ashore. Disappointed at how few provisions his men had been able to procure, he "walked to some of the plantations, but was told there was a general scarcity over the island."

Broughton then walked a mile back to the pinnace, accompanied only by one Ni'ihauan. "I walked unmolested, meeting several of the inhabitants . . . As I had visited twice before, and many of the officers had made shooting parties in the interior without any interruption, I had not the least fear for my own safety." The next day, July 30, 1796, Broughton received some provisions from the man he assumed to be his friend on Ni'ihau, the chief "Tupararo". This 'friend' left the ship saying he had more to give them but that they must receive the rest of the provisions on shore. Broughton must have had some slight apprehension of possible risk because when he sent the cutter to take delivery, "The mate was commanded to go on shore with 2 marines properly armed, another man to barter and the boat's crew with a midshipman to remain off at a grapnel. If anything went amiss, they were to signal the ship."

In less than an hour the officer on deck informed Broughton that most of the Ni'ihau canoes, which had been close around the ship, had gone ashore. Since the weather and the ocean gave no cause for such a retreat, Broughton began to suspect something might be wrong. He gave directions to signal the shore party. At 11 A.M., in response to his signal, he saw the shore party from the 'Providence' strike the tent. Immediately after observing this Broughton heard "a firing from the boat".

At first he thought this a signal to recall those who might have strayed elsewhere on the island. Then a second signal was hoisted for the pinnace to come ashore. Without delay Captain Broughton ordered an officer with marines to go ashore with the pinnace. What they found was that tragedy had struck the original shore party.

Broughton was appalled to realize he had been persuaded by a chief he assumed friendly to send his men into a deliberate trap whose design was murder. His journal laments, "On the return of one of the boats I heard with much concern that the 2 marines were killed; and that the mate, Mr. Cowley, with the botanist, Alexander Bishop, who went to barter, had escaped with the greatest difficulty." The pinnace remained on shore, protecting the dead bodies from the Ni'ihauans "who seemed anxious to get them though they were sunk below the surf."

Broughton was astonished and indignant, for "this unhappy transaction took place without the smallest provocation on our part . . . " He and his officers agreed they must retrieve the bodies and, before proceeding to Kauai to enlist the aid of the chiefs in bringing to justice Tupararo and the other principals in "these horrid murders, we also thought it necessary to make some example on the spot."

Broughton had all the boats manned. He gave directions that the marines "should burn every house, canoe, and plantation within a mile from the beach where the boats were, and should return before sunset." The Ni'ihauans fled the beach as the approaching pinnace fired to clear the shore for landing. By now, Ni'ihau people were enough acquainted with gunfire to drop down on seeing the flash from the muskets, and then to run away. Broughton reports that "the houses were soon in flames, and 16 canoes on the beach were burnt or destroyed."

All this while, great numbers of Ni'ihauans assembled, armed with spears. Two of them had "the ill-fated marines muskets and accouterments. As our people advanced, they fled and so prevented any personal atonement for their treachery." The bodies of the two marines were retrieved from about nine feet of water and at three p.m., after Mr. Mudge left shore, the Ni'ihauans rushed to search for the corpses and "found the grapnel our people had lost in the attack."

Broughton comments that this was as unprovoked a murder as any "that has occurred in these islands." Only at this point in his account does he mention the most extraordinary circumstance that he had aboard Raheina and Timarroe, the two Ni'ihau girls rescued from Nootka by Vancouver. Raheina had asked passage for herself and her companion from Kauai. That morning, Raheina's husband, Tupararo, had lulled any suspicions Broughton might have had by sending his and Raheina's child aboard "that we might see him."

Raheina and Timarroe were evidently "much alarmed by the massacre" which had evidently been planned by Raheina's husband. The two women, relates Broughton, "desired to be sent on shore; which request we complied with, giving each a letter, begging they would entrust them to the first vessel that arrived there but upon no account to let them be seen by the Europeans at Atooi." Broughton seems to have felt that these white men, and particularly the Botany Bay escapee and deserter Hughes, were behind Tupararo's scheme to acquire additional muskets by the murder of the marines. Harking back to the naivete of his feeling of safety his first day on Ni'ihau, when he had strolled alone with a Ni'ihauan (presumably Tupararo), Broughton remarks that "the unhappy event" of the murders made him realize his experience that first safe-feeling day had been, in truth, "a fortunate escape".

News in those days traveled slowly, and sometimes not at all. Such seems to have been the case with these murders on Ni'ihau. They were not known to the next foreign visitors, who came with the same impression of friendliness and safety that Broughton had enjoyed the afternoon before his two marines were killed. Such at least is the impression gained in reading the journal of a young American, Ebenezer Townsend, Jr., who visited Ni'ihau two years after Broughton's disastrous experience.

Ebenezer Townsend was a son of New Haven, Connecticut's most affluent and successful ship builder and ship owner. The ship 'Neptune', on which young Townsend was supercargo, had been fitted out in 1795 for a sealing voyage on which the elder Townsend, a shrewd investor, planned to repeat the recent lucrative sealing voyages undertaken from Salem, Massachusetts and Providence, Rhode Island. He hired Daniel Green, a veteran shipmaster, "a strict disciplinarian and an honest man" according to Ebenezer Townsend, jr.'s journal, to command the 357-ton fast sailing ship and its crew of forty-five "young and sturdy Connecticut men".

The 'Neptune' 's three-year voyage proved profitable beyond the elder Townsend's dreams. They killed and salted ''80,000 seals, taking the furs to Canton where they were sold for $280,000. gross profit," according to young Ebenezer, who was only 25 years old at the time and doing well as supercargo of his father's ship. From Canton, the 'Neptune' was bringing an equally lucrative cargo of "tea, silks, nankeen and China ware" back to New Haven. During the 1796-1799 duration of its round the world voyage, the 'Neptune' passed through the Sandwich Islands where, in his diary, Ebenezer Townsend, jr. describes meeting John Young and Kamehameha on Owhyhee, and calling at 'Mowee', Honolulu, and 'Atooi', before making a brief stop at 'Onehow'.

His entry of the 'Neptune' 's August 30, 1798 stop at Ni'ihau reads: "One of our Indians went on shore to forward the getting of yams, which we found were scarce. I believe a month later we should have found them plenty. We have not anchored and we shall not, as we shall square away for Canton in the evening. We find the trade small at this island but generally a good island for yams. The southern part of the island looks poor but the rest appears pretty well."

Townsend describes the Hawaiians as "an active, well-made people". He comments that "most of the men, particularly the chiefs" disfigure themselves by having knocked out their front upper teeth. As to Hawaiian women, the young man of New Haven saw the *wahines* of 1798 as "very pleasing in their manners and evidently, particularly those that are young and handsome, have the same power over the men that they have in countries more civilized." He did not, however, like their "one forbidding custom of turning the hair up on the forehead and taking the color out with lime, so that there was a streak perfectly white on their forehead when the rest of the hair was very black."

In their stop at Ni'ihau neither treachery nor suspicion of it seems to have bothered Townsend and the 'Neptune'. In general, young Ebenezer's assessment was that "These islanders are neat in their persons, respect their legislators and their laws, are cheerful and obliging to each other." He adds, with the romantic nostalgia of those who view the person and life of "the noble. savage" as ideal and these Pacific Islands a utopian paradise, that "These people appear so happy that I reflect much on the subject . . . "

Turbulent Times

IN 1796 KAMEHAMEHA, who had conquered all the other islands, tried to invade Kauai and Ni'ihau. He was defeated by the rough seas and high winds of the Kauai channel where so many of his fleet of 800 war canoes were swamped and lost, that he was forced to turn back to Oahu. It was a costly disaster, occurring at the wrong time for the ambitious Kohala chief. Many of his warriors drowned. Those who swam ashore on Kauai, were – according to Hawaiian historian Samuel Kamakau – promptly put to death. Returning to Oahu, Kamehameha learned that there were rebellions against his rule fomenting on his own home island, Owhyhee, and on Maui. His determination to conquer Kauai and Ni'ihau remained strong, but circumstances forced him to spend the next few years stabilizing his control over the windward islands. Kamehameha's continuing ambition to add the leeward isles to his kingdom is well documented by various ship visitors of the time. Among these was the British ship 'Margaret', a trader out of Portsmouth England, one of the numerous vessels calling at Ni'ihau in 1802.

The 'Margaret' 's Second Officer, John Turnbull, kept a detailed journal, relating that the 'Margaret' anchored off 'Attowaie' on December 26, 1802. Kauai was the next to last stop on the trader's voyage through the Sandwich Islands. Perhaps

61

she had not taken advantage of the yams available in Honolulu, where Kamehameha, seeing how profitable a trade item this tuber was at the time, had established large plantings of yams and potatoes at three locations in and near Honolulu. Perhaps the 'Margaret''s captain thought Ni'ihau yams would prove superior in keeping qualities to those grown on Oahu. Whatever the reason, it was Ni'ihau yams with which the 'Margaret' wished to provision for the long voyage on to China.

Second Officer Turnbull writes that after the 'Margaret' had been anchored for several days at 'Attowaie', Kauai's King Kaumualii dispatched a message to 'Onehow' informing his people there of the 'Margaret''s impending visit. According to Turnbull, Kaumualii "directed them to treat us with every attention and supply our wants." The Ni'ihauans did exactly that, confirms Turnbull, "for on our making the island, the natives flocked about us, furnishing an abundance of yams at a very moderate rate. We there also laid in a small addition to our stock of salt."

In her four days anchorage at Ni'ihau the 'Margaret' took on nearly three tons of yams. During this time, though "all were eager to be admitted on board", the ship "received none but one of the king's deputies and, through the interest of this great man, two other chiefs." From these chiefs Turnbull learned that the Ni'ihauans "had but little hope of being able to withstand the attacks of their common enemy Tamahamaha" (Kamehameha). They were "stedfastly attached to their lawful king" (of Kauai) "and determined to so remain."

In an earlier stop on Maui, the 'Margaret' had witnessed the size of Kamehameha's force and later, on Oahu, had observed the magnitude of the fleet of canoes with which Kamehameha again intended to attack Kauai. It was said that Kamehameha's watchword as he prepared for this conquest was "Let us go and drink the water of Wailua, bathe in the water of Namalokama, eat the mullet that swim in Kawaimakua at Haena, wreathe ourselves with the moss of Polihale." Another time he spoke of wanting to "surf on the waves of Kauai". To rest on the fine *makaloa* mats of Ni'ihau was probably also one of his ambitions in trying to conquer these last two islands that remained free of his rule.

In June of 1803 an American trader, Captain Richard Cleveland, part-owner and supercargo of the 'Lelia Byrd' and his partner Captain William Shaler brought very special gifts to Kamehameha – the kingdom's first horses. The 'Lelia Byrd' deposited a mare and foal on Owhyhee, and another horse on Maui where the king was in residence, then sailed on to Oahu. Cleveland notes in his journal that "meeting with but partial success in procuring here a supply of yams, we left on the 5th (of July) and passed the following day lying off and on Atoui, the most western island of the group, with no success, and then bore away to the westward."

On this voyage through the islands, the 'Lelia Byrd' carried an ultimatum from Kamehameha to the ruler of Kauai and Ni'ihau. Cleveland comments that "Atoui at this time was independent of the government of Tamaahmaah from whom we were bearers of a message to the king purporting that the ambassador, which had been sent to him, together with one of equal rank, be sent to Waohoo within the space of one month acknowledging him, Tamaahmaah, as his (Kaumualii's) sovereign on penalty of a visit from all Tamaahmaah's forces."

Kaumualii did not come on board the 'Lelia Byrd' nor did anyone from the ship go ashore on Kauai. As a result, Kamehameha's message "was given to one of the European residents who promised to convey it but said it would be disregarded." As concerns this first 'ambassador' sent to Kauai by Kamehameha, Kamakau's account of the matter is that this chief was so well treated by Kaumualii, and given such lavish gifts of lands and wives that he chose not to return to Oahu.

In the spring of 1804 Kamehameha was ready to take Kaumualii's kingdom by force. A great fleet of canoes and several foreign-style ships, equipped with cannons, were gathered on Oahu, ready to launch an invasion of Kauai and Ni'ihau. This time Kamehameha sought to insure success by enlisting the favor of the gods. As special rituals were being conducted by the high priest Hewahewa, a man named Lono-hele-moa came forward to try to persuade Kamehameha to abandon his plan of conquest. Staking his life on what he was predicting, Lono-hele-moa prophesied that if Kamehameha pursued his plan of attack, before his expedition could depart a terrible pestilence would strike his warriors and himself.

In one of those inexplicable coincidences that are impossible to explain rationally, this prophesy was accurate. Before the great fleet could depart, an epidemic of one of the new foreign diseases struck Oahu. The pestilence may have been cholera, or possibly bubonic plague. It proved fatal to hundreds of Kamehameha's people – chiefs and commoners alike. The great Kamehameha himself went down with the disease and for a time his life hung in the balance.

Eighteen months later when Capt. Cleveland's partner William Shaler brought the hurricane-battered 'Lelia Byrd' back to the islands, Kamehameha had not yet given up on attempting armed conquest if diplomatic overtures should fail to win him sovereignty over the leeward islands. As Shaler anchored in Honolulu harbor that September of 1805, his urgent request of Kamehameha was that the monarch take over the 'Lelia Byrd'. Shaler's idea was that the King's carpenters could repair and refurbish the vessel in order to provide naval support to any future invasion of Kauai. What Shaler asked in return for the 'Lelia Byrd' was a 45-ton schooner then being built by Kamehameha's carpenters. The new schooner was a far smaller vessel than 'Lelia Byrd' but it would be large enough for Shaler to send his assistant on with his and Cleveland's cargo while he himself waited for passage on the 'Atahualpa'.

Kamehameha was evidently much impressed by William Shaler for he put at Shaler's disposal a commodious grass house and servants for his sojourn in Honolulu. Their close and confidential relationship is recorded by Shaler in his journal. "What particularly occupied him" (Kamehameha) "at present was the desire of reducing Attooai, the leewardmost of the group, which had not yet fallen under his dominion." Shaler pointed out to Kamehameha that Kauai and Ni'ihau, "being so far to the leeward, there is considerable risk in an expedition against it, as a miscarriage would be attended with almost total ruin on account of the difficulty of returning so far to windward."

This caution might have had some effect on Kamehameha's thoughts for Shaler continues, "He has frequently assured me that his ambition would be satisfied with the king of Attooai's acknowledging him as sovereign and paying him an annual tribute. However this may be, he – like all ambitious men – is determined to have no rival and is making great preparations for the invasion of that island. My ship, when repaired and equipped, will give great respectability to his naval forces."

Until the new schooner which he was giving Shaler in return for the 'Lelia Byrd' should be completed, Kamehameha stored Shaler's valuable cargo of furs and specie in the royal warehouse. No wonder Shaler's journal gives such a positive account of this chief!

As Shaler was about to leave Honolulu on the 'Atahualpa' he was informed by one of Kamehameha's emissaries returning from Kauai of a plot by Kaumualii. The king of Kauai planned to approach Oahu in a foreign vessel, one of such imposing appearance that Kamehameha would come to greet it offshore, as was his custom. Once the unsuspecting Kamehameha should come on board, Kaumualii intended to kill or kidnap him. This disclosure, remarks Shaler, gave "a show of justice to Kamehameha's determination of invading the island."

While Shaler was Kamehameha's guest, the king asked his opinion of his invasion plans, "intending," says Shaler, "that I inform Tamoree of them, hoping through any means to induce him to submit to Tamaihamaiha's terms." In a meeting of chiefs following Kamehameha's demonstration to Shaler of his immediate force of warriors and musketeers, Shaler advised that as to "the war of Atooai", Kamehameha should "use every means to terminate it in an honorable manner by negotiation." Many of Kamehameha's chiefs agreed with this. When the time came for Shaler's departure, Kamehameha presented him with a gift of two beautiful feather cloaks. Shaler's counsel of negotiation must have had some effect for Kamehameha requested him "to use my influence with Tamoree to settle on honorable terms."

Shaler left Oahu on the 'Atahualpa' October 2nd, 1805 and reached Kauai on the evening of the fourth. A ship riding at anchor nearby turned out to be Kaumualii's. Shaler learned that "Tamoree" himself was aboard. This ruling chief of Kauai and Ni'ihau whom Kamakau describes as a 'religious chief' was, says Shaler, "terribly alarmed at first and refused to come on board, but after some hesitation he paid us a visit at about 8 o'clock. After Captain Adams settled with him about the supplies he

wanted, I broached the business of my mission and represented to him the folly of making any resistance to Tamaihamaiha
and the still greater folly of expecting to amuse him by idle tales
of submission to which his conduct constantly gave the lie and
furnished Tamaihamaiha with a pretense for treating him as an
enemy. I stated to him the terms on which he might have peace."

Shaler considered his mission successful for "Tamoree
seemed impressed." He asked Shaler to write a letter to
Kamehameha, a letter which Kaumualii's emissaries would
deliver to Honolulu. In this letter Kaumualii said he agreed to
whatever terms Tamaihamaiha would dictate that would be
commensurate with Kaumualii's honor and personal safety.
Shaler added his own postscript, describing Kaumualii's
'humility' and requesting Kamehameha "to attribute his past
conduct to bad counsel and to deal favorably with him."

Unfortunately there is no evidence this letter was ever sent.
Tension between the two rulers remained high, with Kame-
hameha still not convinced of the feasibility of negotiating
his demands. In 1806, a year after Shaler's counsel to gain
Kaumualii's kingdom by negotiation rather than conquest, trader
Amasa Delano wrote in his journal that Kamehameha was
continuing to contemplate an armed attack on Kauai and
Ni'ihau.

In July of 1807 Isaac Iselin, supercargo of the ship 'Maryland'
relates that his ship carried an ambassador with dispatches from
Kamehameha for Kaumualii. Iselin provides a concise description of Kaumualii, whom the American traders also called King
George. The ruling chief of Kauai and Ni'ihau was, wrote Iselin,
"a fine looking man of about thirty with an excellent European
countenance and his whole deportment more that of a French-
man than a South Sea Islander."

During the next three years there were intermittent
exchanges of gifts and messages between the two rulers. It was
a New Englander, Captain Nathan Winship, one of the early
sandalwood traders, who finally managed to persuade Kaumualii that acknowledging Kamehameha's sovereignty and sending annual tribute would be in Kaumualii's best interests – as
well as that of the traders who were doing business with both
kingdoms. Winship urged Kaumualii to negotiate face to face

with Kamehameha on Oahu. To demonstrate his confidence that Kaumualii would come to no harm at the hands of Kamehameha, Winship left his first mate on Kauai as a hostage, directing that if anything should happen to Kaumualii, the mate would be put to death.

On the trip to Oahu, Kaumualii and his retinue traveled on Winship's vessel, the 'Albatross'. Off Oahu, Kamehameha came out with an entourage of canoes to greet them. The Oahu canoes were filled with high chiefs and priests, resplendent in red feather cloaks. Aboard the 'Albatross' Kaumualii was dressed in magnificent traditional chiefly garb while Captain Winship and his officers were in full dress uniform. Samuel Kamakau says in his account of this meeting that as Kamehameha came on board, Kaumualii grasped his hand saying, "Here I am. Is it face up or face down?"

When Kamehameha protested this inference, Kaumualii announced, "This is my gift at our meeting – the land of Kauai and its chiefs, its men great and small. From mountain to sea, all above and below, and myself to be yours." In what must have been a magnanimous gesture difficult for him to make Kamehameha refused this offer. "I shall not accept your land, not the least portion of your domain." All that he asked was Kaumualii's acknowledgment of his sovereignty and, in addition, the promise that when Kamehameha's successor, his young son Liholiho should visit Kauai, he be favorably received. Kaumualii agreed to both these conditions.

As he went ashore on Oahu, Kaumualii was warned by Kamehameha's trusted foreign adviser, the Englishman Isaac Davis, that some of the chiefs were plotting to poison him. But at the feasting that followed it was Isaac Davis whom the vengeful chiefs poisoned that April of 1810. After several days as the guest of Kamehameha, Kaumualii returned to Kauai, laden with gifts from his host. From then on governance of Kauai and Ni'ihau by their beloved Kaumualii seemed to the inhabitants of those islands to continue much as before. Outwardly Kaumualii ruled as if he were still independent but this chief whom Turnbull of the 'Margaret' considered far superior in every way to Kamehameha was not easy in his mind about the future.

Foreigners, he had learned, had different ruling chiefs who warred against each other for territory and power just as the ruling chiefs of the various islands of Hawaii had always done. The British King seemed to favor Kamehameha. The Americans, Kaumualii had observed, were interested only in trade and profit. The chance to duck under the protection of the ruling chief of all the Russians, the Czar, was welcomed by Kaumualii when an adventurer named Georg Scheffer, who claimed he represented the Russian government, arrived on Kauai in 1815.

It made little difference to Kaumualii that Kamehameha had banished the intrepid Dr. Scheffer from Oahu. Scheffer, who was from Baranov's Russian American Company of Alaska, was furnished with land on which to build two Russian forts on Kauai as well as extensive acreage near the site of the fort at Hanalei. Scheffer's promise, and Kaumualii's fond hope, was that with the aid of the Czar not only could the Kauai chief regain his independence but might be aided in conquering Kamehameha and making the entire kingdom his own.

It all proved a fantasy. On his 1816 visit to Hawaii, Lt. Otto von Kotzebue of the Russian naval vessel 'Rurick' disclaimed any Russian ambitions in Hawaii, denounced Scheffer as an imposter, and recommended his prompt deportation. The Russian flag which had flown above the two forts on Kauai was lowered just as American traders, with whom Kaumualii did a brisk business in exchanging sandalwood for foreign ships and goods, threatened to shoot the flags down.

Scheffer was long gone and Kaumualii's ambitions to break with Kamehameha dissipated by 1819 when Kamehameha died. With the accession of Kamehameha's son Liholiho (Kamehameha II), came the most abrupt and devastating of all changes in Hawaiian society. The power of the old gods, the power of kapu was challenged by the new king– successfully. For women and commoners this signalled unprecedented freedoms. It was Liholiho's mother, Queen Keopuolani, and his father's favorite wife, the powerful Queen Kaahumanu, who persuaded Kamehameha II to himself break the most rigid of all kapus, and do so publicly.

By sitting down to eat with his mother and Kaahumanu, by watching them eat food previously prohibited to women and by himself eating forbidden foods, prepared by women, Liholiho effectively ended the stranglehold of kapu on himself and his people. To modern men and women this does not sound like the radical act of defiance which it was in that time and culture. Even the high priest Hewahewa took part in breaking the kapu, sending messengers throughout the kingdom to announce what had been done. With few exceptions, from Ni'ihau to Hawaii Island the people greeted this overthrow of the old gods by destroying ancient temples and burning or throwing into the sea their sacred images of stone, wood, and feathers.

For almost a year, until the arrival of the first company of Christian missionaries at the end of March, 1820, Hawaiians lived without fear or guilt, free from all the old prohibitions such as that of death to the commoner who did not prostrate himself before even the shadow of an *alii*, or death to men and women who ate together or to women who ate certain forbidden foods.

To the American missionaries arriving off the Big Island port of Kawaihae on March 30, 1820, the news of the Hawaiians' break with what the pious New England protestants referred to as 'heathen idolatry' seemed a sure sign their mission had been directed to the right place at the right time. From Kawaihae their ship, the 'Thaddeus', proceeded to Kailua-Kona, where Kamehameha II was in residence. Their arrival was not welcomed by the king, whose French advisor urged him not to let the missionaries ashore. Hopefully, the weary company on the 'Thaddeus', whose sea voyage from Boston had taken six months, waited aboard for several very long hot days.

It was not their Christianization of his islands that Kamehameha II feared so much as the Americanization that his French advisor warned him might happen. And, of course, without that being the mission's intent, such did come to pass.

Among the passengers on the 'Thaddeus' was one of Kaumualii's sons, George Kaumualii – also known as Humehume. He had spent several years in the United States, serving for a time in the U.S. Navy and lately attending the Foreign Mission School in Cornwall, Connecticut. George Kaumualii was a personable, bright young man who entertained the missionaries on their long voyage from Boston to Hawaii by singing and playing the bass viol. He was much enthused about returning home, and visibly annoyed by the delays and hesitation on the part of Liholiho and his advisor, Jean Ricord, in allowing any of the missionaries – or himself – to leave Kona once they were allowed to land.

It was May before the 'Thaddeus' could take George on to Kauai. As payment for his son's passage from Boston, King Kaumualii provisioned the brig for its voyage on to Canton and, in addition, supplied the captain with sandalwood in an amount worth one thousand dollars. Kaumualii had no way of knowing that for all seventeen missionaries, and their three Hawaiian assistants, the group rate charged for the passage had been only $2500. For Kaumualii, anything was worth the return of a beloved son.

George Kaumualii did not return to Kauai alone. With great enthusiasm, promising them a far warmer welcome from his father than Liholiho had given them, he brought with him two couples from the mission company. King Kaumualii was delighted to have Mr. and Mrs. Samuel Ruggles, Ruggles' sister Lucia Holman and her physician husband, Dr. Thomas Holman on Kauai. He gave them a large tract of land with grass houses at Hanapepe. One would think that with all this, George Kaumualii would continue as a model convert and son. However, he proceeded to dismay both his missionary friends and his father by becoming an alcoholic. Within a few months, he was completely estranged from his father and from the missionaries. He married a daughter of Isaac Davis, the English 'chief' who had presumably saved Kaumualii's life in 1810. With her, and a retinue of one hundred commoners, 'Prince George' retired to a valley where he spent much of his time drinking gin.

This did not alter his father's relationship with the missionaries. Mr. Ruggles, a schoolmaster, was so well liked by King Kaumualii that the people of Kauai and Ni'ihau called him 'Keike o Kaumualii' – the child of Kaumualii. There is no record as to when the missionaries first visited Ni'ihau, but with the frequent coming and going of Ni'ihauans to Kauai, it can be presumed that Ni'ihau soon knew about the new religion, and the book that seemed to the Hawaiians to be the magic key to the new god.

Despite the king's cordial reception of them, it must have been a frustrating time for the Ruggles, and it was indeed a frustrating experience for the Holmans who only stayed on Kauai for eight months. Not only the language but the customs and the culture were foreign to the two American couples. The naturalness of the sexuality displayed by the Hawaiians shocked the puritanical missionaries. The climate was hot, humid, and the rain showers at Hanapepe often torrential. There was as yet no written Hawaiian language and so no vehicle by which to teach the art of reading and writing as Ruggles yearned to do.

In 1821, about a year after the missionaries settled on Kauai, Rev. and Mrs. Hiram Bingham came from Honolulu to visit the new station which the Holmans' successors, Rev. and Mrs. Samuel Whitney had established. In his book, *My 21 Years in the Sandwich Islands,* Hiram Bingham wrote that on his first visit he "found the station there (at Waimea, Kauai) prosperous". He baptized the children of Mrs. Whitney and Mrs. Ruggles, met King Kaumualii and "encouraged the king whom I found teachable and friendly. As I proposed to return from Kauai to Honolulu, Kaumualii took out a handkerchief, bound my hands, and drew me near his side – thus emphatically signifying his wish if not his purpose to detain me as his missionary."

Comparing Kaumualii's commitment with the potential and interest of Liholiho, Kaahumanu, and other prominent chiefs, Bingham judged Kaumualii as exceeding all others in his desire to learn the new religion, and to be able to read and write. Rev. Whitney reported that Kaumualii was also amenable to the new tabus of Christianity, for when Whitney asked the king to not allow the dancing of *hulahula* on the Sabbath, Kaumualii immediately pronounced the Sabbath as a day when *hulahula* was not to be performed on Kauai or Ni'ihau.

In the summer of 1821 Kaumualii informed the missionaries that he was sending the 'Becket' – a brig which he had recently purchased with sandalwood– on a trip to Tahiti, the Society Islands and the Georgias to 'promote friendly intercourse' with those fellow Polynesians. Kaumualii suggested that two of the missionaries might wish to take this voyage, to consult with Huahine based Rev. William Ellis and other London Missionary Society veterans who had been most successful in their

Christianizing endeavors in Tahiti and its adjacent islands of the South Pacific.

The two selected to make the trip were Mr. Ruggles and the Rev. Hiram Bingham. Bingham prudently consulted Liholiho and the two most powerful *alii* in his court – Kalanimoku and Kaahumanu – as to this plan. To his relief they approved of the trip, asking him to deliver gifts from them to Pomare, the ruler of Tahiti. With these in his luggage, Bingham left Oahu for Kauai on July 8, 1821. Also a passenger on this short interisland sail was Queen Kaahumanu's sister, a high-ranking chiefess whom Kaumualii welcomed by having his grass houses, and the area in front of them spread with "the best Ni'ihau figured mats."

Final preparations to leave for Tahiti were under way when John Coffin Jones, an American trader who also served as the United States Commercial Agent in Honolulu, came to Kauai to dissuade Kaumualii from going forward with the voyage. The Boston firm which Jones represented held promissory notes owed them by Kaumualii for ships and cargo. These were to be paid off within the year by delivery of sandalwood. Jones, expressing his concern that Kaumualii was growing old and 'might pop off' at any time leaving his debts unpaid, argued against the Tahiti venture. He managed to convince Kaumualii that the 'Becket' 's proposed voyage would encourage British speculators and traders to come to Hawaii. This, Jones argued, would likely be the result of Bingham and Ruggles making contact with London Missionary Society men like Rev. Ellis. The American traders to whom Kaumualii was deeply indebted would not look with favor on this, Jones warned.

Bingham was dismayed and disgusted by such misguidance on the part of America's representative in the islands, but neither he nor Ruggles could persuade Kaumualii to ignore Jones' advice. At this opportune moment Liholiho arrived, having impulsively made up his mind on a trip from Honolulu to Waialua, Oahu, to change the destination of his overloaded, leaky vessel and a royal party which included the chief Boki and chiefess Liliha. Liholiho's unexpected arrival on Kauai on July 22, 1821 did not in the least alarm Kaumualii who again made the generous offer of his kingdom and all in it. As had his father, Liholiho magnanimously refused, saying, "I have not come to take your islands." The astute Kaumualii immediately dispatched a schooner and a brig to Oahu to inform Kalanimoku and Kaahumanu that Liholiho was safe in Waimea, and that any who wished to join him would be sumptuously entertained.

The two kings relaxed on fine Ni'ihau mats, feasting and being entertained for the next several days until Liholiho's five favorite wives joined him from Oahu. After they arrived Kaumualii took the royal entourage on a forty day tour of Kauai. Bingham and Ruggles made their own exploration of the island at the same time, sometimes and at some places rejoining Kaumualii and Liholiho to travel by canoe. No specific mention is made as to whether, on this grand tour, they also visited Ni'ihau.

On Sunday, September 16th, Liholiho and Kaumualii each went out sailing on their respective vessels, anchoring that evening at Waimea where Liholiho invited Kaumualii to come aboard his yacht, 'Pride of Hawaii'. All unsuspecting, Kaumualii did so. To his chagrin, about nine o'clock that evening, 'Pride of Hawaii' suddenly raised sail and left for Oahu. The Kauai people were stunned, hearing what had happened. The following morning Rev. Bingham, who was in Waimea, recorded the reaction of a chief there who sorrowfully exclaimed, "Farewell to our King – we shall see him no more."

The chief was wrong. Kauai did see its beloved Kaumualii again – but under far different circumstances. On October 9, 1821, he became the husband of Queen Kaahumanu who further cemented her ties to the ruling family of Kauai by also marrying Kaumualii's handsome, seven-foot tall son Kealiiahonui.

In his *Kauai, The Separate Kingdom* Edward Joesting writes that in Honolulu Kaumualii "appeared in a black velvet coat and pantaloons, a woolen waistcoat and white silk stockings and carried a gold watch". Little wonder, comments Joesting, that "Kaahumanu enjoyed showing off her newest trophy as she traveled around the islands. Courteous and dignified in manner, Kaumualii added quality and prestige to Kaahumanu's entourage."

More than any other concrete act of ritual, ceremony, or treaty, this marriage signalled the acquisition of Kaumualii and

his kingdom by the Kamehamehas. Evidence of the tacit assumption that all the islands were now absolutely their domain is that in 1822 Kaahumanu and Kaumualii made an expedition to Nihoa, the small uninhabited islet beyond Ni'ihau. This was a sentimental journey for Kaahumanu, whose ancestor Kawelo-a-Mahuna had composed a mele mentioning that islet:
  "The rain cloud of Kona rises.
  It rises over Nihoa,
  Beyond the base of Lehua
  It pours down and floods the streams."
The mele of Hiiaka also mentioned Nihoa:
  "It rises over Nihoa
  Beyond the base of Lehua."
  On their trip to Nihoa, the royal couple traveled in a foreign vessel piloted by Captain William Sumner, a bluff Englishman who had long resided in the islands. Having 'rediscovered' Nihoa, Kaahumanu made the proud proclamation that it was now annexed to the kingdom of Hawaii – a sign she no longer even considered Kauai and Ni'ihau as separate, or different – an assumption to which Kaumualii must by now have become resigned.
  Not so his son George. In May 1824 Kaumualii died, bequeathing his kingdom to Liholiho. That summer George Kaumualii led a rebellion to try to regain control over his father's two islands. His forces were defeated by Kalanimoku and veteran warriors from Oahu and Maui. The affair was brief but bloody, a disaster for George Kaumualii's supporters, most of whom were killed. He himself, together with his wife and child was captured and exiled to Oahu where he died at the age of 29.
  Even those chiefs from Kauai and Ni'ihau who had not taken part in the uprising, and those who were on Maui at the time for the funeral of Kaumualii, suffered as if they too had been part of the rebellion. All Kauai chiefs were stripped of their lands. Kauai and Ni'ihau were parceled out among chiefs whom Kamakau describes as "the loafers and hangers-on of Oahu and Maui".
  The rebellion took place while Liholiho and his Queen Kamamalu were on a trip to visit the King of England. It was a trip from which they never returned, for in London, both

became ill with the measles and died. When this sad news reached Hawaii, Liholiho's young brother became Kamehameha III. Until the boy monarch became of age, his *kuhina nui* or regent, Kaahumanu, was the real ruler of the eight-island kingdom. The dependent status of Kauai and Ni'ihau was emphasized by her to foreign visitors as is evidenced by the journal of Captain F.W. Beechey of His Majesty's ship 'Blossom' who "touched at Owhyhee to deliver the despatches and packages addressed by the Foreign Office to His Majesty's consul at that island to procure refreshments and water." On May 31st, 1826, Beechey records:

"We took our leave of Woahoo and proceeded to Oneehow, the westernmost island of the Sandwich group, famous for its yams, fruit, and mats. This island is the property of the king and it is necessary previous to proceeding thither to make a bargain with the authorities at Woahoo for what may be required, who in that case send an agent to see the agreement strictly fulfilled. On the 1st of June we hauled in a small sandy bay on the western side of the island, the same in which Vancouver anchored when he was there on a visit of a similar nature to our own, and I am sorry to say that like him we were disappointed in the expected supplies, not from their scarcity but in consequence of the indolence of the natives."

Beechey goes on to describe the island: "Oneehow is comparatively low and with the exception of the fruit trees" (probably breadfruit trees) "which are carefully cultivated, it is destitute of wood. The soil is too dry to produce taro but on that account it is well adapted to the growth of yams, etc. which are very excellent and of an enormous size. There is but one place in this bay where the boat of a man of war can effect a landing with safety when the sea sets into the bay, which is a very common occurrence; this is on its northern shore behind a small reef of rocks that lies a little way off the beach, and even here it is necessary to guard against sunken rocks; off the western point these breakers extend a mile and a half."

Of the Ni'ihauans Beechey remarks: "The natives are a darker race than those of Woahoo and reminded us strongly of the inhabitants of Bow Island. With the exception of the house of the Earee" (*alii*) "all the huts were small, low, and hot; and the one which we occupied was so close that we were obliged to make a hole in its side to admit the sea breeze. We took on as many yams as the natives could collect before sun-set and then shaped our course for Kamschatka."

Pule and Palapala

PRAYER *(PULE)* AND the new magic of an Hawaiian alphabet *(palapala)* soon spread even to remote Ni'ihau. The epidemic of religious fervor was touched off by a number of chiefs – the most prominent among whom was the Regent Kaahumanu.

After Rev. Bingham's wife Sybil nursed Kaahumanu through a serious illness, the powerful chiefess – convinced her life had been saved by the prayers of the missionaries– became an ardent Christian. It was at Queen Kaahumanu's urging that everyone in the kingdom –including the people of Ni'ihau– began to follow the new foreign ways, learning to read, observing the Sabbath, worshipping God and obeying his laws. George Kaumualii's fellow passengers on the 'Thaddeus' had not anticipated such speedy or easy success. Only five short years after their arrival, Hawaii was transformed into a Christian nation. Conversion of spoken into written Hawaiian was equally rapid.

By 1822 the first Hawaiian primer was run off on the mission house press in Honolulu. It was written Hawaiian that was to alter the spoken language in a profound and permanent way. The problem for the mission committee charged with devising a 'standard' form of written Hawaiian was that from island to island the pronunciation varied from the quite Tahitian inflections of Ni'ihau and Kauai to the more Marquesan intonation of the island of Hawaii. T and K, L and R were the thorniest phonetic issues for the missionaries to settle. In 1826, by the democratic vote of conscientious New Englanders, Tamaahmaah became Kamehameha, Tauai was from thence forward written as Kauai and Mauna Roa, the massive volcano on Owhyhee, came to be spelled, and later, pronounced Mauna Loa.

At first adults were the only pupils in the schools set up by mission stations like that of the Reverend Samuel Whitney whose territory included all of Kauai and Ni'ihau. At first parents said their children were too wild to learn to read, but beginning in 1829 a particular effort was made by the missionaries to also gather the children into schools – an effort in which Ni'ihau students were sometimes not too eager to participate. Their school houses were grass huts, as were school houses everywhere in the kingdom. On Kauai, surf boards often did double duty as desks and this may well have been the case on Ni'ihau too.

On his rare visits to inspect their schools and hold church services for them, Ni'ihauans gave a warm welcome to Reverend Samuel Whitney, a native of Branford, Connecticut and his wife Mercy. In addition to teaching school and conducting Sunday services for the large population of his two-island station, Whitney also had to train teachers for the new schools opening everywhere and conduct annual examinations of all the pupils on each island. His annual reports reflect his frustration at being unable to adequately serve the people of Ni'ihau.

In 1833 Whitney wrote: "This small island lies 20 miles west of Kauai. The want of good water, the occasional famines when the people are obliged to leave and the sparse population seem to exclude the hope that a foreign missionary will be comfortably and usefully settled among them. There are on that Island 1,079 inhabitants scattered over a seacoast of 40 miles of dry and barren country. Waimea is rather nearer than any of the other stations, though Hanalei is almost equally accessible and the island could be occasionally visited by a Missionary from these stations."

In his 1833 report he lists ten schools on Ni'ihau. They were of two types: *pi a pa* for those who could not read and a superior kind of school for those who had already learned this magical art. At the more advanced schools on Ni'ihau pupils continued to study reading but were, in addition, taught geography and arithmetic. They were also expected to memorize one Bible verse each day.

In Whitney's Protestant Christian view the worst threat to the spiritual welfare of Ni'ihauans came when, at the close of a period of severe persecution of all Catholics and their Hawaiian converts, religious freedom was enforced by the ultimatum of a French man-o-war and Catholicism was permitted throughout the Hawaiian Kingdom. In his *History of Catholic Missions in Hawaii* Yzendoorn reports that Father Arsenius Walsh, an Irishman who was a member of the French Congregation of Sacred Hearts, arrived at Koloa Kauai on December 22, 1841. In his first few months on Kauai, he established several Catholic congregations, and at Koloa, the mission of St. Raphael the Archangel. According to Yzendoorn, Father Walsh often "cast desirous glances on the neighboring island of Ni'ihau, which on his visits to Hanapepe he could discern on the western horizon as a sharp outlined cloud hanging on the water."

Ni'ihau by then already had a few Catholic converts – a development that much alarmed Reverend Whitney. In his 1841 Mission Station Report Whitney writes, "it is with feelings of deep regret and concern that I often think of a part of our field (the island of Ni'ihau) as almost entirely excluded from my personal labors, and never more so than just now. Owing to the fact that one of the Catholic converts, a woman of extensive family relations and influence has been at that Island scattering Catholic books and setting up a school among her relatives."

The following year Whitney was still distraught over the situation on Ni'ihau which "though included in this station, is but seldom visited and has not received that attention and labour which the wants of the people demand. It is separated from us by a somewhat dangerous channel of Sixteen miles in width which is seldom passed except by natives in canoes. It has a population of one thousand and upwards, among them are nine schools in which are 214 children." Whitney does not make clear how many of these might now be Catholic schools and Catholic students. He remarks only that "Within the past year, the Catholics have gained a footing there. They have a native teacher, who is said to be very zealous, and gaining quite a number of converts to the Catholic faith. It is with weeping eyes that we often look toward the rugged cliffs of that Island and ask what can be done for the wretched inhabitants? With the exception of these on Ni'ihau, there are no Catholics in the district of Waimea."

Towards the end of July, 1842 Father Walsh heard that several canoes were about to depart for Ni'ihau. He hurried to Waimea, where the canoes were waiting, and there called on Kealiia-honui, the son of Kaumualii who, like his father, had been taken as a husband by the late Queen Kaahumanu. After Kaahuma-nu's death, Kealiiahonui had returned to Waimea where he lived quietly, a pious Protestant. When Father Walsh told Kealiiahonui of his plan to travel with the canoes to Ni'ihau, the aging chief requested him to "advise the children there to frequent the schools." When Walsh was informed that Kealiiahonui meant specifically and exclusively the protestant schools, the fiesty Irish priest said he would do all in his power to persuade the children not to attend them!

Walsh arrived on Ni'ihau on July 26, 1842. A convert there, having been informed that the priest planned this visit, had ready a small chapel and presbytery. In it, five days later, Father Walsh celebrated the first Mass ever held on Ni'ihau with, reports Yzendoorn, "a considerable congregation". Walsh remained on Ni'ihau for nearly one month, during which time he baptized more than one hundred men and women. His proselytizing roused the ire of one of Ni'ihau's devout Protestants, a man named Apela Tahitiae, a tax assessor, teacher, and school inspec-tor who also served as a judge. Father Walsh particularly offend-ed this dignitary by taking one of the Catholic converts, Kamaunu, to Kauai for a "fairer trial" – presumably by a Catholic judge.

The reports of Walsh's visit to Ni'ihau so distressed Reverend Whitney that in October he went there himself to see the extent of Catholic proselytism. Whitney spent a week on the island, writing in his annual station report that "I held a protracted meet-ing which was well attended; but the prospects of the people on that Island are exceedingly dark. They are ignorant in the extreme and almost destitute of the means of instruction. The Catholics are rushing in upon them, and leading them by the scores into the delusions of the Man of Sin." This reference was probably to the Pope, although it may have alluded to Walsh himself.

In his 1842 visit to Ni'ihau, Samuel Whitney was also distressed by the condition of the schools there, feeling that they were "very indifferently kept". He is again somewhat vague as to how many schools are on Ni'ihau. "Eight or ten" his report states, but he does not mention how many of these are Catholic schools. He was in a much more optimistic mood when he visited Ni'ihau the following year. After his week's visit there in 1843, Whitney records that he is "delighted with the evidence I saw of the Spirit of God among the people." He had heard rumours before his 1844 visit that several weeks earlier Walsh had again been on Ni'ihau and that a majority of Ni'ihauans had been baptized in the Catholic faith. Whitney was relieved to find that the rumours he heard at Waimea had been greatly exaggerated. "On strict inquiry I learned he had drawn away about 140, including the children of 3 schools which he had quite broken up."

After Whitney returned to Waimea in 1844, loyal Protestants on Ni'ihau sent word to him that some twenty or thirty of these defecting students, and their teacher, had returned to the Protestant fold. Whitney's assessment of the situation was that "There may be about one in ten of the inhabitants of Ni'ihau who profess to be followers of the Pope; but they know little or nothing of the Romish faith. They are in bad savor with the bulk of the people on account of their immoralities, and unless they have a priest to guide them, there is not much danger they will increase."

Quite unaware that he is echoing the distrust felt by Father Walsh, Reverend Whitney blames the deteriorating conditions on that much maligned *kahukula*, Apela Tahitiae, who in his role as judge on Ni'ihau had been challenged by Father Walsh. In his 1844 station report Whitney repeats his fears as to the inroads of "the Papists" on Ni'ihau if someone from the Protestant Mission is not stationed there "immediately". He alleges that "Most of those who have gone to the papists have been driven to them by the wild and wicked doings of our *Kahukula* and his agents in oppressing and robbing the people." Whitney attributes this sad state of affairs to the "present School Laws under which this has taken place."

On his 1845 visit to examine the pupils of the Ni'ihau schools, Whitney was accompanied by a young visitor from Honolulu, Gorham Gilman, who recorded his impressions in a 75 page handwritten manuscript. "Rustications of Kauai and Niihau" – a treasure that has fortunately been preserved in the library of the Hawaii Mission Children's Society and Hawaiian Historical Society. Gilman's account illuminates the changes on Ni'ihau since Turnbull's visit in the 'Margaret', some forty years earlier.

"Makaika", as young Gilman signs his manuscript, had a second companion on the trip, a Mr. Tobey who is described only as a coffee planter from Kauai. On arrival, Gilman and Tobey accompanied Reverend Whitney to a high point on Ni'ihau from which they could see "only a few patches of sugar cane and yams. Descending we walked through the plantations of the people but everything bore the marks of the drought of which the people were complaining." All three visitors were eager to buy the famous *makaloa* mats of Ni'ihau but much to their disappointment they called at several houses and found only a few inferior mats for which the Ni'ihauans were asking what Gilman considered "exorbitant prices".

There were, observed Gilman, no large trees on Ni'ihau – at least none that he saw. He found the houses of the Ni'ihau-ans not only small but "most appear to be very old and uncomfortable. The dogs and pigs consider they have equal rights to them." At the examination of school pupils held by Reverend Whitney, Gilman described the children as "all neatly and well dressed. They appeared cheerful and happy. Some with their parents' clothes on which troubled them some. Others with the pretty native *pa'u* or petticoat of vari-colored tapa."

In 1845 the church was the largest building on Ni'ihau, and then as now situated in a village of some 14-16 houses. A small Catholic chapel was on a nearby hill. Eager to buy 'curiosities' young Gilman pursued his quest for *makaloa* mats. He was taken to a cave where there was a very large mat being woven "for the use of some one of the nobility. It is several yards long and the width in proportion and will be a rich specimen of native work, the figures being neat and regularly worked in."

While Reverend Whitney was attending to his mission duties, Gilman and Mr. Tobey walked on to Keawanui. On the way they saw no houses "and nothing of interest but several shallow water holes containing water so green and brackish it would be very hard to drink." At Keawanui they observed a wedding and then, "resuming our walk we came to the remains of an *heiau* or temple – one of the latest built and so in good preservation. It was the dwelling place of 'Kihawahine', a powerful goddess. The *heiau* was about 150 ft. in length, 10 ft. high, and 10 ft. wide." Their exploration of the island had taken all day. "At about sunset we arrived at the last village, Lehua, at the end of the island from which we hoped to take our departure."

The three visitors spent the night in the schoolhouse of that village. They got little rest for the place was full of fleas. They had hoped to travel on for a brief visit to Kaula, the Bird Island where the Ni'ihauans went at certain seasons to get birds and feathers but high surf cancelled this plan. When the party returned to Waimea, Gilman made his assessment that "Niihau is the most out of the way and least visited of the Hawaiian Islands. The people are not so good looking as those of some of the windward islands. The schools we saw were very good and the scholars appeared well." But, like Reverend Whitney, he was convinced that "the introduction of Catholicism has made a bad tendency among them." There were, he records, about 150 Catholics then on Ni'ihau.

The Rowell Affair

SOON AFTER HIS trip to Ni'ihau with young Gilman Samuel Whitney became seriously ill. He went to Lahainaluna, Maui for treatment and died there on December 15, 1845. His widow, Mercy Whitney, carried on the work of the mission until Reverend George Berkeley Rowell, a member of the 10th Company of Protestant Missionaries, arrived in Waimea with his wife and two young children. Both the Rowells were from New Hampshire, and had come out to Hawaii in 1842.

George Rowell was a handsome personable man, thirty-one years old when he was appointed to succeed Samuel Whitney. Like his predecessor, Rowell was highly popular with the Hawaiians. In 1847, he made his first visit to Ni'ihau, staying there for one week – a visit that came somewhat later than that of a foreign ship which, a letter from the Minister of Interior to the Tax Assessor on Ni'ihau informed that agent in February, 1847, "has permission to visit Niihau". The Captain "has permission to buy food but none of the sailors are to remain on shore nor is the Captain to take any natives on board; no women are to go on board."

Foreign ship visitors to the island were decreasing as the years went by. Perhaps this was due to yams and water being intermittently scarce there or perhaps the nuisance of obtaining a permit from the government to stop there dissuaded ship captains. The occasion of a foreign visitor was still common enough however, so that Rowell sees no need to mention this particular ship in his station report. Nor does he mention the changes in land tenure that began with the Great *Mahele,* the land reform process that had been initiated by the King the year before the Rowells' assignment to the Waimea station.

In September of 1848 Rowell spent another week on Ni'ihau, noting of this visit that "With the death of their veteran (Whitney) and greatly beloved and lamented former pastor, the interest of many of the people in the ministrations of the Gospel died also. Some seemed to have been seized by a kind of desperation and rushed again into many of their vile practices and fooleries and even some members of the church became entangled in them."

The great measles epidemic of 1849 prevented Rowell from making a visit to Ni'ihau during that year, for he could not find a Hawaiian well enough to man his canoe. On his October 1850 trip he notes "a larger congregation assembled on the Sabbath to hear the word than had ever before been known. This was owing to large numbers of Catholics who rushed in and filled the house to overflowing. No part of my audience appeared more interested and attentive than they. In travelling, too, about the island, no part of the population more cordially welcomed me to their houses and to their hospitalities, than the catholics. At the present time both of the catholic schools on Niihau are disbanded for want of competent teachers. The schools generally in the field have been prosperous with the exception of the painful fact that the number of children in the schools is yearly diminishing."

In his 1851 station report Rowell rejoices that "The progress of popery in this field the past year has not been perceptible. On Ni'ihau, which has been its stronghold, it has rather waned than otherwise." He still makes no mention of what for historians would be a landmark event. No longer were the lands of Ni'ihau – or any other island – to be capriciously given or taken back at the whim of a chief. Western style ownership, and western style land titles, deeds, or patents were the result of the nine years of the division of all lands in the kingdom, a lengthy legal process known as the Great *Mahele.*

As part of this land conversion process, one twentieth of all government lands were designated to be used or sold for educational purposes. Those designated school lands which were sold enabled creation of a fund for the support of a kingdom-wide school system. Also five hundred school and church sites were defined and registered – among them presumably the school and church site at Puuwai village, Ni'ihau.

In the nine year process of redistribution of land, the king (as the government) and the chiefs and chiefesses received clear title to their vast acreages. Commoners were given the opportunity to pay a small commutation fee giving them fee simple title to their *kuleana*. In some areas they were also given the chance to buy other lands outright. On Ni'ihau, only one person seized the opportunity to own his *kuleana*. The rest of the island became crown land, the property of the king to whom Ni'ihauans occupying that land must now pay an annual lease rent. Alas! What had been hoped by the monarchy to be a source of revenue never worked out on this island.

From the outset, collecting his rent from Ni'ihauans was a problem for the king and his agents. Ni'ihauans who acquired cash from selling mats or yams preferred to donate it to the church rather than pay the king's agents 'rent'. Only one Ni'ihauan had taken advantage of the Great *Mahele's* opportunity for commoners to own the lands on which they lived. A man named Papapa had paid his commutation fee to the king's agent and in 1855 received a royal patent for his fifty acre *kuleana*. Aside from this one fifty-acre tract, all the rest of Ni'ihau now belonged to the King, who found the island an increasingly frustrating property to own.

His ministers did not, however, at first encourage any would-be buyers. Soon after Kamehameha IV came to the throne there were several attempts by Ni'ihauans and others to buy the entire island. In 1851 a letter from the Minister of Interior to a Hawaiian named Puko states that Ni'ihau (that is, the entire island) "is not for lease or sale." By 1853 the king evidently changed his mind for there is a letter in the Hawaii State Archives, dated 1853, from the Minister of Interior to Reverend Rowell asking if the missionary "would undertake the business of selling the government lands on Ni'ihau."

There is no record of Rowell's reply. He was probably not interested. In the Hawaii State Archives is a letter dated 1855, at last replying to Puko that no lease could be made because the government "has decided to sell Niihau to the residents thereof." But nothing more came of this statement and at about the same time the government refused the request of E. Lihau who applied for the purchase or, if purchase was not possible, the lease of "the coconut grove and salt ponds" on Ni'ihau.

Missionary Rowell was too preoccupied with ousting "Popery" from Ni'ihau, and confronting the new religious competition of Mormonism to busy himself with problems being encountered by the king's agents in trying to collect lease rents from the people of Ni'ihau. Like Rowell, whom they much liked, Ni'ihauans felt spiritual matters to be of more importance. What money they had went to their church. In 1855, a year the king's agent could not collect one penny of lease rental from Ni'ihau, Rowell records proudly that "the contributions of the people of the whole district including Niihau, for benevolent purposes during the year was $462.55."

Rowell made two week-long visits to Ni'ihau in 1855. His only comment concerning these was: "No very uncommon events of good or evil have occurred in the field." Morality – of the strict Protestant variety – was of primary importance to missionaries such as himself, all of whom viewed Honolulu and Lahina as – according to Rowell – "twin hot-beds of vice". With pride, Rowell reports that as to the extent of "use of intoxicating drinks by natives", not one person on Ni'ihau was known to have indulged in alcohol and out of a population of 790 only 377 used tobacco. Rowell obviously agreed with the report of the Ministry for Public Instruction, "the state of public morals cannot be said to be bad in these islands."

As to the status of education on Ni'ihau, in 1854 there were 147 students registered in eight schools. Reading, writing, arithmetic and geography were the major courses. For the first time 53 Ni'ihau pupils were studying Singing. "Singing," said a former missionary who had become the kingdom's Minister for Public Instruction, "is an exercise of which native children are particularly fond; it tends to make the school a pleasant place; to supersede old heathen songs and to wipe out old heathenish ideas; to inculcate refined sentiments".

Sentiments of quite another kind were evidently aroused in Rev. Rowell, not so much by music as by one particular musician. In 1860, after several years of hard work Rowell had completed his ambitious project of building a large stone church in Waimea. An organ had been installed in the new church and Reverend Rowell had proceeded to teach a Hawaiian lady the art of playing it. In the process, he seems to have done far more than make music with her. Gossip escalated. Rumours flew even to Ni'ihau. Rowell's more conservative Hawaiian parishioners were so affronted by the alleged affair that they refused to recognize him as their pastor. For a time Rowell managed to continue his life as a missionary and as a husband and father of seven children as if nothing were amiss.

His station reports were written in the same calm style with no hint of the trouble accumulating for him. He notes, in 1861, as if this is his major difficulty, that "three or four Mormon priests came from Lanai and spent a few weeks in my field." At least one of these Mormons went to Ni'ihau where the 1860 census had reported a population drop to 647. Many of these remained loyal to Rowell, as did a large faction in Waimea. Those who opposed Rowell confronted the loyalists by interrupting services with constant ringing of the bell or other disturbances. When these harassers held their own service, the Rowell faction in turn harassed them. The scandal rocked Kauai and Ni'ihau and rippled on out to the rest of the kingdom.

Through it all, Mrs. Rowell seems to have remained quite serene, tending to her household and her large family of young children as if nothing were amiss in her marriage. Rowell himself gives little indication that his tenure as missionary to Waimea is about to end. His 1861 station report stresses that "The fever of horse racing and other games has so raged a large part of the year as to absorb all the time and thought of the irreligious and the young and destroy in a great measure their inclination to attend religious meetings."

The 1863 Waimea mission station report is signed by acting pastor J.W. Smith. It states "the former pastor has, for his immorality been deposed from the ministry." Smith charges that "those who supported Rowell engaged with him in irregular and disorderly practices" and "were not in regular standing as church members." An act of Censure had been passed on them of which they had been "duly notified."

The resulting factionalism between those supportive of Rowell and those condemning him was so bitter that the Supreme Court in Honolulu was called upon to hear the case. There were many followers of Rowell on Ni'ihau where D.S. Kupahu, one of the young Hawaiian graduates of the seminary in Wailuku, Maui had recently been stationed. Smith writes that Kupahu is "laborious. The people there (on Ni'ihau) wish to have him ordained."

Rowell did not leave Waimea nor did he intend to. His wife, Malvina Jerusha Chapin Rowell, a graduate of Mt. Holyoke Seminary in Massachusetts, must have been a strong and determined woman with a mind amazingly open for her day. She stood by her husband and supported him. When his connection with the American Board of Commissioners for Foreign Missions was severed, the Rowells built a smaller wooden church near the large stone one he had erected in Waimea. George Rowell remained the devoted pastor of a loyal congregation of followers, including some on Ni'ihau. His influence was considerable during his remaining years. Eventually he became the leader of a brotherhood of independent Hawaiian churches.

While all this was going on, the government was preoccupied with trying to collect back lease rental payments from the people of Ni'ihau. The frustration of the king's agent, J. Wahinekea of Hanapepe, is evident from his letter of April 11, 1863 to the clerk of the Ministry of Interior. Having greeted the clerk with "Love to you," Wahinekea writes, "I wish to inform you that I went to Niihau to demand of the natives their rent for the fifth year. The natives said that there was no money to be had belonging to us now. I said how about mats, if you have any on hand let me take them and I will take them to the King, who will buy them. They replied, there are no mats made up now. That was the first time I went in the month of December. In the month of March I went again. This is the amount of money received ($21.50) from the hands of the land agent of the King (on Niihau)."

In his concluding paragraph Wahinekea mentions goat skins which were valuable for export, being used throughout the world to make vellum for binding fine books. "Here are 280 goat skins and 20 from the natives making altogether 300 goat skins. It is coming by the hands of my servant which I am sending you."

Presumably the 20 goat skins were a partial rental payment for Ni'ihau crown land occupied by commoners. That and $21.50 cash were hardly an embellishment to Kamehemeha IV's treasury. The king's canny Scots advisor Robert Crichton Wyllie was a large landowner on Kauai (at what is now Princeville). His hope, which Kamehameha IV now shared, was that somehow soon, they might be able to sell the island.

The Bargain

THE CHANCE FOR Kamehameha IV and Robert Crichton Wyllie to convert Ni'ihau from a worthless asset into good hard cash came in the autumn of 1863 when a family of well-to-do New Zealanders sailed into Honolulu harbor in their bark 'Bessie. The passengers listed on the manifest published in the *Pacific Commercial Advertiser* on October 1st, 1863 were "Mrs. Gay, Mrs. Sinclair, Mrs. Robinson, Miss A. Sinclair, F. Sinclair, J. Sinclair, J. Gay, G. Gay, E. Gay, C. Gay and A. Robinson".

'Mrs. Sinclair' was Elizabeth (Eliza) McHutchison Sinclair, a petite vivacious 63 year old Scotswoman who had spent the previous twenty-three years pioneering in New Zealand. The 'Bessie' had been purchased for her by her oldest daughter Jane's husband. Thomas Gay, an experienced mariner who served as the bark's captain. Mrs. Sinclair's entire large family were aboard, including nineteen-year old James Gay, Captain Gay's son from his first marriage. Except for her youngest daughter Anne, all of Mrs. Sinclair's offspring were old enough to remember their first long voyage – from Scotland to New Zealand in 1839-40. James and Francis, now grown men, were both bachelors. Helen Sinclair Robinson, the oldest daughter, was aboard with her young son Aubrey.

91

Because this family was to play a stellar role in the subsequent history of Ni'ihau, and because over the years the media – especially the press – has tended to misunderstand and misrepresent their history, intentions, and stewardship of the island, I shall digress here to set the record straight so far as family history, and their acquisition of Ni'ihau is concerned.

Eliza McHutchison Sinclair was born April 26, 1800, one of six children of the wealthy, socially prominent McHutchison family of Glasgow. Among other amenities such as a spacious formal garden, their home had a famous aviary. Eliza's childhood was, in one sense, much sheltered but in a deeper and more impressionable way, a childhood in which she observed the fashionable indulgences of the day and their debilitating effects. At dinner parties the ladies were sent home in sedan chairs as soon as the meal was over. The gentlemen stayed to get drunk. From earliest childhood Eliza would get up in the morning and see the gentlemen from the previous night's dinner party stagger from under the tables where they had passed out. She would watch in dismay as they struggled to walk around in the garden until they recovered enough to be able to go home. It was a memory that kept her – and helped her to keep the next few generations of her family – ardent teetotallers.

At eighteen, when she made her debut, Eliza McHutchison was only five feet tall, a slender energetic girl whose deep blue eyes dominated her strong face. Later that year, when she accompanied her father on one of his business trips out of the city, she met Edinburgh-born Francis Sinclair, a Captain of the Royal Navy who was reputed to be the handsomest man in Scotland. Eliza was intrigued by his hero's record in the Battle of Trafalgar, by his good looks, by his 6 ft. 2 inches of height, and most of all by his open personality. At a time when other men of fashion wore their hair in a powdered queue, Francis Sinclair had his dark, curly hair in the new, loose natural fashion. For each of them, the attraction was strong and instantaneous. He was 29 and Eliza 19 when they were married.

Captain Sinclair resigned his commission to take a post in the Inland Revenue Office. They lived first in a small house in the outskirts of Edinburgh where Eliza gave birth to their son George. Before long the couple moved to Sterling, to a large stately house named Bothwell Hall. Here the rest of their children were born: Jane, Helen, James, Francis and Anne. Perhaps it was his naval experience, perhaps part of the adventurous spirit of the times that in 1839 led the Sinclairs to decide to leave Scotland. The government was offering retired naval officers generous land bonuses in the new colony of New Zealand – an offer Francis and Eliza Sinclair felt was too good to miss.

They left for New Zealand in October 1839 with their most precious possessions – their family. Anne, the youngest, was only seven months old. George was 19, Jane 16, James 15, Helen 13, and Francis 6. It was a four months journey around the Cape of Good Hope, past Australia and Tasmania, which was then known as VanDiemen's Land. Eliza was so deathly seasick the entire voyage that the captain of the ship feared for her life. Fortunately her two maidservants remained well, as did the children and, of course, her naval veteran husband. Once the ship docked at Wellington, New Zealand in February 1840, Eliza's vigorous good health immediately returned. Much to their disappointment they were informed when they disembarked that the land they had chosen was being fiercely defended by the Maori. Settlement there now was out of the question. As a result, the family stayed in the charming, "quite settled" community of Wellington for the next three years. It proved a period during which Eliza Sinclair learned much about the Maori, and the Maori in that area came to appreciate her coolheadedness.

One day a group of young Maori from a nearby *pa*, a Maori village, stole all the laundry from Eliza's clothesline. She successfully dissuaded a hotheaded neighbor from pursuing the thieves with a gun. Captain Sinclair was away when this happened but when he returned the following day he went to the chief of the Maori village. The chief ordered the young men to return the stolen linen. He then went to the Sinclair's residence and placed his huge spear, inlaid with abalone shell, at their front door. It was with relief that Eliza learned this was a sign of Maori friendship and protection – a sign she could trust. The chief's spear stayed there just outside the front door until 1843 when the family finally left to explore the coast of the North Island and to survey their hoped-for acreage.

During the three years in Wellington, Captain Sinclair hand-hewed the timbers and personally built a stout sailing vessel, the 'Richmond'. It was sizeable enough to transport his family and their possessions to their area of North Island which they found to be an extraordinarily wild and beautiful place. Each night they anchored and went ashore to camp along one of the deep bays. They had no chief's spear to protect them here. The hostility of the Maori whose lands they had intended to occupy was a constant threat to their lives – a powerful reason to send them back to settle on a tract at Pigeon Bay, near Akaroa (Canterbury). With them went another Scots couple, Mr. and Mrs. Ebenezer Hay. Each family lived in a tent until by July (mid-winter in New Zealand) they completed building a rough shack of wattle and daub. The entire group lived in that until, a year later, farther down the bay, Captain Sinclair built "Craig-forth". He and his sons cut the white pine lumber by hand from the surrounding forest where they also obtained red totara shingles for their new home.

One of the Sinclair's first priorities was making friends with their Maori neighbors. Captain Sinclair soon traded the 'Richmond' for ten cows which he brought overland from Akaroa, he and his sons cutting a trail in order to do so. The pioneer life suited the entire family. At forty-two, her children later remembered, Eliza Sinclair was youthful and vivacious. She learned to handle a canoe as well as a Maori. She thought nothing of walking the 15 miles to Akaroa, where the nearest shops were located. The three years in Wellington had well equipped them for life on their remote Pigeon Bay acreage. The girls as well as the boys could ride, shoot, and sail a boat. They could also make their own clothes, keep house, cook, and even provide themselves with shoes if given leather and tools. Captain Sinclair hewed the timbers to build a new, smaller sailing vessel for coastal supply trips. His sons, helping him, became adept at boat building too.

They needed all such skills, all their courage, and resourcefulness at the Pigeon Bay homestead which lay in the shadow of a mountain that still today is called Mt. Sinclair. While they were first camped there in tents, there were frequent threats of trouble from the Maoris. Captain Sinclair's determined overtures of friendship with these original settlers of New Zealand averted at least one planned massacre. It was never an easy life at Craigforth but Francis and Eliza Sinclair saw to it that the difficulties were balanced by good times. Both Francis and Eliza were staunch Calvinists who frowned on dancing, drinking, and card playing. The family found its own pleasures. Some evenings it could be music. Eliza had a fine piano, one of her prized possessions. Other evenings it was literature. The boys would take turns reading aloud. As they listened, Eliza and the girls sewed. James was particularly fond of the literary evenings for his great passion was not only reading – but writing poetry.

Only three years after the move to Pigeon Bay this idyllic life was shattered by tragedy. In 1846 Eliza Sinclair's husband, her oldest son George and George's best friend, 18 year old Jane Sinclair's fiance Alfred Wallace, left to sail to Wellington for supplies. The weather became stormy soon after their departure. The seas were so rough that evidently the small boat capsized. No trace of the three, or of their vessel, was ever found. Daughter Helen wrote to a friend in Christ Church that "Mother's constant activities keep her from brooding too much on our great loss. She supervises so capably all work at Craigforth, up before dawn and never retiring until late at night, cheerful and encouraging, a great source of strength for all of us."

Laudatory as her daughter's impression might have been, Eliza Sinclair's grief was such that she left Craigforth in charge of a Mr. McIntosh and for two years lived alone in Wellington, Perhaps her old, close friends like the Governor General of New Zealand, Lord George Grey, helped her through this difficult period of adjustment to widowhood. When she returned to Pigeon Bay, Eliza Sinclair was able once again to be a cheerful, encouraging source of strength to her children. They were now of an age to marry and begin their own families. Jane, recovering from her grief at the loss of her fiance Alfred Wallace, married Captain Thomas Gay. Helen married a man some twenty years older than herself – the first magistrate of Akaroa, Charles Barrington Robinson. In 1853, their son Aubrey was born. Helen was reticent about her marital problems but they were such that when Aubrey was one year old, she walked with him in her arms over the fifteen miles of trail from Akaroa to Craigforth. On arrival she announced she had left her husband, that she would never go back to him, and that she was home to stay.

Eliza was distressed by Helen's decision, but she never pressed her daughter for the details that had led her to leave Charles Robinson. As other grandchildren were born, Eliza took great pleasure in them but Aubrey Robinson was always her special pet. Aubrey was nine years old in 1862 when his bachelor uncle Francis and his mother Helen Sinclair Robinson, both of an unusually adventurous nature, persuaded their mother that Pigeon Bay had become too settled to be exciting. Their suggestion was that Craigforth be sold, and that the family emigrate to a country that would give them the pioneering thrills New Zealand had once afforded. British Columbia and California were their suggestions. Although Anne and James were not too keen about the idea, Eliza Sinclair liked it. She felt it most fortunate that her son-in-law, Thomas Gay, was a ship's captain, and charged him with finding a vessel on which the family could make their voyage across the Pacific to find a new home.

Captain Gay decided upon a 300-ton English bark, the 'Bessie', which was purchased 'fully fitted'. On the deck and into the capacious hold went the family furniture, books, and personal possessions. A cow with hay and grain was along to provide milk for Eliza's grandchildren. There were crates of chickens. Some fine merino sheep. Quantities of jams and jellies made at Craigforth. Hogsheads of bully beef. Barrels of apples from their orchards. Helen wrote in her diary – an entry that seems to contradict the story that she was one of the instigators of the move – "It all seems like a dream, mother being at her age the leader for such an undertaking. But she says *it will be done* and we trust her implicitly."

As the day of departure neared, Helen wrote: "Mother was on the jetty from early morning until long after nightfall, forever dashing up and down the gangplank, checking cargo aboard, keeping the workers stepping lively, checking the working gear of the vessel, ordering the crew here and there to make everything shipshape".

At the last minute, Eliza decided her piano was essential to have along to accompany religious services and musical activities at sea. At last the bark was loaded and ready. In April 1863, carrying the gold she received from the sale of her properties, with all of her family members, several servants and a small crew, sixty-three year old Eliza Sinclair set out on a new adventure.

They were sailing up the South Pacific to Tahiti when disaster threatened. An enormous octopus with tentacles fifteen feet in length suddenly emerged from the sea! With a force that caused the ship to list, the monster grasped the mast and the rigging. The family, terrified, stood frozen where they were on the deck until the octopus let go the ship and slipped back into the calm sea. From the whaling vessels that Eliza Sinclair fondly remembered as 'floating palaces' calling at Pigeon Bay in her early days there, she had heard tales of such giant creatures but until this experience she had always thought the whalers were simply telling tall tales.

Tahiti, with its languid tropical air, its palm fringed shores and beautiful interior mountains seemed like fairyland to the voyagers on the 'Bessie'. There was a brief family flirtation with settling in this magical place but on closer inspection they found the level lands of the coast too limited in size for the farming and ranching they intended. There are contradictory reports as to their next stop. Some family accounts insist they anchored briefly in Honolulu on their way to the Pacific Northwest. Other family members insist with equal fervor that the 'Bessie' simply sailed past the Sandwich Islands, noting fine views of Mauna Loa and Mauna Kea on the horizon.

Whichever might have been the case is of no importance. In early June the 'Bessie' arrived at Victoria, on Vancouver Island. British Columbia was a wet and wild country, quite as undeveloped as they had hoped but with dense forests that would make clearing for agricultural use too long and costly an enterprise. The Indians of the region were far different from the Maori of New Zealand. Eliza Sinclair found them "alarming". Her intent was to take a look at California next. However, winter seas were not conducive to easy anchorages at locations like Monterey. An acquaintance, Henry Rhodes, whose brother Godfrey lived in Honolulu, advised the family to avoid California's winter rains and rough seas by sailing to the Sandwich Islands where even the winter weather was warm and pleasant. Family concensus agreed with this and so the 'Bessie' sailed back across the Pacific.

They were welcomed on their arrival in Honolulu harbor by that indefatigable greeter of all newcomers, the Reverend Samuel Damon, missionary of the Seaman's Bethel and publisher of the temperance paper, *The Friend*. It was Reverend Damon who found them a house to rent for the winter, at a location that is now Sheridan Street. They were soon comfortably ensconced there, and much pleased by the friendliness of the town. Among the family's new friends were the British Consul, General Miller; the Thomas Browns, the Herman von Holt family, Mr. and Mrs. Synge, the Judds, and Bishop and Mrs. Staley of the Episcopal faith preferred by Kamehameha IV and his Queen, the former Emma Rooke.

Within a matter of days they were introduced to Robert Crichton Wyllie, a fellow Scotsman with whom Eliza Sinclair was much impressed. Hearing that the family was seeking a ranch site, Wyllie resolved to find one for them in the kingdom. The Sinclairs, he told the king, were exactly the fine kind of new people needed in the islands. In Anne Sinclair's journal is recorded the different parcels which the family were urged to consider purchasing.

In quick succession that October they were offered Kahuku on northern Oahu, Ford Island in Pearl Harbor by Dr. Ford and the lands of Honouli and Ewa, later purchased by James Campbell. Though the Sinclairs were pleased to be shown these properties, none seemed to them to be 'the right place'. They were, however, eager to look further. Anne quotes her mother as having remarked, "Though the land in California was so cheap we knew that country was not yet in a settled condition." After only one month, Eliza Sinclair felt that Hawaii seemed to be a 'more settled community' offering 'a pleasant life'.

A large part of the Sinclair-Robinson-Gay clan's immediate attraction to the islands was the Polynesian atmosphere. They had felt at home with their Maori neighbors in New Zealand. Here they felt an equal affinity and aloha for the Hawaiians. Anne records the family understanding of the Great *Mahele,* the transformation of land tenure that had taken place a decade before their arrival, as having enabled many Hawaiian commoners to take up their small *kuleanas*. This, she wrote, was the reason "it was well nigh impossible to find a large enough tract of land for our purpose." She concluded, "no reasonable person could object to this law as it is a fine thing for the natives."

How or when the idea of offering Ni'ihau to the Sinclairs occurred to Kamehameha IV and Minister Wyllie is not clear, but offer it they did. The previous two years had brought the heaviest rainfalls in history to that island. A Kauai enthusiast himself, and thus partial to the Leeward Islands, Wyllie suggested to James and Francis Sinclair that they take a look at Ni'ihau.

An entire island that could be theirs? Eliza directed her two sons to sail there at once to survey such a good prospect. Wyllie made no mention to them of the fifty acres owned by Papapa, or the provision for school and church lots and harbor areas. What he offered the Sinclairs was the chance to buy all of the island, which he represented to be entirely owned by the crown.

That autumn of 1863 Ni'ihau's lowlands were lush and green. Its several brackish mud flats were brimming freshwater lakes. Much impressed, James and Francis returned to Honolulu to report to their mother that Ni'ihau had everything they wanted, with exactly the kind of isolation they sought. They had no idea, and no one mentioned to them that Ni'ihau was semi-arrid, that the condition in which they had seen it was unprecedented, or that every few years the drought was so severe that Ni'ihauans moved temporarily to Kauai in order to survive.

The Sinclair brothers saw Ni'ihau as Kamehameha IV and Wyllie wished them to see it: an island where they could raise cattle and sheep, build a new version of Craigforth, and enjoy life in a balmy year-round climate.

The initial offer made by the family was $6000. Wyllie was a shrewd bargainer. Not only did he want to unload this burden from the monarchy but he wanted to try to get the best possible price in doing so. He told the Sinclairs that the only terms on which the king said they could have Ni'ihau would be either on an annual lease rental of at least $600 a year or, if they preferred an outright cash purchase, for $10,000 in gold. With no hesitation the family decided to meet the king's price which, according to a long-persistent myth, included Mrs. Sinclair's piano.

On November 30th, in the middle of the transaction, Kamehameha IV died. His brother, Lot Kamehameha, was enthroned as Kamehameha V. Thus land records of the Hawaiian Monarchy for January 23, 1864 read: "Kamehameha V, by the grace of God, King of the Hawaiian islands, by this His Royal Patent, makes known unto all men that he has, for himself and his successors in office, this day granted and given, absolutely in fee simple unto James McHutchison Sinclair and Francis Sinclair as tenants in common, for the consideration of $10,000 paid into the royal exchequer . . " – and there follows a description of the island of Ni'ihau.

The Hawaii State Archives contain an interesting insight into the keen business sense of Kamehameha V. On completion of this sale, his Minister of Interior has an urgent memo sent to the King's agents on Kauai concerning the sale of Ni'ihau and the imminent occupancy of 'the *haoles*'. The agents are directed to quickly go to Ni'ihau, and to round up and kill as many of the goats on the island as possible. Goat skins being a valuable market item, the King evidently saw no reason to leave such an asset for the new owners.

The New Chiefs of Ni'ihau

WITH MUCH EXCITEMENT the family vacated its rental house on Sheridan Street, said Aloha to their friends in Honolulu and sailed the 'Bessie' to Ni'ihau. By late spring they had established themselves in grass houses in the village of Puuwai. Their situation might well have discouraged less seasoned pioneers. No Hawaiian on the island spoke English. No one of the family understood Hawaiian.

They busied themselves getting acquainted with the terrain, exploring coast and interior, and planning which areas of the island to devote to sheep, to cattle, to horse pastures. They chose a home site on the bluff near Nonopapa landing and waited patiently for the building materials they had ordered from Boston to arrive.

Their first caller and closest foreign neighbor was a handsome, middle-aged Scandinavian bachelor from Waiawa, Kauai. Valdemar Knudsen was a graduate of the University of Oslo, Norway and spoke several European languages. After a brief interlude in the gold rush in California, he had sailed on to Hawaii, landing on Kauai in 1851. He quickly learned to speak Hawaiian, a necessity for foreigners settling in the kingdom, especially on the outer islands. It was Knudsen who aided the Sinclairs their first few weeks on Ni'ihau by

101

acting as their interpreter, and by helping to teach them the Hawaiian language.

With his help and their own ingenuity, the family soon began to be able to communicate with their Ni'ihauan tenants. Young Aubrey was the enthusiast, adept at learning Hawaiian and getting to know the island. So too were his cousins – George, Francis, and Charles Gay.

The only one for whom the new life was not easy was Anne, the youngest of Eliza Sinclair's children. Anne had not wanted to emigrate, but to remain in New Zealand and marry James Montgomery. It was her brother Francis, who shared Anne's love for and gift of poetry, who had persuaded her she must relinquish that relationship for the sake of her family. The others were soon much at home on Ni'ihau, but Anne yearned for New Zealand. Night after night she would dream she was in a boat, rounding a point from which she would be able to see their old home, Craigforth. Always, she told her daughter years later, she woke just before Craigforth came into view.

To occupy herself these first months on Ni'ihau Anne channeled her abundant energy into what her daughter, Ida Knudsen von Holt in her memoir *Stories of Long Ago: Niihau, Kauai, Oahu* (republished in 1985 by Daughters of Hawaii, Honolulu) remembered her mother having described as "teaching young and old to speak English, to write a little, and to read the Bible." Rev. Rowell of the Waimea Mission Station was evidently much relieved that a devout Scotch Presbyterian family had purchased Ni'ihau and would now become exemplary models for the Hawaiians there. The Sinclairs must not have heard the scandalous rumours current about Rowell, or else chose not to believe what they heard for Anne wrote in her journal that the family much appreciated the monthly visits of Rev. Rowell, "who had charge of the Niihau Mission." She adds that "We became very good friends and helped him all we could."

One day Eliza Sinclair discovered that one of her silver teaspoons was missing. Remembering her success with recovering her stolen linen from the Maori during her early days in Wellington, she went to the headman of the village and told him she suspected one of the children might have taken the spoon.

Immediately he lined up all the children in Puuwai. With a stern gaze he informed them that he had a magic glass which enabled him to look into the privacy of their minds and hearts, to know everything they were thinking and everything they might have done.

He then held a shard of looking glass to his eye and went along the line of children, peering through it at each one in turn. As he approached one small boy with his 'magic glass' the child began to tremble, and then to cry. Before the chief even tried to see into this child's heart, the boy took the missing spoon from his pants pocket. After he received a long lecture about what a terrible thing he had done to the 'new chiefs' of Ni'ihau, the spoon was safely returned to Mrs. Sinclair. From that time on, the possessions of the family were respected as kapu, which the possessions of chiefs had been since the legendary days of Ni'ihau's settlement by Polynesians from Tahiti, BoraBora and other islands of the South Seas.

In 1864 travel between Kauai and Ni'ihau was usually made either in one's own canoe, as paying passenger in a whaleboat rowed by Hawaiians or by chartering a small sailing vessel. The whaleboat was a most uncomfortable way to go, but it took only four to six hours. Rev. Rowell on his visits, and Valdemar Knudsen on his more frequent trips to assist his new neighbors, used this when they could not find a ride in a canoe. To sail to Ni'ihau from Kauai could, on the occasion of light airs, take as long as three days! Having experienced one such three day trip, Anne Sinclair preferred to endure the relatively minimal four to six hours of extreme discomfort in the whaleboat.

When the family first purchased their island, a Hawaiian named Kapahe was running a whaleboat from Kalalau, Kauai, bringing taro and poi to Ni'ihau as well as providing passenger service back and forth. When the Sinclairs decided they should buy their own whaleboat, Valdemar Knudsen recommended they hire Kapahe to be their captain.

A native of Kauai, Kapahe was one of those veterans of the wild periiod described by the missionaries when the art of murder was cultivated in the Waimea area. As a young man he had belonged to a group called 'The Stranglers'. After he killed a man belonging to the rival gang, 'The Clubbers', Kapahe decided to change his ways. He bought an old whaleboat and long before the Sinclair family purchased Ni'ihau, he began taking poi and taro there from Kalalau. The legends of Kapahe's strength are many. Once he was shipwrecked on a trip when he sailed from Kalalau with a load of taro and an elderly Hawaiian couple who wanted to visit Ni'ihau.

In the middle of the channel they were caught in a sudden gale, a northerly that came roaring down on them. Under the battering of the mountainous waves, the old whaleboat began to break up. There was nothing to do but to swim towards Ni'ihau, which the three of them began to do. They could make little headway in the turbulent seas. Since Kapahe was younger and much stronger than they, the old couple urged him to leave them behind. At first, he would not do so. Then he decided he might best swim to shore to get help and come back to rescue them. He told them this, and encouraged them to try to stay afloat, but as he swam away he could hear the two of them singing a hymn. He knew by this that they had given up.

All night Kapahe swam with the gale. At last at dawn he felt the sharp edges of a reef under his feet. He staggered ashore, thinking he had reached Ni'ihau. He was so exhausted he could not even look at his surroundings but immediately fell asleep on the beach. When he woke, he saw that he was not on Ni'ihau but on the small uninhabited island of Lehua. Back into the ocean he went to swim across the treacherous rough channel separating Lehua from Ni'ihau. The tide and strong current carried him up the coast until he came ashore at Kii.

Valdemar Knudsen's recommendation of Kapahe to the Sinclairs was based on Kapahe's tremendous sense of responsibility for his passengers and by the Hawaiian's prodigous strength as a swimmer. Without hesitation Kapahe agreed to work for the new owners of Ni'ihau who, with their own whaleboat, captain and crew could now go back and forth to Kauai as they pleased. Other whaleboats continued to provide passenger service and deliver poi, taro, and other wanted items to Ni'ihau. Ni'ihau people had always been and continued to be frequent travelers back and forth to Kauai and, on occasion, to the bustling centers of Honolulu or Lahaina, Maui.

By winter, 1864 the family had moved from their temporary quarters at Puuwai into what they named "The House" – for it was the only foreign style dwelling on Ni'ihau. There were, eventually, nineteen rooms built in the airy tropical fashion of the day with connecting open passageways and porches. Nearby they planned a carriage shed, servants quarters, and warehouses. In the meantime, the conversion of the island into a large ranch proceeded. The fine merino sheep, and the few milk cows they had brought with them from New Zealand were long since ashore, adjusting to their new environment. Francis had taken charge of purchasing substantial numbers of sheep and cattle from the kingdom's big ranches – such as the Parker Ranch – on Hawaii. Horses were an essential– and fine ones were readily available in the kingdom, for horses and horse breeding had rapidly become popular in the sixty years since the first horse– a curiosity to Hawaiians of that day –was landed on the Big Island by Captain Richard Cleveland.

The new owners of Ni'ihau were not in any way the recluses that popular mythology often insinuates they were and are. One of their numerous early visitors remarked that the Sinclair men could ride, rope, and lassoo "as well as any native Hawaiian" – remarkable not only in this visitor's eyes but in the eyes of the Ni'ihauans was that the Sinclairs readily acquired the art and skill of surfboard riding "which it has been said to be impossible for foreigners to acquire." It is amazing that James Sinclair should have been able to surf for he suffered intermittent ill health, the result of an accident back in New Zealand when a tree had fallen on him.

Once they were settled ashore, had purchased their whaleboat and hired Kapahe as captain of it, the family no longer needed their bark 'Bessie'. Captain Thomas Gay left to take the vessel on what Ida Knudsen von Holt's memoirs relate as a trip to Australia to sell it. Unfortunately, the voyage ended in tragedy – the untimely death of Jane's husband, Captain Gay. Mrs. von Holt's information from her mother concerning the death of Anne Sinclair Knudsen's brother-in-law was that "After consummating the sale in Sydney he unfortunately contracted pneumonia and died." *The Friend* in its August 1865 issue carries this notice however, "Died – On the 9th of February, suddenly, on board of the bark 'Bessie' at Newcastle, New South Wales, Capt. Thomas Gay, on the voyage to the Sandwich Islands, deeply and sincerely regretted by family and friends."

That March, several weeks after Captain Gay's death, his widow gave birth to their daughter Alice, the first white child born on Ni'ihau. It was a year of mixed grief and joy for the Sinclair family. For Jane Sinclair Gay, the deep grief of losing her husband was assuaged by the birth of their daughter. Eliza Sinclair mourned the loss of a son-in-law, rejoiced at the birth of another grandchild, and was delighted by Francis' decision, later that same year, to return to New Zealand to marry his cousin, Isabella McHutchison, and bring her to Ni'ihau.

Anne was somewhat bitter about this, considering the choice Francis had persuaded her to make in not staying back in New Zealand and marrying James Montgomery. By now, however, she was being courted by Valdemar Knudsen, who shared her love of poetry, her interest in botany, her zest for riding and exploring the beaches and mountains of Ni'ihau and Kauai. On one occasion Knudsen brought along William Brigham, a botanist gathering island flora for the Harvard collection. Brigham, who was later head of Bishop Museum in Honolulu, much enjoyed his visit to Ni'ihau and he too was much attracted to Anne Sinclair. He even asked Valdemar Knudsen to arrange a return visit so that he might ask Anne to marry him! Since Knudsen intended to propose to Anne himself, he was not enthused and evidently did not make Brigham's return possible.

It was on one of Knudsen's frequent trips to see Anne Sinclair that his life was saved by Captain Kapahe of the family's whaleboat. Knudsen was returning from Ni'ihau to Waimea. Kapahe as usual was at the helm, with a crew of sturdy Hawaiians manning the oars. As they took their time coming through the rough surf off Waimea, Knudsen announced he would get there faster if he jumped overboard and swam to shore. Nothing Kapahe said could dissuade him. Into the ocean he went!

The distance to the beach had not looked that great from the whaleboat. Once in the sea, however, Knudsen found it was a distance impossible for him to cover. He swam as fast and hard as he could, but in the surf he could make no headway. After a time he was so exhausted he was on the point of giving up. Suddenly he felt something crash against his right side. A shark? Fearfully he turned to look. It was the big muscular body of Kapahe who had jumped overboard to make sure the stubborn Scandinavian got safely ashore. With his powerful arms Kapahe pushed Knudsen ahead of him until they were on the beach. He left his passenger there, then turned back through the surf and swam out to the whaleboat again.

In 1866 Anne McHutchison Sinclair announced to her family that she and Valdemar Knudsen had become engaged. Much as he liked Valdemar Knudsen as friend and neighbor, it seems that Anne's brother Francis was not enthused about her marrying him and leaving the bosom of the family. They were then living all together in "The House" on Ni'ihau. Grandma Sinclair, James, Francis and his bride, the widowed daughter Jane (whom her niece refers to as Jean) Gay and her children, Helen Robinson and her son Aubrey, and Anne. In her memoirs Ida von Holt comments "it seems to our modern way of thinking almost unbelievable they could all live happily together". But, she adds, Grandma Sinclair was "so devoted to her family she always wanted them near her. She had a way with her that made everyone do as she wished . . . even the Hawaiians called her 'Mama' ".

Although these may well have been forgotten over the years, with the Sinclair's as with most families, there must have been stresses, strains, undercurrents of envy and flare-ups of anger at times as well as the periods of harmony remembered by Anne Sinclair Knudsen's daughter.

There is an inference of such a flare-up in 1866 when Anne Sinclair told the family of her engagement. Francis is said to have remarked, "Is it because I have married that you are leaving us?" Ida von Holt relates that the family felt Anne was "cruel to leave them and want her own home though, as they thought highly of Valdemar Knudsen, they had no real reason for objecting to her marriage, and were glad of Anne's choice." For her wedding, Eliza Sinclair announced she was giving Anne her share of her projected inheritance in cash – a most substantial gift.

The wedding took place on Ni'ihau on February 12, 1867. There is no record of whether they were married by the family's old friend, Reverend Rowell, now dismissed from his original missionary post, or by Rev. D. Kupahu – who in July 1866 had been ordained and installed as the first (and only) fulltime pastor ever assigned to Ni'ihau.

It was that same year, 1867, probably after the wedding, when Captain Kinney of the 'Nettie' dropped anchor at what he called 'Cook's Harbor' on Ni'ihau. Ninety years earlier, Cook's surgeon, William Ellis, had done a lovely watercolor of the grass houses along this shore. There were still, Kinney observed now, four such Hawaiian *halepili* and, in addition, one *halepili* warehouse. On the beach he was greeted by Ni'ihauans who had ready for trade an abundance of sweet potatoes, onions, pineapples and finely done rush mats – the famous *makaloa* mats that on his 1845 visit Gorham Gilman had found too expensive to acquire.

When Captain Kinney came ashore the second morning of his 1867 call at Ni'ihau, he found all the Hawaiians were busy constructing a raft to land the lumber which the 'Nettie' had brought. The consignment was to "Messrs. Sinclair for the purpose of making additions to the hospitable mansion." Once the lumber was on shore, the rafts were to be used to load bales of wool and cotton which the Sinclairs had produced on their island. Captain Kinney's mention of cotton is interesting. This is the only indication that cotton – which during the American Civil War had been a favorite crop throughout the kingdom– was once grown on Ni'ihau.

As to the ready labor of the Ni'ihauans in all this stevedoring, Captain Kinney comments that "it seems the practise if not the right to demand feudal serice by the lord of the manor from the natives still exists, and at his call all the available population came forth." He does not mention that the size of the 'available population' was now less than half the number who had been residents of Ni'ihau before the Sinclair's purchase of the island. Only three hundred Hawaiians remained as families who worked in some capacity for Ni'ihau Ranch or the Sinclair household.

On his walks ashore at Ni'ihau, Captain Kinney saw many "natural plantations of pineapples. They grow everywhere over the island, spontaneously with no other culture than that of nature. They are the juiciest and best flavored of any in the tropics." Kinney describes "King's wells – two tanks of cool water cut out of the basalt" on a hill with a magnificent view. Later he visited "The House" and reported that one gets "a warm Scotch welcome even without letters of introduction to the Sinclairs". Their residence much impressed the Captain of the 'Nettie'. "The situation of (Sinclair's) house is very beautiful and commands extensive views. It is on a long cape-like ridge on the northwest side of the island that terminates in sand dunes. Trees only are wanting to give it that rural air."

By 1867 Francis Sinclair had become well versed in Hawaiian as had the rest of the family. James was not in the best of health. It was Francis whom Eliza Sinclair asked to manage Ni'ihau Ranch and acquaint their tenants with the privileges and prohibitions under which Ni'ihau people might remain on the Sinclair's private island. These conditions are recorded in the reports of the Church of Ni'ihau, originally written in Hawaiian and half a century later translated into English by territorial forester Charles Judd, for the Hawaii Mission Children's Society Library.

The Church of Ni'ihau had been formally established, with D. Kupahu as pastor, on July 15, 1866. Meetings were held in two places – in the government schoolhouse at Puuwai on Sunday mornings, and at the house of a member in Nonopapa Sunday evenings. Since American Board of Foreign Missions support had been withdrawn from the Sandwich Island mission stations, the Hawaiian Evangelical Association had been formed of which the Kauai association was part. Each church was now self-supporting, including the Church of Ni'ihau.

Kupahu notes in his 1867 report that things are improving under the new ownership, recollecting that "Sunday was not entirely peaceful in the past months at times when many whaling ships came to Niihau. If this was on a Sunday, the day became a day for gadding about for everyone and Sunday was not peaceful. Because the haole people of Niihau knew of this disturbance on Sunday, the police were ordered to watch even the ship's crews and to expel the people of the island from getting near the sailors. After the whalers went away, disturbance on Sunday is scarcely known at this time."

There were several competing sects on Ni'ihau in 1868. Kupahu lists one of these as "the Rowell religion" and states that "the majority of the Hawaiians of this Island are of this religion in which they are tenacious". There were also many Catholics, whose leader was a layman named Stephen. A few Ni'ihauans had become Mormons. For a time a considerable number followed the preaching of a Kauai prophet, Kanepalaka. Only 30 were actual members in good standing of the Church of Ni'ihau.

Kupahu was most grateful to the example of the 'haole', (the Sinclairs) who frequently attended church services on Sunday and whose young people also came to Sunday School. Attendance at this much improved when Francis Sinclair announced that all children, including those of Catholic families, must go to Sunday School at Puuwai. Reverend D. Kupahu seems to have been a hard worker, and most dedicated, but for some reason he did not find favor with Francis Sinclair. His 1868 report ends with a section headed "Concerning my Being Discharged". He writes: "I am through with my services as pastor of the church of Niihau. I do not intend to return there in the future because of being discharged by the owner of the land but if perhaps some member of this Association (the Hawaiian Board) thinks of asking me this question, 'Why were you discharged?' or some similar question then I shall reply that this is a hard question to answer because this is the question I placed before the owner of the land with the question, 'What are the reasons for my being discharged?' No answer has been given me. Only the statement (from Francis Sinclair), 'I do not want to tell. We do not wish to discuss it. This is final.'"

Kupahu was replaced by a lay leader, Deacon A. Kaukau. It is his report, under the subhead 'The work of F. Sinclair', which describes the conditions under which the 327 Ni'ihauans remaining on the island must agree to live – or leave. 'The Hawaiians are very grateful for their haole chief in several ways," Kaukau writes and then lists what they are grateful for. First, he states that April "is the month for sheep shearing. That is the time when 3,000 or more sheep are slaughtered." Inferring that at this season Ni'ihauans are premitted to eat as much of the mutton as they can, he adds that the entrails are thrown into the sea for the sharks. The 'haole' also gives permission "to collect the tallow. Each family has from one to two barrels and are thus well supplied with tallow every year."

Further, Kaukau elaborates, "F. Sinclair gave graciously an eighth of the whole island of Niihau as an open country where the horses of the people may run. He gave them the posts and boards for the horse pasture from the uplands to the sea at Keawanui. He also gave freely lands for planting sweet potatoes – 2 planting places at Pukeheke and below Kamalino – perhaps 100 or more acres." And in contrast to the chiefs of the old days, the people are free to "gather fish surrounding Niihau; there is no disputing about fish like in the days of the konohiki (the king's agent)."

In order to enjoy these privileges and perquisites, however, Ni'ihauans had to agree to observe a number of rules. Kaukau enumerates these in his church report. "F. Sinclair will punish persons indulging in sexual gratification and drinking liquor. The Government will punish persons who drink outside of their house lots. Sinclair will punish the persons who drink liquor inside of all the houses, if discovered."

The second rule concerned church attendance. "F. Sinclair and his family regularly go to church services and he urges the Hawaiians to come to the church services. He marks the children that do not attend Sunday School and punishes them if they always stay home. Therefore his Sunday School is full throughout the year." Kaukau is full of praise for these conditions which were nothing other than the contemporary puritan social morality the protestant missionaries had always tried to urge on the Hawaiians.

It was only now that the family learned they did not own the whole island. Francis Sinclair, who had become fluent in Hawaiian, spoke at this meeting to all the people of Ni'ihau, detailing the rules which they must agree to obey if they were to remain on the island. He was appalled when old Papapa announced that none of what the *haole* said applied to him – he was his own master, living on his own land. Proudly Papapa showed the 1855 royal patent to his fifty acres.

Relating this story many years later, Valdemar and Anne Knudsen's son Eric says of his grandmother and uncles, "They thought they owned the whole island, but behold – they did not. It was not enough that they had thousands of acres and this old man had only a few. It was the fact that they couldn't get those also that took all the joy out of owning the rest. Before long it seemed as if the value of the old man's little holding exceeded in value all the rest of the island."

Changes

ERIC KNUDSEN DOES not flatter his own family in his account of how his uncles, aunts, and grandmother acquired this last fifty acres of what they had assumed was all theirs. In his most fascinating book, a collection of radio talks given by him and later published as *Teller of Hawaiian Tales* in Honolulu, 1945, Eric writes that the Sinclairs tried to buy Papapa's small acreage but he refused to sell. It seems as if he couldn't have been much in the way but the trouble was no road could be laid out, no fence could be built without in some way having to cross Papapa's land.

Every member of the family had tried to persuade the old couple to sell. No luck. The Papapa's continued to live contentedly in their little grass hut on their fifty acres, with no need to pay attention to the 'rules' that the new chiefs demanded the rest of the residents of the island follow.

At their wit's end, the Sinclairs enlisted the aid of Valdemar Knudsen to handle the matter. Knudsen was astonished when his brother-in-law, Francis Sinclair, told him they were willing to pay as much as one thousand dollars for the fifty acres in question. He agreed to do what he could, and asked that a deed be prepared for the Papapa's signature, and that one thousand silver dollars be supplied him to pay the couple should he succeed in buying their land for the family.

112

When he had the deed, and one thousand silver dollars securely wrapped in a cloth bag, Knudsen rode off to the Papapa's *kuleana*. In the old couple's grass house he piled the dollars one by one in shining piles to tempt them. That did not work.

Knudsen scooped up the dollars from the table. He piled them one by one again and as he did so, he suggested that by taking the money the couple would be able to live well on Kauai. "In Waimea valley the natives live alongside a beautiful running river of sparkling sweet water," he told them. "The women go out in it and catch shrimps and *oopu* and swim in it. All the valley is full of taro and the *pake* makes poi twice a week. Coconut trees grow along the banks and you can have all the *hau hau* nuts you want for the asking!"

A second time, the Papapa's refused.

Patiently, Knudsen scooped up the silver dollars. Patiently he piled them one by one a third time. As he piled the dollars he tempted them in a different way, saying, "In the village of Waimea there is an old whaler named Salem Hanchet. He has opened a store and in it you can buy new holokus made of bright colors. All the well dressed women of Kauai wear them! For the men, he has good top-boots and denim pants."

But still the old man refused to be lured out of his land.

"That's too bad," said Knudsen. "This is a lot of money. You could live in ease the rest of your lives. But that is your affair, not mine! That is all. Aloha! I go." And for the last time he scooped the silver dollars back into his bag.

As he finished, the old woman sprang to her feet. "Stop!" she cried. "Those dollars are mine! Bring out your deed. Here, you stupid old man!" she accosted her husband. "Are you crazy? Sign the deed and I will sign!"

This he did, and when both had signed, Valdemar Knudsen handed them the bag of silver dollars, took the deed, and left.

"So," concluded Eric Knudsen in his marvelously skillful telling of this story, "the thorn was removed and both families were happy."

By now the 'brimming lakes' and 'lush green pastures' Francis and James had seen in their 1863 visit had regressed to mud flats and semi-arid grasslands. Rainfall had diminished to its normal minimum. Within a very few years Eliza Sinclair moved to the Makaweli, Kauai property she had purchased – 21,400 acres of land formerly held by the King's late sister, Victoria Kamamalu. Eliza still loved Ni'ihau. In summers she stayed there and most of the family, as always, stayed with her. Captain Kinney's 1867 impression of having received "a warm Scotch welcome" was one experienced by all foreign visitors to Ni'ihau. As to Hawaiians visiting the island or Ni'ihauans leaving for extended visits to relatives and friends elsewhere, there were no restrictions. Ni'ihau was anything but a 'hermit' island.

In the late 1860's and early 1870's Mrs. Sinclair imported a succession of tutors to educate her grandchildren, both on Ni'ihau and at Makaweli. On Ni'ihau, the family entertained a remarkable variety of visitors including the aforementioned William Brigham of Harvard. On several occasions a man-o-war anchored off the bay and the captain and officers made "The House" their headquarters. Lord and Lady Brassy, cruising the world in their yacht, stopped off at Ni'ihau and were royally entertained. The British Commissioner, his wife, and daughter were among the family's many visitors. "All enjoyed the pleasures of island life, horseback riding, swimming, surfriding and roaming the beautiful shores which were covered with exquisite seashells," recollects Ida Knudsen von Holt.

Her impressions are substantiated by a Ni'ihau visitor (anonymous) who wrote with enthusiasm in the October 1870 issue of *The Friend* of her (or his) September 1870 visit:

"On the island of Niihau the Sinclair's have, I think, their full heart's desire. I never was more pleasantly disappointed in regard to any place. Viewed from Kauai, it presents a most uninteresting appearance which is very deceptive. It is about 20 miles long, and five or six wide, containing over 60,000 acres of land. The greater part affords most excellent pasturage, especially for sheep. It is a strange fact (and I was informed by Mr. Sinclair it was true) that *kikania* (a troublesome burr) would not grow on the island. Were it not for this fact, the wool would deteriorate in price. In one of my rides about the island, I was shown some subterranean caves, in which were growing with great luxuriance the breadfruit, hau, and many other trees. This

was within a stone's throw of the ocean. There are many delight-
ful rides about the island. I never spent ten days more pleasantly.
A person enjoying hunting and fishing can there find sport such
as I have not seen in any other island of the group."

In her seventies, Eliza Sinclair was as active as ever, taking
a shrewd hand in running the family business, doting on the
Knudsen's growing family, riding horseback daily – often with
her grandson Aubrey, who was as wild about good horses and
riding them as was his grandmother. By 1872 Francis Sinclair,
his wife Isabella, and young George Gay were the only family
members now living permanently in "The House". The others
resided at Makaweli on Kauai, in the spacious home Eliza
Sinclair had built on that extensive acreage. Like many *kamaaina*
of their day, the younger members of Eliza's family were ardent
travelers. Even the grandchildren were acquiring a cosmopolitan background. Anne Sinclair Knudsen and her husband took
their young ones on frequent trips to Europe.

For the Knudsen children, however, their favorite destination continued to be Ni'ihau. Eric writes of his great joy
whenever Kapahe, the big Hawaiian captain of the family's
whaleboat, delivered an invitation from Grandma Sinclair for
the Knudsens to come spend a few days on Ni'ihau. In answer
to one such invitation, Anne Sinclair Knudsen assured Kapahe
she would have herself and the children at Pupu Pakai – a small
landing place on the shore below Kekaha, in time for a proposed
3:00 A.M. departure.

When that day came, with much anticipation the Knudsens
reached the landing place well ahead of time. How disappointed
they were when Kapahe told them plans had to be changed.
Though it was summer, the rough seas of a *kiu* (the stormy
conditions more common to winter gales) had come up during
the night. Since there were to be young children aboard, Kapahe
had decided to postpone departure. Disappointment gave way
to relief when he told them the postponement was only to be
until daybreak. "Then," he told Anne Knudsen, "if a wave
washes a child overboard, he can be rescued."

At last dawn came and everyone boarded. "The old whaleboat was heavy in the water and we made slow progress," Eric
Knudsen recalled. Just outside the landing place they met a

boat from Waimea, loaded with Ni'ihau people and their possessions. The Waimea boat asked Kapahe if it could accompany him, and he agreed. As the two boats reached the middle of the channel, the seas became mountainous. Looking back, those on Kapahe's boat could see that the second vessel was being swamped in one gigantic wave!

Anne Knudsen was appalled to see a mother and her two and a half year old child washed overboard, with the mother showing concern only for an iron pot she clutched in her arms. When Anne called out that the woman should rescue her child, the Ni'ihau woman only laughed. "My child can float but this iron pot cannot!" she replied and kept her arms and eyes on the pot. A few moments later, the Knudsens – to their great relief – saw the tiny child come paddling over the crest of a second great wave. She and her mother – and the pot – were safely hauled back aboard their boat, the child laughing as if the whole adventure had been the greatest fun. Such, commented Eric Knudsen, was the way in which Ni'ihau people felt totally at home in the roughest seas.

Like her young brother Eric, Ida Knudsen von Holt reminisces in her memoirs about those happy times of her childhood when the whaleboat would land the family at Kii. Her cousin George Gay would be waiting for them, along with a number of Ni'ihau cowboys. As the whaleboat approached the beach, the crew tossed ropes to the waiting cowboys who then hauled boat and passengers up onto dry land. Coffee was bubbling on a campfire. While the grown ups were enjoying their first – and long awaited – cup of morning coffee, George would hurry out to the reef with his rod and line. In one cast he would haul in a *moi*, clean it in one of the tiny pools, and have it broiling over the fire by the time a second cup of coffee was in demand.

It was a two hour drive by horse and carriage from Kii landing to The House. On the way they passed what Ida Knudsen von Holt remembers as "lovely rolling grassy plains where countless sheep roamed". As the carriage pulled up at The House, Grandma Sinclair would rush out to greet them. At 74, she was, recalled her granddaughter, "beautiful and fascinating in her dainty dress with her lace cap showing

Lehua Island. Niʻihau in background.

Niʻihau as seen by Cook's surgeon, Wm. Ellis, 1778.

Thatch-front cave dwelling, 19th century.

courtesy Kauai Museum. **Mrs. Francis Sinclair and Family at Makaweli House, 1893**

Seated l. to r.: Francis Gay, Mrs. George Gay, Mrs. Sinclair, Mrs. Charles Robinson, Mrs. A
Robinson with Aylmer, Mr. Aubrey Robinson and Sinclair.
Standing l. to r.: Eliza Gay, Francis Sinclair, Mrs. Francis Sinclair and Mr. Wodehouse.

courtesy Kauai Museum.

Captain Thomas Gay.

courtesy Kauai Museum.

Francis Gay.

Aubrey and Alice Robinson, Cecilia and Eric Knudsen, Sinclair and Selywn Robinson, Anabel and Harold Gay, 1906.

House Party arriving on S.S. Kinau, Nonopapa, July 1908.

Mrs. M. Faye catches an eel. July 1908 house party.

courtesy Auckland Institute and Museum.

Francis Sinclair photo of Ni'ihauans, 1885.

courtesy Auckland Institute and Museum.

Another Francis Sinclair photo of Ni'ihauans.

courtesy Auckland Institute and Museum.

Fishing, Ni'ihau. Circa 1885.

courtesy Hawaii State Archives.

Waiting for the steamer. Nonopapa Landing, circa 1910.

Shipping cattle, Ni'ihau. Early 20th century.

Loading sheep, circa 1916.

Last grass house on Ni'ihau. Kawaihoa, 1908.

Niau-Kanahele wedding on Ni'ihau.

Ni'ihau School.

The House, Kiekie. 1908.

A Puuwai Home.

under her shirred silk bonnet."

Such summer visits were spent swimming, riding, roaming Ni'ihau's beaches collecting shells, and – as the Knudsen children grew older – surfing. The family had built a grass house on the east end of Ni'ihau at Kawaihoa. Often the Knudsens would spend several days there. Fishing was excellent from nearby rocky ledges. Cowrie shells could be found in abundance.

The regular full-time residents of The House – Francis and Isabella Sinclair – must have enjoyed these summer visits too. Isabella was engaged in collecting botanical specimens, painting watercolor sketches of the plants, and preparing a collection that eventually became a book: *Indigenous Flowers of the Hawaiian Islands.* Francis' desire to spend his time writing poetry and short stories had to be postponed. These years on Ni'ihau he had little time for other than business correspondence.

In the Hawaii State Archives are copies of his numerous letters to the Ministry of Interior. They are brief and to the point. Under the Hawaiian Monarchy a bureaucracy flourished that was no less cumbersome than the modern bureaucracy of the state of Hawaii. In every district the government had appointed agents to grant marriage licenses, agents authorized to perform marriages, agents to acknowledge 'instruments' (whatever officialese that might have been), and among others– agents to take charge of labor contracts. On Ni'ihau the government agents, with one exception, were Hawaiian appointees. That one exception was George Gay, who was the agent authorized to issue marriage licenses on the island.

In 1873, on the eve of a trip during which Helen Robinson intended to take him to Boston for medical treatment, James McHutchison Sinclair died. He was 48. His obituary in *The Friend* is terse. "James McH. Sinclair of Niihau, late of Craigforth, Canterbury, New Zealand, died at Makaweli, Kauai."

Helen and James had planned their trip to include taking young Aubrey Robinson, Eliza, Francis, and Charles Gay to America to complete their education. After James' death, Valdemar and Anne Knudsen assisted Helen in taking the four teenagers as far as Salt Lake City, a trip they made from the coast largely by stagecoach.

The following year Francis Sinclair, born a British subject in Scotland, became a naturalized citizen of the Hawaiian Kingdom. The record in the Hawaii State Archives shows that in 1874 through D. McBryde of Kauai, for the sum of five dollars, Francis Sinclair had obtained a copy of his oath of allegiance to the Hawaiian king.

1874 was a year of great changes in the Monarchy. In February the gentle Lunalilo's short reign ended in death. The legislative assembly, after a heated contest between Kamehameha IV's widow, Queen Emma and Colonel David Kalakaua, elected Kalakaua as King. There is no record of any preference Francis Sinclair might have had in this unusual election.

Among the items of the next few years filed in the Hawaii State Archives is the March 15, 1883 letter sent by the Minister of Interior relative to "F. Sinclair's request" for a government subsidy to bore artesian wells on Ni'ihau. The government was evidently not willing to invest in a privately owned island, no matter how desperate the owner's need for a larger and more dependable water supply.

Francis Sinclair was impatient to have one of the younger generation return to take over the management of Ni'ihau, but he had to wait ten years before he could be free of that responsibility and pursue the writing he yearned to do. When that day finally came, in 1883, another time of extensive change began for the island of Ni'ihau.

Gay and Robinson

WHEN HE RETURNED to Hawaii at the age of 31, Aubrey Robinson had a degree from Harvard University, had finished law school, and traveled extensively throughout the world. After a decade away, Hawaii was more than ever his choice of the place where he wished to spend his life. He and his cousin Francis Gay had always been as close as if they were brothers. They had grown up together in their grandmother's household, where they had the cultural stimulation of such guests as writer Isabella Bird Bishop, a Victorian traveler who was the first woman in Hawaii to adopt the outrageous new costume of bloomers. Aubrey and Francis shared school memories as well, both with the tutors Grandma Sinclair imported to Ni'ihau and Makaweli, and later at Rev. Dole's boarding school on Kauai. Together, also, Aubrey and Francis had gone on to complete their education on the Mainland soon after the death of their Uncle James in 1873.

On Aubrey's return in 1883, the two cousins formed the partnership of Gay and Robinson to operate the family properties and adjoining tracts of leased lands. It was a time when Sir William Renny Watson, the Scotch entrepreneur, was as eager to acquire plantations as he was to sell island planters his modern Glasgow-made mills to grind their cane. In addition to his

119

knowledge of law, Aubrey Robinson had a natural talent for business. Negotiating with Sir Wiliam Renny Watson, he made an arrangement most profitable to Gay and Robinson. They leased 6000 acres of their land to Watson who ran it as Makaweli Plantation, cultivated by the Hawaiian Sugar Company. The remaining 2000 acres of good Makaweli canelands were cultivated by Gay and Robinson. The cousins used their upland acreage as a ranch, on which they ran 1000 head of Devon cattle. Ni'ihau too was a ranch operation, as it had been since the family's purchase of the island.

Of all the family properties, Ni'ihau was Aubrey's special interest. To his grandmother's delight (in her eighties Eliza Sinclair went riding daily) Aubrey Robinson imported a number of pureblood Arabian horses, some of which he kept at Makaweli and others which he took to Ni'ihau. For Ni'ihau, this heralded a new era. From his travels in Europe, India, and Asia, Aubrey Robinson brought home many ideas about changes he wished to bring about for the betterment of the island – and, so he sincerely believed – for its people. He was a young man well ahead of his time, an innovator and a conservationist.

In June, 1884 his close relationship to his cousin Francis Gay took on the new dimension of brother-in-law when he married Francis' younger sister Alice Gay, who had been born on Ni'ihau. At the time of Aubrey and Alice's wedding, their uncle Francis and his wife Isabella had not yet left the islands. The Francis Sinclairs were still at Makaweli where, one month before the wedding of Aubrey Robinson and Alice Gay, Isabella Sinclair signed the completed manuscript of her *Indigenous Flowers of the Hawaiian Islands.*

By February 1885 she and Francis were in London, overseeing the printing of what is now recognized as a classic study of indigenous Hawaiian plants. The aloha of Isabella and Francis Sinclair for the Hawaiians of Ni'ihau and Kauai is clear from Isabella's dedication of her manuscript: "To The Hawaiian Chiefs and People who have been most appreciative friends and most lenient critics, this work is affectionately inscribed."

In her introduction, Isabella modestly points out that hers "is not by any means a large collection considering that the flowering plants of the islands are said by naturalists to exceed

400 varieties. But the enumeration was made some years ago, and it is possible that many plants have become extinct since then." She goes on to cover such diverse matters as the effect on Hawaiian flora of climate, destructive agencies, habitats, discusses the Hawaiian vernacular names formerly generally known to the Hawaiian peoples and laments the difficulties of flower painting in the Tropics.

Long before its 1885 publication, Isabella Sinclair document- ed the authenticity of her 44 colored plates, each with one unnumbered page of text, by sending herbarium specimens of each plant to the Royal Botanic Gardens, Kew, England. The Director, Sir Joseph Hooker, encouraged her to publish her work and assisted her in this when she and Francis came to London in 1885.

Sampson Low, Marston, Searle and Rivington of London published the book which merited unusual notice for the work of an amateur botanist. There was a brief review by James Britten, editor of the *Journal of Botany* who commented, "Mrs. Sinclair does not profess to be a botanist but she is evidently an observer as is shown not only by her drawings but by the simple descrip- tions that accompany them." In Berlin another review appeared, written by the reporter for *Plant Geography of Europe.* Nearly seventy years later an in-depth review of *Indigenous Flowers of the Hawaiian Islands* appeared in *Pacific Science,* volume VIII, 1954. Dr. Harold St. John, dean of Hawaii's botanists, named his review "Hawaiian Plant Studies 23". After lauding Mrs. Sinclair as a gifted artist and extremely keen observer, Dr. St. John commented that "even today Mrs. Sinclair's book has more color plates of Hawaiian plants than any other book."

In February 1885, the year that Isabella Sinclair's book was published, an event that would add a unique component to Ni'ihau's population and history occurred in Honolulu. The vessel 'City of Tokio' landed the first large contingent of Japanese contract laborers – more than 900 men, women, and children. Among these was a young man named Asahina Umekichi (in the Japanese style of last names given first). His contract was taken up by Francis Gay, and Asahina – ignorant of any language other than his own native Japanese – was provided passage to Kauai.

For the first few months, Asahina worked at Makaweli as a ranch hand. He was a hard worker, and a quick learner. His later recollections, told to his son, retired Honolulu dentist Dr. Noboru Asahina, were that 'Mr. Gay' was most kind and helpful, a genuine friend. As soon as Asahina began to speak Hawaiian, he was taken to Ni'ihau – probably the first Japanese ever to live on that island. His son, more than a century later, remembers that "My father used to tell me how good he was at setting fence posts on Ni'ihau. First, he told me, you put plenty of gravel in the post hole, and some water around the dirt – then pound! pound! pound! until that post is really firm into the ground."

As he became more fluent in Hawaiian, Asahina was used as a handyman and houseboy – cleaning 'The House', serving guests, and on occasion driving the carriage for 'Mr. Gay'. Aubrey Robinson took advantage of Asahina's cultural background. The range of Asahina's jobs, his three years on Ni'ihau, included making an experimental planting of green tea. To Aubrey Robinson's keen disappointment, neither the quality of the soil nor the amount of rainfall was right for the tea bushes to flourish. Only at Makaweli did the tea plants from Ceylon do well.

When his contract was completed, Asahina left Ni'ihau to return briefly to Japan. He had been asked by Francis Gay to find a contact in Japan who might wish to import the fine wool of Ni'ihau sheep. Asahina did his best, but no one in his home islands was interested. During the time he was in Japan, he used the money he had saved from his three year labor contract to apprentice himself to a dentist in Tokyo. No dental schools existed then. A man learned his profession by watching, helping, and then working under the tutelage of a master. When his apprenticeship ended, Asahina returned to Honolulu to become the first Japanese dentist in the community. It was due to a mailman's error that, soon after his return to Honolulu, his name was changed from Umekichi to Dr. Mumekichi Asahina.

His son, who also became a dentist in Honolulu, believes that his father's brother may have followed him to Ni'ihau. Whether or not this was so, from 1888 on, after the original Asahina's departure, there seems to have been at least one and sometimes several Japanese working for Aubrey Robinson in 'The House' on Ni'ihau.

The wool which Dr. Mumekichi Asahina tried to find a market for in Japan was the major product of Ni'ihau. Once it was baled and ready, the wool must be lightered from shore out to cargo vessels which on rare occasions lost the entire valuable shipment at sea. One such was a schooner named the 'Thunderer' that got the cargo of Ni'ihau wool no farther than Waimea Bay.. Eric Knudsen tells how, as soon as the 'Thunderer' was fully loaded at Ni'ihau, the captain of the vessel – a *haole* – ordered his Hawaiian crew to sail first across the channel to Waimea, Kauai. There he let them go ashore, a permission he soon regretted for it was several days before he could gather them all back aboard.

By the time he did so, the weather turned bad. Departure was impossible – but so was safe anchorage. Great swells pushed the 'Thunderer' and its valuable cargo of Ni'ihau wool inexorably towards a reef that spreads its teeth across Waimea Bay. When the schooner went up on this reef, the Hawaiian crew jumped overboard and swam ashore through the surf. The captain, who was an older man, stayed with his ship. From shore, a throng of people watched him tie himself to the mainmast as the schooner slowly broke to pieces under him.

One of the shore watchers, an eighteen year old girl named Mele, asked one of the crew why the captain did not also swim ashore.

"That *haole* cannot swim!" she was told.

"But why doesn't someone go save him?" asked Mele.

The crewman shrugged. "We are all tired. We just managed to get ashore ourselves through that surf."

At this Mele stripped off her holoku, dropped it on the beach and entered the ocean. With strong sure strokes she swam out, ducking under each wave that slammed toward shore until she reached the wreck. The old captain was terrified, a hopeless look on his face.

Mele untied him from the mast and coaxed him into the water, urging him to trust her to get him safely ashore. Then, pulling him on with one arm, Mele swam the old man back through the boiling surf to the beach.

Gratefully the old man reached into his pocket. He had only one small coin, which he handed to her.

Mele refused. "Keep it. You need it more than I do. Besides, what I did was only fun!" And with that, putting on her holoku, Mele walked quietly away.

Shipwrecks were not uncommon for vessels plying near Ni'ihau. In 1886 a small steamer, the 'Planter', left Waimea in the late evening of January 27th. The steamer was coming in for a landing at Ni'ihau the following day when she crashed into a boulder as she approached Kii landing, on the eastern end of the island. Passengers and crew took a small boat and made their way ashore. The Captain delayed leaving his vessel and as it sank he was washed overboard but rescued by a Ni'ihauan. Such excitement was not uncommon for an island now used not only to strange human visitors but to all kinds of new fauna.

From 1884 on, in addition to raising fine merino sheep, Aubrey Robinson was pasturing short-horn cattle on the island. He had imported a variety of game birds, including Mongolian and Chinese pheasants and quail. Most of these he released at Makaweli but a few had been brought to stock Ni'ihau. Captain Cook, Lord Vancouver, and Archibald Menzies would have been delighted that Aubrey Robinson was also adding to the food plants of Ni'ihau. He was, in the last few years of this nineteenth century, planting a number of improved varieties of mango, pear, mangosteen, zapote, and star apple. Many of his trees came from China, India, Mexico and other countries he had visited.

Whaleboats were still used to travel between Ni'ihau and Kauai but, in place of the old sailing vessels, interisland steamers now served Ni'ihau on a regular basis, taking Ni'ihauans off to visit relatives elsewhere and bringing relatives and friends from other islands to visit them. Aubrey and Alice Robinson delighted in hosting groups of their friends at fishing parties and week-long summer outings on Ni'ihau.

Over the years, no one had enjoyed summer outings on Ni'ihau more than Eliza Sinclair, who died on October 16th, 1892 at the age of 93. Her obituary in *The Friend* tells how "she arrived here with her family 29 years ago and purchased the island of Niihau for a sheep ranch, from Kamehameha IV for $10,000, settled at Makaweli, which large tract she subsequently purchased and where she has lived ever since she arrived here, never having left Kauai except for a short visit to Niihau."

This latter statement was of course inaccurate. It had been quoted from the obituary of Mrs. Sinclair in the *Pacific Commercial Advertiser.* As to survivors, *The Friend* reports that only two of her children are still alive. Anne Sinclair Knudsen, who "now lives in this city" (Honolulu) and "a son, Francis Sinclair, now living in Alameda, California." In addition, says the obituary, she is survived by "several grand and great-grandchildren residing here and in California." The remainder of the obituary is devoted to an assessment of Eliza Sinclair's long life.

"Mrs. Sinclair was a most remarkable woman of Scotch birth, possessed of an active business mind which enabled her to be the ruling spirit and manager of her large property. She always enjoyed remarkably good health in her mountain home at Makaweli." She had been alert and active until "a few weeks since she had an attack of grip from which she recovered, but it left her so weak and helpless that she felt it was of no use to make any effort to recover and prolong life in such a helpless condition. Then, calling her grand-children and friends to her bedside, she bade an affectionate farewell to each, closed her eyes and expired . . . apparently with no pain but with a bright hope of eternal glory in the spirit land."

The tribute ends with the notation that "Mrs. Sinclair has been a constant subscriber to *The Friend.*"

Eliza Sinclair's death came in the final months of the life of the kingdom in which she had made her home since 1864. Political unrest had seethed in the islands for a decade, with intense rivalry between British and American interests, each vying for control. Queen Liliuokalani, a strong willed and independent woman, was known to favor the British and had her own firm ideas about her constitutional monarchy. Where the Sinclairs, Robinsons, and Gays stood in the critical matter of loyalty to the Hawaiian monarchy is documented only by a news item that states in 1892, the year of his grandmother's death at Makaweli, Francis Gay was appointed by the Queen to her commission planning a Hawaii exhibit for the World's Columbian Exposition to be held in Chicago in 1893.

That commission, along with all other governmental functions of the monarchy, was ended in January 1893 when a powerful group of American businessmen staged a bloodless coup with the assistance of the American Consul in Hawaii, and a show of naval forces from an American man-o-war which 'happened' to be in Honolulu at the time.

For the next five years, 1893-8, Hawaii was to be governed as a Republic by this clique of businessmen whose aim was to have Hawaii annexed as a United States Territory. Ni'ihau was sufficiently distanced from the political upheaval so that the everyday life of the island was not disrupted, but the Hawaiians of Ni'ihau must have shared their countrymen's emotional desire to restore their Queen, or at the least to be allowed to continue as an autonomous Hawaiian nation.

Throughout this hectic period the social summer outings, the visiting of Hawaiian friends and relatives to those on the island continued. Tourists were easily able to visit Ni'ihau as is evidenced by an April, 1893 article in *Paradise of the Pacific* titled "Lanai and Ni'ihau – Two Interesting Islands Seldom Visited By Tourists". The author began with the recommendation to tourists that the trip to Ni'ihau was most pleasant and worthwhile. "Niihau lies to the southwest of Kauai whence it is reached by an agreeable passage by steamer, or the traveler whose time is valuable can cross the narrow passage that separates it from Kauai by the ever convenient whale-boat. The islet has an area of about 70,000 acres or something over 100 square miles. It was once more thickly populated, but is now little more than a large sheep ranch, more than one half the land or 40,000 acres being the property of Gay and Robinson, the owners of the Makaweli Estate on the island of Kauai, and the population consisting chiefly of shepherds and employees of that firm." The writer of this 1893 article seems not to have been aware that Gay and Robinson was a family partnership of two grandsons of Eliza Sinclair, whose family owned all of Ni'ihau.

The major portion of the article mentions the interesting things the visitor may see and acquire on Ni'ihau. "A fine grass, which is indigenous and is not to be found elsewhere, though closely resembling the Guayaquil (Ecuador) grass used in the manufacture of Panama hats, was formerly woven into 'Niihau mats' which are quite noted for their great delicacy and softness. These mats were woven in different designs and colors and were really beautiful. They are now very rare and of late years the price – which formerly ranged from five to eleven dollars or so a piece advanced to an exorbitant degree when the industry was abandoned."

This last phrase sounds as if the Hawaiians abandoned making *makaloa* mats. The truth was that thirty years of sheep grazing around the swampy areas where the sedge once flourished destroyed the plants from which the mats were made.

What was available in 1893 was a unique Ni'ihau product which the article recommends tourists buy: Ni'ihau shell necklaces. "Shells of great beauty and of many varieties are found upon the shores and those with a reddish coral color are gathered by the not-over-industrious natives, and being strung into necklaces and similar ornaments are disposed of to fellow countrymen and to foreigners. Considerable taste and ingenuity are displayed in the manufacture of these pretty articles, and as tourists are, as a rule, ready to pay liberally for curiosities, the natives derive a considerable income from their sale."

The last sentence was perhaps the most intriguing to readers. "There are (1893) more grass houses on Niihau than any other island of the Hawaiian group."

The Mystery of Mystery Island

THE GRASS HOUSES of Ni'ihau were the last vestige of a native Hawaiian culture that, having been discouraged by American missionaries since 1820, was now given what in 1898 could have been a fatal blow. There was a widespread opinion that the Hawaiians themselves, whose numbers had diminished from an estimated 400,000 in 1778 to fewer than one tenth that by 1893, would soon become an extinct race. There were many Hawaiians who agreed that they were a variety of Polynesians who might not survive far into the twentieth century.

A counter-revolution by those loyal to the Queen failed. Then, throughout the islands, the small remnant of native Hawaiians and their supporters banded together to protest the American takeover of their government, petitioning the President and the Congress of the United States to restore to them their rightful independence and sovereignty. Rightfulness was not the consideration in the 1898 decision made by President William McKinley, nor was it the motivation of the Americans who had usurped power and put Liliuokalani under house arrest in Iolani Palace. What now guided Hawaii's political future was business interests, the need for Hawaiian sugar to be assured duty free entry into American ports.

128

None of this turbulence seems to have been noticed by a young woman from Lansing, Michigan who became quite close to the owners of Ni'ihau during her visit to Waimea, Kauai in 1894. Miss Florence Boyer's brother, Reverend Virgil Boyer, had recently been appointed the first minister of the newly organized Waimea Foreign Church. Aubrey Robinson and his wife Alice were active members and supporters of his congregation. In a letter written to her niece many years later, Florence Boyer told how the Robinsons had hired her to teach their two older sons, Sinclair and Aylmer. She had affectionate memories of these two small boys and of their parents, reminiscing how the Aubrey Robinsons had wanted her and her brother to have a memorable, and comfortable trip to see Ni'ihau. To that end they had chartered a steamer to come from Honolulu to Kauai to take Rev. Boyer and his sister, and the Robinson family, on an excursion to that still very Hawaiian island. "It was like a story book!" wrote Florence Boyer in a letter which is now in the Hawaii State Archives.

Among Miss Boyer's other vivid memories of her year in Hawaii was her trip at Christmas time to Honolulu, where she was the Christmas dinner guest of the President of the Republic of Hawaii, Sanford Ballard Dole, son of the Rev. Dole whose Kauai boarding school Aubrey Robinson and Francis Gay had once attended. She was thrilled by the dinner party, where she was 'beau'd' by a young Mr. Rowell whose grandfather had been the controversial missionary for Kauai and Ni'ihau.

Miss Boyer was back in Lansing Michigan when Hawaii became a United States Territory. President William McKinley, pushed by the need to acquire Pearl Harbor as a permanent coaling station for the Pacific fleet, finally gave his approval to President Dole's annexation request. Jingoism was running high in America. War with Spain was at hand. Cuba, Puerto Rico, Guam and the Philippines were about to fall under the dominance of the United States. Hawaii's fate was fortunately different. At annexation in August 1898, the islands were promised that they would soon be upgraded from territorial status to full partnership in the union as an American state. At the time, no one guessed that it would be sixty-one years before this promise was fulfilled.

That August in the official ceremony on the grounds of Iolani Palace (which the provisional government had renamed the Executive Building) the Hawaiian flag was replaced by the stars and stripes. With deep emotion, and the chants of lament once reserved for the death of a ruling chief, the Hawaiian people relinquished the tradition of more than a thousand years of independence and autonomy.

As had the shift from Monarchy to Republic, the change to territorial status had little actual effect on Ni'ihau. Under the Organic Act passed by the Congress of the United States in 1906 Ni'ihau's traditional relationship with Kauai was preserved. It was now part of the County of Kauai. The legal changeover for this private island was minimal. There were no immigrant labor contracts, which under United States law were now illegal. Except for crown lands, which were taken by the new government, land titles granted by the kingdom were honored by the Territory. As it had been since 1864, Ni'ihau was private property. But as to emotional change – the Hawaiians of Ni'ihau must have lamented as did their fellow Hawaiians in Honolulu who wept when their beloved flag was struck.

Aubrey Robinson treasured the Hawaiian-ness of his island but made no immediate moves to protect it. Well into the early years of the Territory, the hospitality of the Robinsons kept Ni'ihau open to relatives and friends like the Judd's of Honolulu and the Waterhouse's of Kauai. Julia Waterhouse Damon Rodenhurst, born in 1907 on Kauai, was told by her parents that before her birth, every summer they were guests of Aubrey and Alice Robinson at wonderful fishing parties on Ni'ihau.

By 1915 however, the private island settled into the isolation that was to mark it through most of this century. Whether the reason was that old recurrent problem of drought and a minimal water supply for residents and visitors, or the lack of any transport beyond the uncomfortably limited space on the Robinson whaleboat, the half century of "warm Scotch hospitality" ended. Those who came to Ni'ihau, including relatives of the Hawaiians living there, were able to do so only by the specific permission of Aubrey Robinson, a permission that imposed time limits on any visit and severely restricted the number and kind of visitors. The island was no longer served by regular stops of the interisland steamships. Tourists were no longer welcome. The summer parties diminished to small, quiet family affairs. The era of Ni'ihau's reputation as a 'forbidden island' began.

This was not the result of any personal arbitrariness, as some surmised. Aubrey Robinson, like his uncle Francis Sinclair before him, had made every effort possible to find and develop new water resources for the island. In 1899 a complete well-boring plant was shipped to Ni'ihau but no significant artesian wells were found. The only solution was to try to keep the Ni'ihau population at a level commensurate with existing supplies of water. Aubrey Robinson determined that one hundred and thirty inhabitants were as many as the island's water resources would support.

In 1910 the territorial census recorded 208 inhabitants of Ni'ihau. By 1919, Aubrey Robinson had reduced the number of residents to 130 by transferring families to Makaweli, applying the same solution to the lack of water that ancient Hawaiians had themselves once used.

The conservation and reforestation of the island was another major concern of Aubrey Robinson. The wild goats whose catholic appetites did so much damage to Ni'ihau vegetation were no longer hunted for their skins, as had been profitable in the days of Kamehameha IV. By 1917 Aubrey Robinson had managed to eradicate the total population of Ni'ihau goats. Had he been alive to hear this, Francis Sinclair would have been much pleased.

Francis died July 22, 1916 on the Isle of Jersey, England. He had spent the last 31 years of his life creating stories and poems as he had always wanted to do. His obituary in the *Honolulu Advertiser* describes him as "planter, rancher, author and poet" – which in turn he had been. He lived fully until his death at 83, residing in a number of places. At first he and his wife Isabella had settled in Alameda, California after their return from the London publication of her book. "During later years," says his obituary, "Mr. Sinclair resided in London, devoting his time to literary work. Among his works are "Ballads and Poems From the Pacific", "Under Western Skies", and "From the Four Winds". Most of Francis Sinclair's stories and poems dealt with what he knew best – Hawaii and the Pacific.

By 1916 many of the indigenous plants painted and loving-
ly described by Isabella Sinclair during her husband's years as
manager of Ni'hau were extinct. But Aubrey Robinson had done
much to replenish vegetation on the island by planting some
5000 seedling ironwood and kiawe trees annually. The seedlings
were raised in a nursery at Kiekie, grown in bamboo joints which
were split at the time the seedlings were placed in the ground.
Thorny kiawe, the algaroba that in California is known as
mesquite, flourished in the dry climate and poor soil of Ni'ihau.
. The successful growth of ironwoods and kiawes were two
of the many changes noted in 1929 by Territorial Forester Charles
S. Judd, who had visited Ni'ihau thirty years earlier.

His first trip had been as a young boy with his family,
attending one of the Robinson's Ni'ihau outings. His return in
1929 was in the company of his brother, Governor Lawrence
Judd, on the first official visit of a territorial governor to Ni'ihau.
Charlie Judd had seen a number of villages in 1899. Now, in
October 1929, Puuwai was the island's one settlement.

According to a front page article in the *Star-Bulletin*, the
members of the gubernatorial delegation visiting Ni'ihau on the
U.S. Lighthouse tender 'Kukui' that autumn with Territorial
Governor Lawrence M. Judd were the High Sheriff of the
Territory of Hawaii, the Territorial Forester (Charlie Judd), the
Adjustant general, the Chief of Staff of the Hawaiian Depart-
ment of the United States Army, the president of the Territorial
Senate, the United States Marshal in Hawaii, the Director of the
United States Experiment Station at Honolulu, and Territorial
Senator Charles Rice from Kauai.

The 'Kukui' anchored off Kii. A launch brought the visitors
ashore. There they were greeted by Aubrey Robinson's son
Aylmer – "a trim, smiling young man" who had graduated from
Harvard in 1910, spent a postgraduate year working on Oahu,
and then returned home where, in 1922, he became manager
of Ni'ihau. The initial reaction of the visitors, as recorded by journalist Henry Dougherty was that "at once we were struck by the
atmosphere of yesterday. No telephone wires. No garage. Not
an automobile in sight."

Also welcoming the party as they came ashore on Ni'ihau
were Aylmer Robinson's 'venerable' Scotch foreman, John

Rennie, and about a dozen Hawaiian cowboys who seemed, according to Dougherty, "a little shy of their callers but there was a friendliness in their greeting that was genuine." Dougherty's account and that of Charlie Judd (published in the "Hawaiian Forester and Agriculturist" of 1932 (vol 29, p.5-9) differ in various minor details. Charlie Judd wrote that as soon as they came ashore, the party was "served fruit, oatmeal, and coffee by a Japanese steward in a white jacket." This was in the dining room of the "rambling ranch buildings at Kii, which were shaded by a few windswept ironwood, tamarisk, and juniper trees."

Henry Dougherty remembers the breakfast menu as having been "a generous outpouring of ham and eggs and papaia, pineapple and other fruits, plenty of butter and gallons of coffee." They had already eaten breakfast on the 'Kukui' an hour before landing, but, said Dougherty, "we fell to and did justice to this home-cooked breakfast being offered on our island of mystery." So far as I can determine, this is where the myth of the 'Mystery Island' began – with Dougherty's first using it in his news story and, later, as the title of an article about the trip in *Paradise of the Pacific*.

After breakfast, the group mounted spirited Arabian horses that at first gave novice rider Dougherty a few qualms. He preferred that challenge over the alternative of riding in the "old, thin-rimmed buggy" that, according to him, "rumbled along in our wake, a potential ambulance for the weary or injured." Led by Aylmer Robinson and his sturdy Ni'ihau cowboys, the men rode thirty miles across the island to Puuwai. Again, the descriptions of the ride as written by Dougherty and Judd are quite different – Dougherty with a romantic eye and phrase, Judd with the calm observation of the naturalist.

Judd's description reads: "The highlands of the east central portion closely resemble the Waimanalo pali, not so high to be sure but more verdant. The sandy plains under the cliffs were spotted with groves of thrifty kiawe trees and a ground cover of low, wild ilima bushes in full bloom. Farther southward extensive and closely cropped meadows of *manienie* grass were interspersed with large groves of algaroba trees. These grassy fields, level as a billiard table, resembled huge polo fields. Occasional clumps of coconut trees bent their graceful tops under the burden of closely packed clusters of nuts. A lonely loulou palm tree in a swale marked the site where once stood a native grass hut."

Judd is much pleased that "not one undesirable weed was to be seen anywhere and it was always my understanding that the Robinson family used to lease the adjacent government island of Lehua for the sole purpose of eradicating the lantana upon it to prevent its seed being carried by birds to Niihau." Judd mentions seeing turkeys, an occasional peacock, many cattle and sheep, as well as "flocks of plover which seldom hear the sound of a gun." There had been frequent rains that summer so "the foliage of the trees and hue of the meadows were a brilliant green." Together with the presence of the "contented domestic animals" this gave the area, in Judd's eyes, "every appearance of a well-groomed English park," which extended mile after mile with the highlands on the left and the sand dunes and ocean to the right of the travelers.

Dougherty's account is far more flamboyant in giving us a picture of what they saw in their long ride across Ni'ihau. "Stretching away were undulating plains, covered with kiawe trees. To the south were the barren rocks towering like deserted castles. Ahead of us were the level grazing lands. We passed thousands of sheep. Wild plovers fluttered up from the grass and shot ahead of us. Startled turkeys gobbled and chattered. Soft-eyed gentle cattle sniffed and shook themselves lazily as the horses hove in sight."

He notes what Judd seemed not to have noticed, or perhaps felt not important enough to record. "A long sinuous line of pipe streaked down the serrated ridges and over the rocks, then into the lowland below. It carried water from the only spring on the island – a temperamental spring that gushes a fitful stream at fitful intervals mostly during the winter season."

Like Charlie Judd, he mentions riding through "Thousands of turkeys in a kiawe forest enclosure." Then, "on and on over sand dunes, over rounded hills covered with high grass, through miniature valleys and then we burst into a fine level country where palm trees, ironwoods and kiawes provided shade for thousands of fine cattle. Small lakes were dotted here and there – artificial reservoirs constructed to catch and impound the flood waters from periodical rains."

"To the east of the party rose rugged hills, seared and ragged and parched by super-brillant suns– and to the west the plain rolled away, unfolding before us like green carpets, ending in white hillocks that denote the seashore. These white hillocks were gorgeous, even more impressive than the billions of tons of sand that have made the Barking Sands areas on Kauai famous. Some of the deposits were as white as snow, and in the brilliant sunlight they were hills of diamonds or cut glass."

"We crossed these plains and came into the sheep country and again literally thousands of live things ran helter-skelter from the open spaces into the shelter of the trees and the hillocks. Sheep! Sheep! Milling in every direction– spreading away in droves – a panorama of wild life not easily forgotten."

At Puuwai village the weary horsemen were greeted by some 90 Ni'ihauans, "more than half the population of 160 souls," says Dougherty. He then gives details that 69 Ni'ihauans were gathered in front of the church, which was in the center of the village. "It was a big day in their history," comments the reporter, emphasizing that it was the first time Ni'ihau had been honored by the visit of a territorial governor. Again he reports what is most striking about this very different Hawaiian island, compared to the rest of the Territory in 1929. ''No telephone wires. No garage. Not an automobile in sight!''

In 1864 Eliza Sinclair and her family had lived for a time in the grass houses of Puuwai. Sixty-five years later these have all been replaced with wooden structures, each with the 'tin' (corrugated iron) roof common to plantation Hawaii. Dougherty describes the village's "small houses, spick and span, set back from the road in large grounds. Plenty of air, plenty of garden space provided the rains are generous." Each home had a 1000 gallon water tank. The group had been informed by Aylmer Robinson that "water is a problem which is why when the population goes above 160-180 some are asked to volunteer to move to Makaweli. Those who leave seldom return and if they do are a disruptive influence with their idea of life in the world outside Ni'ihau.

The only modern convenience on the island in 1929 was an electric generator that provided light for the Robinson's ranch house. "Life on Niihau while not necessarily primitive, is certainly not up-to-date," observed Dougherty. He took a romantic, idealized view of what he saw at Puuwai. "There are no noises, no reason to hurry unduly, no bartering or bickering or trading in order to earn a living. An honest day's work brings its reward – and judging by the smiling faces that greeted the governor – work is plentiful, wages are satisfactory, and happiness is the result."

There was no post office on the island. There was neither jail nor policeman for there was no crime. The Robinsons carried out Francis Sinclair's strict prohibition as to alcohol and there was as well a prohibition on the sale or use of tobacco. "A few residents smoke," Dougherty learned. "They acquired the habit while visiting elsewhere in the territory – but they smoke surreptitiously and never in the presence of the owners of the island." In 1929 there was little chance of 'visiting elsewhere'. Dougherty states "there are no ships that sail from the island's precarious ports – only a whaleboat puts out for Kauai during 'election periods' or for holidays."

This gubernatorial visit to Puuwai, important as it was, lasted just one hour. Much of the time was spent inside the schoolhouse which was next door to the church. Like other public schools in the territory, it was supported by government funds and – as was regrettably all too common in plantation and ranch communities on other islands before World War II, the education provided Ni'ihau's 29 pupils was minimal. Only four grades were taught. "After that," says Dougherty, "the boy students go to work on the ranch. The girls are very much sheltered. They either assist their mothers in housework, engage in Niihau reed-mat making, shell lei making, or get marrried." The inclusion of mat-making suggests that Niihau mat-makers were now using a substance other than the long extinct sedge grass that once made their mats unique.

At Ni'ihau School, Edward M. Kahale presided as teacher, religious mentor and singing master. Above the blackboards hung a picture of "the late President Teddy Roosevelt. There are also old-time sketches or paintings of American schoolhouses of forty and fifty years ago." The children were well dressed. "There is no general store or any other kind of store in Niihau."

An occasional peddler came by whaleboat to the island but the colorful dresses worn by the Ni'ihau schoolgirls were "importations from Chicago mail order houses or from Waimea on Kauai. The colors ranged from pink to bright blue hues. A few of the girls had, for the moment, donned store shoes for the occasion."

Governor Judd gave a brief talk to the school children and then came out to the school house steps "and spoke to the populace. U.S. Marshal Oscar P. Cox acted as interpreter, although nearly all present understood English." High Sheriff John Lane, Colonel L.W. Oliver, Marshal Cox, Territorial Senators Robert Shingle and Charles A. Rice were other speakers. Lane and Rice spoke exclusively in Hawaiian and they kept their listeners roaring with laughter. Others of the party were Colonel P.M. Smoot, Willis T. Pope, Charles Judd and -" adds Dougherty, "your correspondent."

About half way through the speeches the girls wearing store shoes began to remove them, returning to bare feet with "befitting smiles". When the speeches ended, Governor Judd led everyone in singing 'Aloha Oe'. Kahale, the teacher, then stepped forward and led the "Star Spangled Banner" which, the governor remarked later, "the residents of Niihau knew better than did the visitors."

After three cheers, the party again mounted and galloped on two miles to the Robinson home which Dougherty describes as "a fine old fashioned wooden mansion with spacious grounds, plenty of barns, and with a general air of fifty years ago contentment and happiness." On the grounds W.T. Pope of the U.S. Agricultural Experiment Station found olives, old ironwoods, tall Norfolk Island pines, large Arizona citrus, green flowered moneypod, native palm (loulou), hala (pandanus) and striped century plant. Charlie Judd's observation was that "at Kiekie, the Robinson's ranch house, the party was served coconut milk and a luncheon. Niihau turkey was the main dish. The sprawling one story house was in a setting of ironwood trees, century plants, pine olive, siris, and cactus. It was," says the forester, "a glorious day."

During lunch Aylmer Robinson told the visitors that at the time on Ni'ihau there were 750 shorthorn cattle, (not the thousands of Dougherty's exuberant estimate). Dougherty was correct however in his 'Sheep! Sheep!' everywhere. There were, confirmed Robinson, 10,000 sheep on the island. In addition there were numerous turkeys– at least one of whom had given his life to provide the governor's party a sumptuous lunch. Aubrey Robinson had imported peacocks to strut on his private domain, and constructed many aviaries around 'The House'. The island and all its livestock and game was run by a manager, a foreman, and thirty cowboys. Charlie Judd saw Ni'ihauans in 1929 as "an industrious and contented people speaking nothing but the Hawaiian language". The island itself seemed to him larger than on his boyhood visit. He and Dougherty both shared the feeling that in 1929, Ni'ihau was operated along the same lines as an English baronial estate.

Dougherty's conclusion: "Everywhere the life of the island is idyllic. There are no rasping noises. No railway train whistles, no honking automobile horns, no radios, no barking dogs, no factory sirens."

What seems strange in retrospect is that although the owners showed this reporter everything on the island, and he talked freely with the people there, he wound up firmly planting the phrase 'mystery island' in the minds of other islanders, and in the island media, where it has lingered ever since. But the only real mystery, it seems to me, is why Ni'ihau– which was made open and available to him, with no prohibitions whatever – was a mystery to Henry Dougherty!

The First Week of the War

IN 1936, THE headlines of Kauai's newspaper, *The Garden Island* and those of the Honolulu papers mourned the death of 83 year old Aubrey Robinson. For the next half century Robinson's isolation of Ni'ihau and its Hawaiians from outside contact were to be given a negative interpretation by those who did not know the island nor understand that minimal water resources and lack of public transport accounted – for the most part – for Ni'ihau's inaccessibility. The rights of private ownership to an entire Hawaiian island were to be held increasingly suspect in the fifty years from 1936 to 1986.

Few in the territory appreciated what Aubrey Robinson's stewardship of Ni'ihau had accomplished. Water resources and population had been kept in balance. Those who romantically hanker for the pattern of Hawaiian tradition ignore the basic improvements of modern times. No longer was Ni'ihau abandoned in time of drought. A once barren island had been forested. In 1936 the men of Ni'ihau were all assured of employment, housing and such perquisites as free poi, mutton and beef and all the fish they could catch. Medical care on Kauai was provided those Ni'ihauans who needed it. In 1936 conditions and wages for Ni'ihau families were much the same as those prevailing throughout plantation Hawaii. These too were being called into question throughout the Territory, a labor struggle that was to be interrupted and at the same time assisted by the war that began five years after Aubrey Robinson's death.

Aubrey Robinson's estate, valued at three and one half million dollars, was left to his four sons who, like their father, were all Harvard graduates. Aylmer, (born in May, 1888) graduated in the class of 1910. So did his older brother Sinclair (born in May, 1886). After graduation Sinclair Robinson spent a year on Oahu, working first as overseer and then as timekeeper for Oahu Sugar Company. Having thus served his internship, the family brought him home to Makaweli where, after six months as assistant manager, he became manager of Makaweli Plantation. In 1916 Sinclair also became a partner in the family firm, Gay and Robinson.

Aubrey Robinson's third son, Selwyn graduated from Harvard in 1916. He came home to Kauai for a few months to work as bookkeeper for Gay and Robinson, then went back to Harvard for a year in the Graduate School of Business Administration. World War I was in full swing. Selwyn volunteered and from 1917 to 1918 served as staff sergeant with the Second Hawaiian Infantry. On his return to Makaweli in 1918 he was made assistant manager of Gay and Robinson, with the additional responsibility of managing Ni'ihau. In 1922, when Selwyn married, Aylmer, who remained a bachelor all his life, took over Ni'ihau.

Lester, the youngest of the four boys, was born in 1901. He graduated from Harvard in the class of 1924 and spent the following year as a management trainee with Libby, McNeil and Libby. In 1925 he returned to Kauai where he became farm manager at Makaweli. From 1927 on he assisted Aylmer in the management of Ni'ihau. Neither brother lived full-time on the island. They commuted two or three times a week on the family sampan.

Neither Aylmer nor Lester were there on December 7, 1941 when a Japanese fighter plane, crippled during the Pearl Harbor attack, made a crash landing on the outskirts of Puuwai. On the 45th anniversary of the attack on Pearl Harbor, December 7, 1986, a four part feature in the *Honolulu Star-Bulletin* detailed this "One-Week War on Niihau Island". Burl Burlingame, *Star-*

Bulletin writer, researched the forty-five year old story with much care, finding the memories of Ni'ihauans not always agreeing on certain points, and articles from the period sometimes contradicting each other. Nonetheless he did a superb job of piecing together what is probably the most reliable – and well written account of what some have called the Battle of Ni'ihau.

Early the morning of December 7th, ranch hand Hawila Kaleohano, a Kona Hawaiian who had come to Ni'ihau in 1930 and married Mabel Kahale, noticed planes flying over the island. Later, around noon, he had just come home from church services, and was standing out in his yard when he saw a plane with the round red symbol of Imperial Japan zooming down out of the sky. Earlier in the year, as part of territory-wide precautions urged by the military in Hawaii, areas of Ni'ihau where planes might be able to land had been ploughed into deep obstructive furrows. From the air, a Japanese pilot named Nishikaichi had spotted the level ground around the Robinson house at Kiekie, but chose instead to land in the yard of the Kaleohano house, just outside Puuwai.

Burl Burlingame's superb description puts us in Hawila Kaleohano's boots as the zero fighter plane, a Mitsubishi A6M2, landed seventy-five feet from where Kaleohano was standing. The plane "hit the ground and bounced directly at him. A wire fence snagged the splayed landing gear and fuel tank, tearing them off. The engine plowed into the rocky soil, folding back the windmilling propellor blades like damp straws."

Kaleohano plunged through the cloud of red dust, smoke, and flying pieces of hot metal to jump up on the plane's wing. The pilot, who was fumbling to loosen his seatbelt, saw Kaleohano and reached for a pistol. The Hawaiian gave him no chance to grasp it. Kaleohano, whose strength was such that he could easily heft a whole sheep on his shoulders, seized the pilot and bashed his head against the dashboard, then tossed the unconscious pilot to the ground.

War, Hawila Kaleohano had heard, was being talked about. Aylmer Robinson had told everyone why the furrows must be made on the level plains of the island. Prudently, Kaleohano grabbed the pilot's Nambu 41 pistol. He jumped down from the plane wing just as Nishikaichi regained consciousness.

Motioning to the pilot to get to his feet and walk ahead of him, Kaleohano took his prisoner inside the house. As the pilot seemed intent on destroying a bundle of papers in his uniform pocket, Kaleohano took them from him – an act that later that week was to lead to a night and morning of terror on Ni'ihau.

By now a number of Kaleohano's neighbors had rushed over. All the rest of Sunday and all Sunday night they took turns keeping watch over the prisoner. Monday was Aylmer Robinson's day to come to Ni'ihau. Kaleohano and his friends felt sure Mr. Robinson would know what to do about the Japanese pilot! So, soon after daybreak, they took Nishikaichi to Kii landing, fifteen miles from the village. There they were joined by the two residents of Ni'ihau who were of Japanese ancestry. Ishimatsu Shintani, the beekeeper, a man in his late sixties, had been on Ni'ihau for many years. He was married to a Hawaiian woman. The second Japanese on Ni'ihau was thirty-seven year old Yoshio Harada who had come three years ago to work as a storekeeper, taking charge of all the supplies kept in the various warehouses.

Like his wife, the former Irene Tanaka, Harada was a Hawaii-born nisei. However, he had spent several unpleasant years in California where the discrimination against Asian-Americans had made him wonder why he thought of himself as American. In California he could not swim in public pools, could not attend the same movie theaters as whites, was forbidden to own property or to marry a white woman. He was relieved to return to the relative paradise of Hawaii which, while restricting job opportunities to Japanese Americans, and denying them social equality, had a day to day atmosphere that was far more palatable. The Haradas, and their daughter Taeko, loved Ni'ihau. Mrs. Harada had a good job here too, working as housekeeper at the Robinson home in Kiekie.

As pilot Nishikaichi began speaking to him in Japanese that Monday morning at Kii, Yoshio Harada had mixed feelings. Old Shintani evidently felt no such tug of ethnic affinity for as the morning passed without Aylmer's arrival, the beekeeper went on home. The pilot cleverly played on the Haradas' sympathies for anyone or anything from Japan. He kept talking to Harada until the nisei felt the urge to help in whatever way he could. Nishikaichi was confident that a submarine would soon surface and rescue him. When he told the Imperial Japanese Navy of Harada's kindness, Harada would receive many honors for in Imperial Japan no group of fighting men was more revered and rewarded than naval aviators – the modern samurai.

Kaleohano and the other Ni'ihau men at Kii kept watching the horizon for Aylmer Robinson's boat. Nishikaichi kept watching for a Japanese submarine to surface. Both were disappointed. That evening, Kaleohano took the pilot back to Puuwai to be guarded during the night. The Haradas remained in their own small house near Kiekie. Probably Yoshio and his wife did a lot of talking, perhaps arguing, that night. As dual citizens, their loyalties pulled in both directions. What should they do?

The next morning, the Ni'ihauans brought Nishikaichi back to Kii Landing. Tuesday passed as had Monday – no sign of anyone. The Japanese submarine would never arrive. It was on far more important missions – hovering ready to shell shore installations at Kahului harbor on Maui and at Hilo on the Big Island, a mission carried out with little success later that month. Nor would Aylmer Robinson be able to reach Ni'ihau, for martial law had been declared in the territory and all sea traffic forbidden to any except the military.

Tuesday and Wednesday passed. By Thursday the pilot knew he had won the support – however reluctant it was – of Yoshio Harada. During the week, in case he should be taken to Kauai as a prisoner, Nishikaichi had torn off his patch and insignia, and tossed them out into the ocean. He kept telling Harada that it was urgent the papers be recovered as soon as possible from Kaleohano. He must also be helped by Harada to destroy what was left of his plane. On Thursday Nishikaichi convinced the Haradas that they should let him spend the night with them, rather than make the long trip back to Puuwai. Irene was compassionate. "Let him sleep on a good bed one night," she suggested.

The invitation relieved Kaleohano and his neighbors. They were tired of having to cope with the pilot. Thursday evening, at dusk, they left Joe Kanahele and Hanaiki Niheu at Kiekie to guard the prisoner. Everyone else went on home to Puuwai.

Now Nishikaichi could carry out his plan, which he had discussed with the increasingly nervous Harada. Early Friday morning he had Harada persuade the two guards that he and the pilot needed to go to the Apiary to see old Shintani. Against his better judgment, with great reluctance, Shintani agreed to go with them back to Harada's home where the pilot and Harada outlined their plot, and what Shintani's role must be.

The conversation took place in Japanese. Sitting listening to the four of them talk around the Haradas' kitchen table, Joe Kanahele announced he was bored. He was going outside and try his luck fishing. That left only one guard, Niheu. When Harada told Niheu that the pilot wanted permission to go to the outhouse, Niheu said, "Sure!" He followed Nishikaichi and Yoshio Harada out the door.

On the way to the privvy Harada pretended to have just remembered something important he must check for Aylmer Robinson. Before going to the outhouse, he told Niheu, he must ask them all to come along for a moment to the honey warehouse. All three men went inside the dark, sweet-smelling building where the kiawe honey that was one of Ni'ihau's exportable products was stored. Niheu's attention strayed to the bright world outside and in that instant, Harada whipped out the Nambu 41 pistol that had belonged to Nishikaichi. Nishikaichi had a double barrelled shotgun. Both weapons were pointing at the startled Niheu.

The tables were now turned. Niheu was a prisoner. They locked him in the warehouse without bothering to tie him up. Then they went to retrieve the papers which old Shintani had agreed to get from Kaleohano. What the pilot and Harada did not know was that Kaleohano had long since hidden the papers in his mother-in-law's house, near the school, and that Shintani – after first pleading for the papers, then offering two hundred dollars for them (an immense amount for Ni'ihau) – had given up and gone home.

They had made a mistake in not tying Niheu's hands. As soon as they left Kiekie, Niheu went upstairs in the warehouse, opened an unlocked window, and jumped down two stories to the ground. Then he hurried, avoiding the road that he knew Harada and the pilot would take to Puuwai. At the village

Niheu tried to warn everyone. Some listened and fled, as did old Shintani. Others simply went into the church.

Niheu was correct in his surmise about Harada and the pilot taking the road to Puuwai. What he did not know was that they were using his horse and wagon to make the fifteen mile trek. It so happened that soon after the two Japanese left Kiekie they met Niheu's wife and her four children, returning by horse and wagon to Puuwai. Nishikaichi commandeered the horse and wagon at gunpoint, forcing Mrs. Niheu and three younger children to get down and ordering teenage Loisa Niheu to stay astride the horse which was pulling the wagon. At the outskirts of Puuwai, they let the terrified Loisa go. Then they went on to Kaleohano's place where Kaleohano's eight year old son told them his father wasn't home.

By now, most of the villagers had fled. Kaleohano was in his outhouse, where he stayed for the time being. When Harada and Nishikaichi left the house to go to the plane, Kaleohano fled. Nishikaichi shot at him, but the bullets hit the privvy and missed the fast running Hawaiian.

Nishikaichi was furious. He and Harada stalked through the village, kicking open doors and ransacking every house to try to find the missing papers. When they came to the house of old Mrs. Huluoulani, she refused to budge or to be frightened. She gave Yoshio Harada a brief lecture on the wages of sin and then turned back to her Hawaiian Bible. When the frustrated Nishikaichi fired several shots into her ceiling, she kept her eyes calmly on the text in front of her.

The fruitless search for the papers took much of the day. At dusk, Harada and Nishikaichi captured two cowboys – Kalanipio Niau and Koahakili Kaliimahuluhulu. The pilot, through Harada, ordered them to dismantle and bring out the two machine guns, which he had previously unbolted from the plane floor. At gunpoint, he forced the two men to hoist the guns and the cartridge belts into Niheu's wagon. Harada convinced him it was wise to let the two men go to alert the villagers as to what would happen if Kaleohano and the papers weren't handed over.

By midnight Harada and the pilot had taken the wagon with its load of machine guns to a rise that overlooked Puuwai.

From there, Nishikaichi began firing a white-hot hail of tracer bullets over the rooftops of the village. It appeared at first as if his strategy worked. Harada, who was anxious to prevent any bloodshed, told the pilot that the villagers were screaming in Hawaiian at Kaleohano to hurry up and give up the pilot's papers or they would all be killed.

Kaleohano – who later became a minister on Kauai – was a stubborn and intensely moral man. Ignoring the screams and pleas of his neighbors he saddled his horse and galloped off in the darkness. His destination was Mt. Paniau, the highest point on the island where the time honored emergency signal to Makaweli could be sent using a kerosene lamp and reflectors. When he arrived, Kaleohano found that several of his neighbors were already there, and had been signaling Makaweli for a long time with no response of lights from the Robinsons.

Some insist that this signal was a bonfire, but with the dry conditions and the flammability of kiawe which forested the island, this would not have been a likely option. Some say that pigeons were used to carry messages back and forth but that on this occasion, Aylmer Robinson had taken all the pigeons back to Makaweli with him on his trip the previous week. Whatever the signal was from Mt. Paniau, Kaleohano arrived there to find others had already sent it – and received no reply from Makaweli. They of course had no way of knowing the whole territory was under severe blackout restrictions!

Kaleohano and several of the men decided the only thing to do was to hurry on to Kii at the northeast end of the island, take a lifeboat and row to Makaweli. This they did, passing Kiekie where a frightened Irene Harada had locked herself and her daughter Taeko in the Robinson house.

Back in Puuwai, Harada worried about his wife, whom he was sure was worrying about him. He and the pilot captured Koahakila Kaliimahuluhulu, tied his hands behind his back, and ordered him to run to Kiekie and tell Mrs. Harada her husband was not coming home tonight until he found Kaleohano. The unwilling messenger set off at a run, but as soon as he was out of sight he swerved down to the beach where his family were hiding. There he met Benihakaka Kanahele who wanted to know what was going on. Kanahele had been gone all week on a hunting trip for wild pig. When Kaliimahuluhulu told him, Kanahele– one of the strongest men on the island – decided that the two of them should go back and capture Harada and the pilot. By now, of course, someone had untied Kaliimahuluhulu's hands.

As they approached Kaleohano's house they could hear the two Japanese smashing things inside. The machine gun cartridges were in the wagon. Good! This was a positive first step! The two Hawaiians scooped up the cartridges and ran back to the beach. At least there would be no more maching gun firing tonight. Realizing that Harada and the pilot were still armed with a pistol and shotgun, Kanahele agreed it was wisest to wait for daylight to try to do anything else. From the beach they could see the glow of flames. Harada and the pilot had set fire first to Kaleohano's house and then to the downed plane.

December nights on the beaches of Ni'ihau can be chilly. The people of Puuwai shivered with cold in the dark hours before dawn. They were all hungry. Kaliimahuluhulu's wife and Ben and Ella Kanahele volunteered to go into Puuwai to find some food. They reached the village about seven o'clock Saturday morning – only to be surprised by Harada and the pilot. Harada told Mrs. Kaliimahuluhulu to return and tell the others that if Kaleohano and the missing papers were not brought to the pilot at once, all the villagers would be killed.

Hearing this she walked away, and then, frightened, broke and ran. Nishikaichi was in more of a hurry, far more desperate than his queasy accomplice. He put his Nambu pistol at Ella Kanahele's head and commanded Harada to send Ben Kanahele to find Kaleohano – 'or else.' The pilot's actions, the tone of his voice, the way he held the pistol at Ella's head left Kanahele no doubt as to what 'or else' meant. He pretended to go off into the forest, and kept calling Kaleohano's name. Looking back from the cover of the trees, Kanahele saw Harada put down the shotgun and the pilot stick his pistol in his boot.

All that went through Kanahele's mind was that Harada, a good man, was not likely to kill any of his neighbors. What must be done was to get the pistol away from the pilot before he killed someone. At this point, Ella Kanahele and the pilot were standing near a stone wall. Quietly Kanahele walked back and began whispering to Harada. At this the pilot shouted something in Japanese which Harada nervously translated. The gist of it was that if Kaleohano and the papers weren't found soon, Nishikaichi was really going to kill everyone – starting with Kànahele and his wife.

As Nishikaichi handed the shotgun back to Harada, and bent to get his pistol, Kanahele jumped him. As he did, the pilot managed to pull the trigger of the Nambu. A .25 caliber bullet entered Kanahele's chest under the left side, then tore out through his ribs in back. It missed any vital organs, but it stopped the big Hawaiian in his tracks. The pilot was raising his pistol to fire a second shot when Ella Kanahele grabbed his arm. Nishikaichi wrestled away from her. Harada grabbed her, trying to keep her away from the pilot and his pistol.

This galvanized the wounded Kanahele. He grabbed the pilot as Ni'ihau cowboys grab a live sheep – by the neck and leg. The pilot screamed. The pistol went off, hitting the edge of Kanahele's left thigh. Ella Kanehele was still struggling with Harada as her husband lifted the pilot and with all his massive strength smashed him against the stone wall, crushing his skull. Burlingame adds the detail that "Kanahele drew his hunting knife and in one quick flashing slice slashed the pilot's throat the way wild pig was killed on Ni'ihau."

Allen Beekman, in his meticulous *The Niihau Incident* (a 1982 publication of Heritage Press of the Pacific, Honolulu) gives this same detail. Others there say no, it was Mrs. Kanahele who finished off the pilot after her husband had felled him. She broke free of Harada, picked up a rock, and heaved it down to split open the pilot's head.

Nothing had happened the way Nishikaichi had said it would. In a panic Harada saw only one avenue open to him – the *harakiri* of his ancestors. He picked up the shotgun and placed it against his belly. Ella Kanahele grabbed his arm so the first shot went astray. Just then Kanahele collapsed. Ella rushed to her husband. Harada again pushed the shotgun at his belly, blasting into his vitals with the second barrel. In agony, he fell backwards between Kanahele and the dead pilot.

Mrs. Kanahele ran screaming for help. She had no sooner left than her husband staggered to his feet. According to

Burlingame, Harada pleaded with Kanahele to stay with him, and help him, to not let him die alone. "I don't want to die here with you," Kanahele is reported as saying and he limped home to the village.

That afternoon at three o'clock Kaleohano and the others in the lifeboat reached Kauai. They had no way of knowing that the battle of Ni'ihau was already ended. By the time a launch with mililtary aid got to Ni'ihau, the bodies of Nishikaichi and Harada had begun to decompose. Ben Kanahele's wounds had been cared for, Hawaiian style, and all of the villagers were moved back into Puuwai.

Alone at Kiekie poor Irene Harada and her daughter waited, weeping, until on December 14 nisei Lt. Mizuha of Kauai, thirteen enlisted men, the six Ni'ihauans from the whale boat, Aylmer Robinson, and Port Allen Harbormaster Eugene McManus arrived to rescue the people of Puuwai. They found everyone in church calmly holding services as usual.

"Where's the Japanese?" asked the rescuers.

"*Make.* Dead," they were told.

Later, in private correspondence (now in the Hawaii State Archives, uncatalogued item) Aylmer Robinson wrote that as to this December 1941 incident, "the Hawaiians handled the situation splendidly and earned the commendation of the Army commanders but the accounts that have appeared in the press have left much to be desired in the way of accuracy."

Never The Same Again

BY EARLY JUNE, 1942 Irene Harada had been taken from Kauai to internment in a camp on Oahu. Old Shintani was on his way to be interned for the duration in a camp on the Mainland. Army Intelligence had retrieved much of interest from the wreckage of the Japanese plane, which had not suffered the fire damage Nishikaichi hoped. The last of the plane's aluminum body parts had been fashioned into saddle decorations by Ni'ihau's resourceful people who were getting used to the wartime traffic of planes overhead and the sight of naval vessels checking the island's coastline. It was early June when the first contingent of G.I.'s arrived to guard Ni'ihau.

Although he well understood that the continuing threat of Japanese invasion made the military presence on Ni'ihau a necessity, these newcomers were a source of much anxiety to Aylmer Robinson. He was as fierce a protector of the Hawaiian-ness of the island as his father Aubrey had been. On June 17, 1942 Aylmer brought his old friend L. David Larsen, manager of Kilauea plantation on Kauai, to Ni'ihau to 'discuss land matters'. Fortunately for us, Larsen recorded his week of experiencing life on wartime Ni'ihau in a journal meant to share his experiences with his wife.

The typescript, available in the Hawaii State Archives, gives us the first detailed description of the island since the 1929 accounts of Henry Dougherty and Charlie Judd. Like them, Larsen possessed the art of using words to paint vivid pictures, but his word portraits are of a Ni'ihau that, because of wartime conditions, would never again be the idyllic and old fashioned place which the 1929 visitors had admired.

Two weeks before Larsen's arrival, the first motor vehicles had arrived on Ni'ihau with a contingent of the 165th regiment, who brought in four jeeps by landing craft. On the day of Larsen's arrival, the *haole* boys of the 165th pulled out leaving only a unit of 13 members of the Hawaiian 299th Infantry, consisting of some Hawaiians, some Chinese, and a few Portuguese boys from Kauai.

It was Larsen's first trip to the island. His immediate impression on landing at Kii was that the Ni'ihauans were a larger people than other Hawaiians. They were extremely friendly and gave handshakes all around as he came ashore. Without a word from Robinson they began unloading the sampan's freight to a flat car which a tractor-trailer pulled up a short track 500 ft. from the beach to a small warehouse. "No one in particular seemed to be the boss and except for 80 lbs. of poi, the boxes of salmon, crackers, flour, taro, sweet potatoes, soap and a few miscellaneous canned goods which were distributed to the proper owners, the warehouse was quickly filled." Larsen wondered at the consignment of two barrels of poi to the main house where only he and Aylmer would be staying.

"Quite a novel experience in this day and age" was the trip from Kii Landing to Kiekie which he and Aylmer Robinson made in a two-seated covered carriage drawn by two good-looking horses.

Their destination was the sprawling old residence that had been built in 1864. It had been expanded over the years to three separate houses interconnected by numerous verandahs and covered passageways. In the yard, at a discreet distance, were servants quarters, warehouses, a carriage shed in which were stored six carriages, a honey house, and several houses "whose purpose I have not yet discovered." What impressed Larsen most about Kiekie was its "magnificent view of the small island of Kaula, 25 miles distant."

His first day on Ni'ihau, Larsen was invited to cross the island by Army jeep with a young sergeant. "I was astounded at the extent of the place. There are miles and miles of pasture with tall grass and scattered kiawe trees. A large part of the time the ocean was not even visible and from all appearances we could have been on a vast continent. The mountains on the north end are always within sight. They are the part of Niihau generally seen from Kauai. The highest point is some 1200 ft. above sea level. Then there is Kawaihoa – the hill at the southern extremity – which also is visible from Kauai in clear weather." . .

Riding along in what was one of the first automobiles ever brought to Ni'ihau, he described "a low flat area of good pasture land ranging from one to two miles in width. Then between the main mountain range that is invisible from Kauai and the small mountain at the southern tip, there is a vast area of flat lands some four to five miles in width, broken by two low hills of volcanic origin and some sandstone hills near the Southern end. Geologically the place is very peculiar. All over the flat pastures of red soil and over the sandstone flats at the Southern end are scatterings of large smoothish boulders. They look as though they had been erupted from time to time, but there is no apparent center of eruption."

In the middle of the island he saw the two large mud flats that are shown on the map as lakes. "After rainy weather they are said to be covered with water. At present, there is only a little salt water towards the center. Along the entire East side of the Island there are numerous similar mud flats or lakes, although much smaller." Larsen mentions seeing "numerous sand dunes and beaches."

As the jeep lurched across the island, it bounced and bumped over the furrows which had been made in early 1941 against any possible air invasion by Japan. To his great dismay and considerable discomfort (he had left Kauai on the sampan at 4:30 A.M. after an even earlier breakfast) Larsen was not served lunch that first day.

His second day, he went with the cowboys to round up turkeys. "There are thousands of turkeys in the pastures. They are driven into temporary corrals, gathered into wagons, brought to headquarters (Kiekie) for fattening on ground-up kiawe beans and cactus leaves." He mentions that "there are also peacocks running wild all over the island."

The large number of cowboys for the relatively small size of the operation of Ni'ihau Ranch puzzled him. In 1942 there were 45 cowboys on the payroll. The total population of Ni'ihau at the time was 180, which Larsen was informed was an increase of 40 persons over the previous decade. Aylmer Robinson explained why the size of the workforce: "When a native son gets to be 15 or 16 he just naturally goes to work." Larsen found that the cowboys of Ni'ihau – and their families – "talk Hawaiian exclusively. Some of the older ones understand but little English." He was impressed by Aylmer Robinson's fluency in Hawaiian.

The honey industry on the island interested Larsen. The honey bee had first been introduced into the Hawaiian Islands in 1853 and by now, less than a century later, beekeeping was one of the profitable enterprised on Ni'ihau. Some 1200 cases (80 tons) of Ni'ihau honey were exported annually in addition to several tons of wax. Each case weighed 130 lbs. Larsen saw Benjamin Kanahele, the 51 year old Hawaiian who had killed the Japanese aviator, pick up two cases of honey with the utmost ease and carry them from the wagon down to the beach to load on the ship. Larsen, who was 56, could not lift a single case!

In his manuscript, Larsen details what he judges to be the tremendous contribution of the Robinsons to the war effort. Evidently, throughout the rest of the territory, others had requested reimbursement for machinery and labor to furrow the level areas as asked of them by the military. No such request was ever made by the owners of Ni'ihau who, says Larsen, "not only transported troops and supplies back and forth between Kauai and Ni'ihau in their sampan and furnished camp sites for soldiers as well as some buildings to be used as headquarters, but they even lent the soldiers horses to ride. The ranch wagons and horses on Ni'ihau were put at the disposal of the troops when they needed to move supplies back and forth from the landing to their camp on the opposite side of the island." Also, on several occasions, Aylmer Robinson had sent out Ni'ihau men to hunt wild pig to supply fresh pork for the soldiers.

However hospitably he had treated them, Aylmer let out a sigh of relief when the last of the *haole* soldiers left the island. According to Larsen this was because "The Robinsons have made it a point to keep the Island as Hawaiian as possible and until the war came along they have certainly been successful at it." Aylmer believed that there were on Ni'ihau in 1942 only one or two quarter whites and one one-eighth white, "all of whom originated as migrants from other islands". These people, married to Ni'ihauans, were still regarded as 'outsiders' after more than thirty years residence on Ni'ihau.

The frequency of ship visitors in the eighty-eight years between the overnight 'fraternization' of Cook's men with Ni'ihauans and Aylmer's great-grandmother's purchase of the island were either not known to or discounted by the Robinsons. As to the Hawaiians of Ni'ihau, the custom was to identify the heritage of the mother. From a practical Polynesian viewpoint, who really knew who one's father might have been!

According to what Aylmer Robinson told Larsen that June of 1942, while the white soldiers were on the island, Ni'ihau-ans did not allow their women folk on the beaches to pick the plentiful small shells they used in making the exquisite shell leis for which Ni'ihau is famous. Some of the white soldiers told Larsen as they left that "there was little fraternizing between themselves and the natives. The girls would run inside whenever a soldier appeared on the village street." Larsen's doubting comment on this is, "Tell that to Ripley!"

Larsen himself saw just one Ni'ihau girl whom he consider-ed a real beauty. While he continued during his week's stay to admire the "almost unanimously large and powerful", magnifi-cent physiques of the Ni'ihau men, his observation as to the majority of the women was that they "are typical Hawaiian, most of them fat and not very good looking."

That first night at Kiekie he was introduced to an old Ni'ihau custom. Whenever the Robinsons were there all cowboys coming to the house before or after work were fed dinner. A sheep was slaughtered and cooked for the first night, not overly much for forty-seven people whose appetites were large. Larsen began to understand why two barrels of poi were consigned to the house where only Aylmer and himself were staying. He remarked how "The cowboys lounged around the yard eating when they pleased and taking great pleasure in conversation with one another, then riding their horses home to Puuwai after dark."

What Larsen had observed on his arrival – the cooperative working together of the Ni'ihau cowboys intrigued him enough to ask Aylmer Robinson about it. Yes, he was told. All work on the island was done on this cooperative basis. "Aylmer tells me that he never gives direct orders but asks if they can do this or that and asks them how it should be done. He says this is the best way to get work and a sense of responsibility out of Hawaiians." Base or minimum pay on Ni'ihau was then $2.00 a day.

By his second day Larsen had learned that on Ni'ihau "only sissies eat lunch". However, at 2:30 in the afternoon, when the cowboys he accompanied came to a stand of coconut trees, he was interested to see that they lost no time in getting off their horses and fairly running up the trees. Everybody indulged freely in soft coconut meat and milk – and then started off again. There were, the cowboys told him, only a few small coconut groves on Ni'ihau. The stand which they passed that day looked weak to Larsen but was, the cowboys told him, typical of the coconut trees on their island.

At dinner time that evening Larsen waited getting more and more famished. Aylmer Robinson did not appear so finally Larsen dined alone on mutton chops, stewed mutton, poi, sweet potatoes, taro, string beans, lima beans, stewed tomatoes, fried bananas, stewed peaches and milk. One of the cowboys cooked and served. On inquiry, Larsen found that this cowboy really didn't like to cook but that Aylmer had asked him to this time. The man told Larsen that most of the cowboys took turns being cook whenever the Robinsons asked them. (Irene Harada had evidently not been replaced as housekeeper and cook).

From the cowboy serving as cook that evening Larsen learned that Ni'ihauans still planted sweet potatoes "when the weather is right" and raised papayas, bananas and sometimes melons. They neither used nor liked green vegetables. Their staple poi was a perquisite, free to each family. Ni'ihauans paid for the flour, pilot crackers, and miscellaneous canned goods that Robinson sent over on the sampan, but there was no freight charge. As to meat, the Robinsons gave out beef and mutton on holidays, special occasions or "when an animal gets hurt". However, wild pig were plentiful. The Ni'ihauans ate a great deal of pork which they dried in the sun like jerked beef.

In 1942 no refrigeration of any kind was available on the island although The House at Kiekie had a small generator used to provide electric lighting. The rest of the island, in 1942, depended on kerosene lamps. Food storage was no problem for fish, plentiful in the surrounding waters, was eaten the day it was caught, or else – like the pork – dried in the sun. Opihi and limu, other favorite foods were picked whenever they wished to eat them. A number of cows and calves were kept in the pasture near Kiekie. Anyone wanting milk could milk these cows but, Larsen was told, Ni'ihauans preferred to use canned milk – even for their babies.

Both tobacco and liquor were forbidden on Ni'ihau. "Coffee is never brought over for the Hawaiians," Larsen notes, "but Aylmer says they manage to get it through other channels. He says he disapproves of it on account of their feeding it to the babies if they have it available. They are allowed to order tea however."

Larsen describes Puuwai at length. "The homes are widely scattered . . . among kiawe trees and cactus thickets and rocks. The area between these yards is used for tethering horses at night or when not let out into the adjoining pastures. Many of the stone walls are covered with night blooming cereus. In the middle of the village is the church, sited picturesquely among old kiawe trees in a spacious yard surrounded by a cereus-covered stone wall." When Larsen declined an invitation to attend church on Sunday, he was told that "On Niihau we always go to church" – and he went.

In the Ni'ihau Church, women all sat on one side, men on the other. Aylmer told Larsen that each Ni'ihau household has a prayer meeting both morning and evening every day. "Church," said Aylmer, "is the only place where the Niihau children are not afraid of the *haoles*." Their parents discipline them by the threat, "If you don't behave we will tell the *haole* on you!"

In church, Larsen saw two *hapa* Japanese – one was a son of Beekeeper Shintani and was married to a Ni'ihau girl. Aylmer also pointed out to Larsen a one-fourth Japanese family descended from a Japanese who landed on Ni'ihau "from a shipwreck many years ago" and married a Ni'ihau girl. It was at church that Larsen saw the beautiful *'ehu'* Hawaiian girl who seemed to him as graceful as a shy faun.

He remarks in his journal, "The whole set up here is so precious and naive it sounds like a fairy tale. They have kept Hawaiian and Christian – perhaps more Christian than Hawaiian and I am sure there is nothing else like it anywhere else in the world. Their isolation and uniqueness is preserved by the rule that if they wish to leave the island even to go to Kauai they must receive permission to do so from the Robinsons, and if they wish to have guests from off-island, similar permission must be granted – the latter being most rare."

On a horseback ride with a cowboy one of his days on the island Larsen again describes Ni'ihau as it looked in 1942, "There are no native forests in the mountains. Mostly it is barren grasslands and rock lands and cactus, except for some tree planting that the Robinsons have done to prevent erosion. Occasionally there were a few wili wili trees and in a few places some Naio– false sandalwood. The chief drawback of the mountain country is lack of water. In places water development has been undertaken quite successfully. In other areas cactus is spread and used as a water supply for the stock."

In riding around the southern part of Ni'ihau, he noted that "A large part of this end is made of sandstone with a scattering of lava boulders. In some places along the shore lava boulders were imbedded in the sandstone many feet below the surface. There were numerous beaches and some perfect spear fishing places where I could see large blue *uhu* swimming about in the clear water. There were signs of former habitation in several places. One place, Pahau, contained the remnants of an old Hawaiian village – a broken down temple or church and lots of small stone platforms indicating houses. I was told this was once a leper settlement."

Hanaiki Niau, the cowboy accompanying Larsen, told him a Ni'ihau version of the legend of Puhi Ula who came from Tahiti. This great eel was crawling ashore on Ni'ihau to catch two children when he was discovered and cut in two by a warrior.

"At one place," relates Larsen, "we passed a couple of wooden houses and the remnants of a mor modern village. This was Kaimalino which until a few years ago was occupied by some ranch hands. To me it seemed ever so much better for a Hawaiian habitation than their present village – it being along the seashore with many very likely looking fishing places. All over this end of the Island were scatterings of the Hawaiian spider flower. Niihauans call it *pilo* and use the roots for a poultice for treating fractures. They say that pounded with salt it is very effective and keeps down inflammation."

"Kawaihoa, the hill at the southern extremity of Niihau is most interesting as it is of volcanic origin and protrudes from a flat area of solid sandstone. Very evidently it was a separate island once. At the foot of the hill there is a perfect little bay, Keanahaki, where the Robinsons have a beach house which from all indications is out of use." Here, in no time at all, Larsen picked up enough glass balls to fill a burlap sack.

"At one beach Niau (the cowboy) stopped for *moi* and with only one throw (of his net) snagged ten nice big ones." At Larsen's suggestion Niau cast his net a second time over the large school of fish the Ni'ihauan refused, saying, "Enough".

During the day Niau gave Larsen small bits of casual information about island life. Sundays, as Larsen had surmised, were exclusively devoted to church and rest. Ni'ihauans gave no thought to the automobiles and trucks that were common on the other islands. They had their own transportation – some 400 horses on the island. Each cowboy owned four horses plus one for his wife and one for each child over eleven. As to dogs, there were none on account of the sheep.

It was with sadness that, at week's end, Larsen returned to Kauai – a sadness for an island whose idyllic way of life was obviously about to be changed. He was quite right! Almost one year to the day after Larsen's visit, the June 19, 1943 edition of the *Honolulu Advertiser* caught readers' attention with a headline that proclaimed: "Once isolated Niihau greets Army, joins nation's war effort". A subhead further grabbed attention. "Natives learn of Beer, Jeeps, From Soldiers at Outpost." The article, by *Advertiser* staff writer Laselle Gilman, pronounced that Ni'ihau was "Hawaii's hermit island no longer. The war – and the Army – have revolutionized Niihau."

Gilman lists the changes which David Larsen had feared were taking place. "Since December 7, 1941," writes Gilman, "The modern world of jeeps, radios, movies, electric lights and bold-eyed strangers in uniform has invaded that legendary baronial estate which is the Territory's farthest-west inhabited island . . . Life on Niihau has been radically altered."

Since Laselle Gilman had never been to Ni'ihau his descriptions leave one wondering as to what was his source of information for what he calls the "broad green grasslands" on which are pastured "perhaps 1,000 cattle, 15,000 sheep, and herds of fine Arabian horses." He is quite correct, however, in his statement that "Nothing on Niihau was ever modernized before December 7. Many of the people were born and died on the island without ever leaving it; they had little interest in outside affairs; and envied no one."

He reports that the Army had never been welcome on Ni'ihau but "welcome or not it promptly moved in and stayed there from that day (December 7, 1941) on." Evidently Gilman had forgotten about Ni'ihau's terrifying first week of the war when nobody answered their distress signals and they had to cope with the war having landed in Kaleohano's backyard.

Gilman's public assessment of the impact of the first contingent of mainland G.I.'s on Ni'ihau matched the private observations of David Larsen. "These *haole* soldiers had strange manners and customs and a strange way of speech, larded with profanity. They kidded the shy young Niihau girls openly and told the wide-eyed boys tall stories about the Mainland. They showed Niihauans moving pictures and let them listen to jam sessions on the radio." Gilman does not make clear that these 'haole soldiers' were replaced after two and a half weeks with 'local' G.I.'s who understood the meaning of *kapu*. In 1943 traffic between Ni'ihau and Kauai was relatively heavy although, remarks Gilman, "you've still got to be a Somebody with pretty urgent business there to get an invitation."

Enter The Politicians

LORAN, AN ACRONYM for long range navigation, was developed just in time to meet the wartime need for aiding heavy military traffic across the Pacific. The November 12, 1943 decision to set up such a system based in the Hawaiiian islands and archipelago was made by the Joint Loran Planning Committee of the Joint Chiefs of Staff in Washington, D.C.- a decision that would bring more strangers to Ni'ihau for the duration of the war and, as it turned out, on into the 1950's.

During the rest of November and much of December 1943, a site selection team made up of representatives of the chief of Naval Operations, the Army Air forces and the Air Service Command surveyed the islands to determine the best locations to build the chain of Loran stations.

The survey team recommended building one monitor station on the island of Kauai, a single slave station at Upolu Point on the Big Island, a double master station on Ni'ihau and a single slave station at French Frigate Shoals. The Robinsons readily gave their permission to build the station on their island. After all, it was wartime and it is probable they assumed the installation would be temporary.

The double master station on Ni'ihau was the first to be built. On March 21, 1944 the Coast Guard's newly created

Construction Detachment C. Unit 80, sailed from San Francisco under the command of Lt. Commander Frank L. Busse, who was later succeeded by Lt. Commander Merton Stoffle. At Sand Island in Honolulu the detachment and supplies essential to build the station were transferred to the 175-foot twin screw steam propelled cutter 'Walnut'. Since this vessel had a draft of thirteen feet, and since the landing sites at both Kii and Nonopapa necessitated a shallow draft vessel, LCM's (Landing Craft Mechanized) were obtained from the Navy Amphibious Section at Pearl Harbor. 7-D Caterpillars and their operators were furnished by the Army to negotiate the heavy sand formation at Nonopapa Landing.

Kii Landing, with its larger stone dock and more sheltered anchorage would have been easier for bringing materials ashore, but its distance (23 miles from the station site on the south-western shore of Ni'ihau) was prohibitive. Nonopapa was only 8 miles from the area chosen by the military survey team and agreed to by the Robinsons – a site halfway between Keelinawi and Leahi Points. On April 27, 1944 the 'Walnut' hove to in deep water well off Nonopapa Landing. The LCM's began off loading but heavy ground swells and the coral formations there presented such undue risk to men and materials that after landing two tractors and a two-and-one-half ton truck, operations were temporarily suspended.

Not until May 4th did the weather improve. Beginning that day, and continuing through May 5th and 6th, some 85 tons of equipment and supplies were brought ashore on the LCM's. During those two days forty enlisted men and two officers, Lt. Cmdr. Stoffle and Lt. Paul C. Edmunds, were also landed on Ni'ihau. The 'Walnut' returned to Sand Island leaving 42 new users of the island's limited water supply – 42 new *haoles* who knew little or nothing about Ni'ihau's isolation or the lifestyle encouraged by Aylmer and Lester Robinson.

By July 22nd, 1944 the Ni'ihau Loran station with its radio tower, control building, and living quarters was completed. System accuracy tests of this and the other quickly constructed Loran stations in the Hawaiian chain were conducted until November 8, 1944. On that date Ni'ihau's station, and those on French Frigate Shoals, Kauai, and Upolu Point, Hawaii were turned over to be commissioned as part of the command of the District Coast Guard Officer of Hawaii's 14th Naval District.

The Ni'ihau Loran station was commissioned as CGIRS, Unit 205. It was, like the other stations, to prove as useful in the first years of peace as it had been during the war in the Pacific. Its isolation in wartime was to be expected but after VJ Day, the Coast Guard contingent on Ni'ihau remained – a changing complement of enlisted men and officers, usually assigned for an eighteen month period. In 1946 they were bitterly vocal about the hardships of being stationed on Ni'ihau. That July reporter Ernest R. May of the *Honolulu Advertiser* interviewed the men of the Loran Station during a visit to Ni'ihau by a Territorial Senate Committee. Back in Honolulu later that week, the reporter expressed the Loran detachment's views in his headline: "Niihau called Alcatraz by Military Garrison".

Reporter May began his story with the statement that "Military personnel stationed on mysterious Niihau have only one kind word to say for the lonely hump of volcanic rock and coral. This is it – 'The only thing we like here is when we get our mail from the states.'". May goes on to inform his readers that evidently, prior to the establishment of the Loran Station, the military had signed an agreement with the Robinsons that GI's would observe Ni'ihau's prohibition of alcoholic beverages – including beer, that no such beverage be kept or used in the barracks, that the Coast Guardsmen (and the wartime detachment of GI's) not have any intercourse, social or otherwise, with the people of Ni'ihau, and that the military personnel not attend Ni'ihau church services or other civilian social functions on the island.

The officials who brought Reporter May along on their trip to Ni'ihau did not have in mind a friendly visit such as Territorial Governor Judd had made to the island seventeen years earlier. Except for the members of the press who came with them, the 1946 visitors were members of a Territorial Senate Committee headed by part Hawaiian Francis Ii Brown. Political sentiment in Hawaii had begun to swerve. Brown and his colleagues were imbued with a social welfare enthusiasm that marked most politicians in the islands after World War II. They were, frankly and openly, on an investigative mission. Later, the senators said they had been denied access to the Ni'ihauans although, in the August 2 edition of the *Advertiser* a picture taken by the press photographer who was along on the senate trip showed what the caption said was a "typical Niihau family".

Access was certainly not the right word to describe this contact. Mrs. Kaohelaulii and three of her teen age daughters were evidently reluctant to have their pictures taken. They refused to give the photographer their names. The photograph had been taken "after lengthy persuasion" as the Kaohelaulii's watched the cavalcade of visitors pass by their home in Puuwai village. "All Hawaiians on Niihau object to being photographed, feeling they are being used for 'exhibition purposes' ". Aylmer Robinson is quoted as saying when he was asked to identify the family. He refused, saying only that they were a 'cowboy' family – as, of course, were all the families on the island.

The exciting stories about the Battle of Ni'ihau that had taken place the first week of the war had stimulated reader interest in this one island of the territory where ordinary visitors were not permitted. The 1946 visit of the senators was a story that the *Advertiser* strung out for several days of what the editor's note called "a series of exclusive Advertiser articles on Niihau, the island where time stands still." The August 2nd article, accompanying the photograph of the Kaohelaulii women, was headlined "Niihau Facing Inroads of Modern Living Trends". This, Reporter May intimated, was going to be the probable result of the visit of the "six-man investigative committee of the Territorial Senate" whom May portrayed as being eager to "transplant the benefits of modern science and transportation" to this island. His August 3rd story was headlined "Isolated Niihau Like 17th Century Island".

May made much of what cowboys on Ni'ihau were paid, reporting that "information given the Senate group is to the effect that the average wage is about $1.50 a day or more." Aylmer Robinson said "The pay scale starts with employees ten years old and older. The standard day is eight hours and overtime is paid." This was quite in line with wages paidd cowboys on other islands. Throughout the Territory, especially during the war, children ages 10 and sometimes younger were employed on the plantations. On Lanai, children working in the pineapple fields were paid only a few cents a day.

Access to more than a grade school education was limited in most rural communities in those territorial days. Ni'ihau School was not too far off the 1946 norm for small remote rural areas in offering only grades one through five. Its two teachers were paid by the Department of Public Instruction who continued to hire unqualified and under qualified (as well as under paid) teachers for Hawaii's country schools. In cowboy communities like Puuanahulu on the Big Island a one room school had one teacher handling grades one through six. The plantation era assumption had been that to maintain an adequate labor force, too much education should be discouraged – particularly in rural areas of the Territory.

Ni'ihau's school building had been built by the Robinsons at their expense. As a physical plant it was comparable to that of many other small rural schools in the territory, no better but certainly no worse either. Yet, the reaction of the Senators visiting the two-room Ni'ihau School in 1946 was that it was urgent a new public school house be built by the Territory.

In answer to queries about Ni'ihau church, which was on the school grounds, the senators were told that "the church has become indigenous with a Bible reading pastor selected from among the more proficient Niihauans."

Amusement? Of course, the committee was told. "Niihauans fish the surrounding seas with nets and spear and hunt wild pigs. There also are more gentle amusements such as singfests in the church and various games such as croquet, which are procured from Chicago mail order catalogs." The statement of Aylmer Robinson that "traditional Niihau isolation is based as much upon the desires of the inhabiting Hawaiians as upon the inclination of the management" was discounted by most of the senators and by the reporter accompanying them.

According to the Advertiser's August 4 article, which bore the 'Alcatraz' headline, the Senators – and the reporter – were kept away from any but minimal contact with the people of Ni'ihau. At least one myth about the island was dispelled in May's concluding article of that date: "Reports that anyone who leaves Niihau is never permitted to return are not correct, according to military personnel on the island." They are quoted as having told the reporter that "At least two men, one an internee" (probably old Shintani, the beekeeper) "and another a man who was drafted for army services, have been known to return in the past five years."

This latter reference is questionable in light of a 1946 statement made by Kauai Draft Board Chairman Andrew Gross. When challenged as to why nobody had ever been drafted from Ni'ihau, Gross replied, "They've been called up according to schedule and most have been fine physical specimens. We send them to Honolulu for physical and mental exams and the Army sends them right back. There's a language barrier and they can't pass the literacy test. It's a shame!" Gross put to rest recurrent rumours in the territory that during the war Aylmer Robinson had arranged to have his ranch hands deferred as agricultural workers. "I don't remember that there were any requests for exemptions from the Robinsons at any time," Gross said. "All the farm, ranch and plantation workers were treated alike by the Board."

If there was a World War II veteran on Ni'ihau in the summer of 1946, the territorial senators and their press entourage did not get to meet him. Nor did they see old Shintani. They charged they were hurried through the village by Lester and Aylmer Robinson who told them very few residents could be contacted on this particular day because "the people are out in the hills working". The school was closed because "the two teachers are away". The church was not open because "the minister isn't around". One frustrated senator voiced his annoyance at being whisked back to the ranch headquarters for a 'luau' which, he later announced with sarcasm, turned out to be sandwiches and coconuts served on the back steps of the ranch house.

At Kiekie the photographer was told the ranch buildings were off limits to the press cameras "because the war years have not permitted proper maintenance of the buildings." At an attempt to photograph one of the six old fashioned carriages, Hawaiians quickly grabbed the shafts and pulled the vehicles into a dark carriage house. Only two hours after their arrival on the island, the irate senators boarded the Robinson's sampan for the return to Kauai. They were to make some extremely strong recommendations to their fellow legislators next session about changes the Territorial government must make on Ni'ihau. Primary among these were recommendations that the 1947 Territorial Legislature install some type of modern communications between Ni'ihau and the other islands of the Hawaiian chain; that the Territorial Board of Health be mandated to station a territorial medical representative on Ni'ihau, and that an adequate school program be initiated, with qualified teachers.

Reporter May's series on this visit began the day after publication of an interview with a Hawaiian woman pastor, Reverend Ella Wise Harrison, who spent three weeks on Ni'ihau that same summer. Her assessment of "Niihau's people as simple and dignified" appeared in an *Advertiser* article written by Keyes Beech published August 1, 1946. Ella Wise, a pastor of the Church of the Living God, had been the guest of friends and relatives in Puuwai. She informed the reporter that on her arrival she had met Sinclair and Aylmer Robinson who welcomed her to "go where she pleased and do as she pleased". Daughter of the late John H. Wise, professor of Hawaiian Language at the University of Hawaii, Ella Wise' comment to the reporter on her return to Honolulu was that "Niihau is something my father used to dream about – a part of Hawaii for Hawaiians only, where their native culture and ways can be preserved, where the race can stand apart and retain its dignity and individuality."

She explained that "Niihau's children are sent to junior high school on Kauai" and that, as to health care, "the people are taken to Waimea, Kauai when they need to see a dentist. When someone becomes ill he is taken to Waimea to see the doctor. The doctor's bills are paid by the Robinsons, the people pay for their own dental care." She described Niihau children as "fat and healthy" with as many as "seven or eight youngsers in a family". She was most impressed by the fact that on Ni'ihau "all of them speak Hawaiian fluently, which most Hawaiians on Oahu and other islands have forgotten."

In subsequent coverage of Ni'ihau by the press, it was the Senate Committee's negative experience which surfaced in numerous articles over the next few years. Neither the Senators nor Ella Wise seem to have been aware of the major problems on Ni'ihau in 1946. An infestation of maggots was attacking the Merino sheet and a blight on panini cactus, which Ni'ihau

Ranch used for cattle feed, had reduced the usual carrying capacity of 1500 beef cattle on the island by "several hundred head". The combination of these posed questions about the ranch being able to continue its full economic support of the Ni'ihauans.

Such a concern was never expressed by the Senators on their return to Honolulu. Instead, they made fervent speeches about Ni'ihauans being denied the right to own property – this in 1946 when the majority of plantation workers in the territory did not and could not own their own homes, but lived in largely substandard 'camp' housing.

In November of 1946 the Coast Guardsmen on Ni'ihau reported that the spotlight of publicity occasioned by the visit of the senate committee had already stimulated change on the island. "A shiny new truck has been brought to Niihau and another is on the way." Formerly, the only truck on the island was that belonging to the Coast Guard. Some Ni'ihauans had also received permission to get gas refrigerators and the first had already arrived. The twelve men remaining at the Ni'ihau Loran Station reported that "the larger part of the fraternization ban continues but some of the Niihau men have become quite friendly to the Coast Guard." The Coast Guard now provided communication with Kauai in case of emergencies but Aylmer Robinson was taking steps to install radio-telephone equipment in anticipation of the time when the Coast Guard might move out.

The report of these changes did not alter the politicians' determination to launch a crusade that was to persist for the next thirty years. "The Niihau people are only permitted to own horses!" they alleged – an allegation that was quite true, and a necessity for an island where with one exception there were only wagon roads and horse trails. Evidently for some years before the war Kauai County had paid Ni'ihau Ranch $500 annually to maintain the road to the school. This funding stopped when someone reminded the county that the road was on private property.

The political crusade to change Ni'ihau over into the image of what the politicians felt it ought to be was launched in the 1947 session of the Territorial Legislature. Special Committee

Report No. 4 pronounced that, as regards Ni'ihau "the entire community is out of step with our local and national concept of the freedom of the individual and of government by the people, of the people, and for the people. No one born and brought up on Niihau would have an opportunity of decent survival in the competition of free men which exists elsewhere in these Hawaiian Islands and in the Union generally." Out of the dim and distant missionary past the senators revived the specter of religious intolerance, claiming that on Ni'ihau, "even in such a primitive community it is intolerable that spiritual solace and guidance, the administration of the rites of the church of their choice, should be denied the tenants, and that such is the case, the adherents of the Roman Catholic Church know only too well." This is the first allegation in eighty years that there may still be 'closet Catholics' on Ni'ihau.

The report continued: "In short, your committee finds that either directly or by implication, three of the four freedoms, to wit, freedom of speech, freedom of religion, and freedom from fear either by name or in essence, are unknown upon the island of Niihau." Committee members Francis Ii Brown, Francis Sylva, John B. Fernandez, C.A. Crozier, Charles M. Silva, and W. H. 'Doc' Hill ended their report with eleven specific recommendations. First was that "sufficient land be acquired by condemnation or otherwise to provide for the establishment of a school up to and including the eighth grade, together with cottages for resident teachers and a cottage for visiting officials or employees (of the Department of Public Instruction)."

A public landing and pier was also sought, "by condemnation or otherwise" of the necessary property required. Title to roads leading from such a public landing to the 'government center' (the school) was advocated. A small landing field for airplanes was to be built on land to be 'acquired' from the island's owners. The committee wanted a resident Hawaiian speaking nurse for Ni'ihau, one who would be under the jurisdiction of the Board of Health. They urged acquisition of land for a small hospital or dispensary, and a district courthouse and police station. They recommended appointment of a district magistrate and police officer.

They wanted radio and telephone communication established between Ni'ihau and Kauai and the other islands. As to freedom of religion, they recommended sufficient land be acquired to build "a small church or churches" to accommodate the members of several faiths and that "a law be enacted which would penalize the practice of forbidding the visiting of the tenants by their spiritual advisors and administering to such tenants the rites of the several churches to which they belong."

During the 1947 session, Representative Flora Hayes of Kona and Buster McGuire made a trip to Ni'ihau to look into conditions there themselves. Both spoke Hawaiian. Mrs. Hayes returned saying "everybody seemed perfectly happy and contented." She praised the excellent manners of the Ni'ihau children, "the result of rigorous training the two-room school." To her, Ni'ihau 1947 was like Kona had been in 1927. It made her nostalgic to see a community where the hectic pace of modern life had not yet appeared.

In March 1947 Representatives Tom Ouye and Matsuki Arashiro of Kauai and Joseph Kaholokula, Jr. of Maui introduced a bill that would have empowered the Commissioner of Public Lands to condemn a sufficient area on Ni'ihau for construction of a training school for juvenile delinquents. Plans for the facility and its operation were to be prepared by the public works department of the Territory. The bill passed first reading and then, fortunately for Ni'ihau, it died.

The same week that this bill was introduced, Senator Harold Rice, who said he had visited Ni'ihau, charged in one of the legislative sessions held in Iolani Palace that school books on Ni'ihau were kept locked up and that the students there learn only from the Bible.

Nothing much resulted from all the legislative furore of 1947. An article in the May 5th *Advertiser* stated that probably because of it there was "A possibility that the 'iron curtain' of private ownership may rise even more in years to come and bring the secluded island of Niihau into current world affairs." They evidently deduced such far reaching effects from the decision of School Superintendent Loper to send the two Ni'ihau teachers to Kauai to observe "more recent teaching techniques and methods." Loper also announced that in the near future he to add grades 7, 8, and a third teacher to Ni'ihau school.

Kauai's Charlie Rice, when he appeared before the Senate on April 23rd "as a representative of the people of Niihau" brought a petition (in Hawaiian) signed by 62 Ni'ihau residents asking that "the people be left as they are". Under extensive questioning by legislators, Rice admitted that the publicity given to the Senate committee's visit, and its report to the legislature, had already done the island some good. He emphasized that the petition from the Ni'ihau residents opposed a public schoolhouse (evidently by this they meant a new building), a road, a wharf and an airport as recommended by the Senate committee on the grounds that "this will bring bad influences into our lives."

In July, Clarice Taylor of the *Star-Bulletin* wrote at length of her interview with visiting Ni'ihau teacher Mrs. Miriam Hanaike, who had come to Honolulu to enroll her daughter Mary, 17, in the University of Hawaii Teacher Training Course. Mrs. Hanaike was herself a graduate of Iolani School and, according to Clarice Taylor, spoke beautiful English. She was the mother of eight children, and told the reporter that the other Ni'ihau teacher, Hannah Niau, was rearing a family of thirteen. Their hope was that Ni'ihau girls, perhaps their own offspring like Mary Hanaike, could be encouraged to come to Honolulu to take the teacher training course and return home to Ni'ihau.

What about the recommendations made by the Senate investigative committee? Mrs. Hanaike replied, "Niihau people cannot understand why the politicians should make such a fuss about their way of life on Niihau." She told Clarice Taylor that many Ni'ihau men were working for Interisland and Matson Navigation Company, that there were Ni'ihauans living and working in California and that ties with those relatives remained strong.

"Marriage is just as exciting to a Niihau couple as any other young couple in the world," said Mrs. Hanaike. "They make a boat trip to Waimea Kauai to take out their marriage license. Then they are either married in Waimea at the Hawaiian church or return to Niihau and are married by Ernest Kaohelaula, our licensed pastor there. Such weddings are followed by a luau, a general celebration." Mrs. Hanaike does not make special mention of the fact that Ni'ihau girls often became the brides of Hawaiians who were not Ni'ihauans. In such cases, the couple sometimes settled on Ni'ihau.

When she was young, Mrs. Hanaike recalled, "Women had their babies Hawaiian style with a midwife. Now (1947) if a young mother wants a *haole* doctor a message is sent to Kauai and Dr. Burt Wade will come over. Dr. J.M. Kuhns makes a regular monthly trip to check on everyone's health. Nowadays the young mothers follow instructions given by Dr. Wade or Dr. Kuhns so the old Hawaiian methods are dying out."

What about language, Clarice Taylor asked this teacher from Ni'ihau.

Mrs. Hanaike's answer was that "The school teaches both English and Hawaiian. English is taught with the use of public school textbooks furnished free of charge by the county of Kauai. They are the same ones used in other public schools in the Territory. Niihau children have no Hawaiian text books," she commented. "They speak Hawaiian at home and want to speak Hawaiian at school. They learn Hawaiian (written) by studying the Bible and Hawaiian hymnals furnished by the Hawaiian Evangelical Association. There is no conflict about religious education on Niihau for it is assumed the Bible should be taught in school." She added that singing hymns was the favorite school diversion. "Boys and girls both have guitars and ukuleles."

While Mrs. Hanaike was being interviewed in Honolulu, Dr. Charles L. Wilkes, Jr., president of the Territorial Board of Health gave statistics that seemed at odds with her placid picture of motherhood on Ni'ihau. According to him, Ni'ihau's infant mortality rate over the past eleven years was 130 deaths per 1000 live births while that of the rest of the Territory was only 46 deaths per 1000 live births. He cited lack of prenatal care and insufficient childbirth supervision as responsible for the high death rate of Ni'ihau babies. Whether or not Dr. Wade or Dr. Kuhns responded to this criticism was not made clear.

In 1947 his fellow politicians chose not to listen to Charlie Rice's plea to "think twice before you force anything down the throats of the Hawaiians. There are no crimes so don't saddle them to a district magistrate." He showed his own colonial point of view, well intended though it might have been, in his statement that "The Niihauans are good cowboys and no one could ever ask for a better maid than one of those Hawaiian girls from Niihau." He contended that "Hawaiian herbs are better medicine than white man's medicine" although, he reminded, as had Miriam Hanaike, that a doctor visited Ni'ihau once a month. His parting shot, with which many in the Territory agreed, was "You are spending hundreds of thousands of dollars to rehabilitate Hawaiians in other areas. This is free, so leave them alone!"

The Eye of the Beholder

IN 1951 ONLY the cluster of abandoned quonset huts memorialized the eight years of Coast Guard presence on Niʻihau. The Loran station there was no longer essential, a decision that must have been a relief for the Robinsons. The island was suffering a prolonged and unusually severe drought. The fewer users of Niʻihau's precious water supply, the better.

Neither the 1951 demise of the Loran Station nor the continuing drought is mentioned in the exuberant article written in December 1953 by Jean Keale, a Niʻihauan who was a student at Honolulu Christian College. "Life on Niihau is very much the same as on any other cattle ranch on the other islands," she wrote in her article entitled "New Year on Niihau" which was published in *The Hawaii Weekly* of December 27, 1953. She told how the cowboys work with the cattle. In the rainy season Niʻihauans plant their potatoes and other garden crops. Each family raises bananas, sugar cane, pineapples, and water melons. Corn is also popular. On weekdays the men work. The children go to school. On Sundays everyone attends church. Humdrum? Not at all in the eyes of the first girl from Niʻihau to graduate from Kamehameha, an education she hoped would enable her to become a teacher at Niʻihau School.

173

It was obvious she was eager to return home. For her the concerns of the 1947 Senate Investigating Committee were largely irrelevant. How could they understand her island, and her people or assess how they felt and what they really wanted after only one visit of two hours! Almost deliberately she repeats the word 'normal' as if she doubts readers from other islands understand what 'normal' means.

"In our life which is so normal for us there is one special week. That is New Year's week and it is a week of celebration. As the church is so much a part of our lives, it is a week of worship." It is also a time when they celebrate the exploits of a famous pig hunter who lived on Ni'ihau more than a century ago. "We call him Keoki. I'm sorry I do not know his real name but I know his story!"

Keoki was the strongest, best rider and hunter on the island. He could snare a pig with a rope quicker and more surely than any other man. He was proud of what he could do and after a successful hunt he would walk boastfully before the other men of Ni'ihau. When others asked God for help in what they did, Keoki scoffed. "Does God find the pig for me? No! I find it. Does God kill the pig? No. I kill it! I do not need to ask for help."

Then came a bout with a gigantic wild boar who looked, said Keoki, "like a devil". For the first time in his life the arrogant hunter called for *kokua* – help. A thick fog hung over the mountain that day and in trying to dodge the ferocious tusks of the boar, Keoki misjudged his footing. He fell backward over a cliff edge, plummeting sixty feet down to a ledge. Fortunately the ledge was at the entrance to a gulch that ran back into the mountain so when his friends heard his cried for help, they could make their way to him. Gently they carried him back to his village. His wounds were severe, but with the prayers of his friends and the skillful application of Hawaiian herbs, he finally recovered.

One year passed before Keoki was well enough to go on another hunt. Before he did so he made a special prayer of gratitude for having been rescued. And this time he hunted not for himself but to make a New Year feast to show gratitude to his friends and neighbors. Each year thereafter he did the same, so long before his death an annual festival of the New Year was established. Because of Keoki's gratitude there was a service of worship in the church. "Today on Niihau," concluded Jean Keale, "we celebrate New Year's in this fashion. We have a week of feasting and worship. The children learn Bible verses. Entire families prepare to conduct parts of the services with hymns and scripture." It was, in 1953, still "a festival of thanksgiving."

Ten months after the publication of this article, Jean Keale fulfilled her ambitions. She was back on Niʻihau, where she was one of the teachers welcoming the first visit of the territory's School Commissioners. Superintendent Clayton F. Chamberlain, who had visited the school on two prior occasions later told *Garden Island* reporter Joe Arakaki that "Niihau School has made tremendous strides in the last year." He attributed this to the addition of grades six through eight which the return of Jean Keale as a third teacher had made possible.

In 1954, the year that Jean Keale returned home as Niʻihau's third teacher, Niʻihau School was visited by the Territorial School Commissioners. These appointed officials seemed pleased with what they saw on the island as did the group of tax appraisers who visited Niʻihau the following summer. In August 1955 J. M. Coney, Tax Assessor and Collector for the Fourth (Kauai) Taxation Division of the Territory of Hawaii, Edward Medeiros, Tax Administrator, Edward Morishige, Building appraiser, Charles Kiilau, land appraiser, Manuel Andrade, cashier, Wallace Tanaka and John Hamano, tax clerks made a Robinson-approved trip to Niʻihau. Since this comprised practically the entire staff of the Kauai tax office, one might have suspected a junket had it not been for the work the men accomplished. They spent two days appraising 183 buildings including dwellings, water tanks, warehouses and other farm units.

The group arrived on Coney's sixty-five foot fishing boat, the 'Kolomana', on which some of the tax people slept each night. The others spread their sleeping bags on the beach. Tax Assessor Coney told an inquiring *Star-Bulletin* reporter that "the people of Niihau were very hospitable and seemed quite contented". He remarked that "the workers there lived in very comfortable homes". One of the highlights of the trip for him and for his staff when the appraisal work was completed was a weekend of fishing in the waters around

Ni'ihau and Lehua Island. Their catch? Nineteen kawakawa, four ulua, three mahimahi and an ahi.

One of the reasons Charlie Rice had given as to why the district courthouse and police station recommended by the Senate Committee should not be built on Ni'ihau was that for the past century there had never been need for either. Ni'ihau people were both godfearing and careful to obey the rules set down by the Robinsons. They were a law abiding community. So that same year of the tax appraisers' visit, it was a historic occasion – albeit an unpleasant one – for two Kauai police officers to arrive to apprehend a criminal on Ni'ihau.

The man they were after was a son of Ishimatsu Shintani, the old beekeeper. Thirty-two year old Levi Shintani was a former Oahu prison inmate who had recently been living in Kekaha, unemployed and homesick to see his parents and his home island. He had not been back there, nor seen his father since 1939. He knew that with his record it was not likely the Robinsons would let him return. His yearning for home over-came him one Saturday night and he went to Waimea Bay and stole a thirty foot sampan. Levi had never in his life operated a boat, but that did not deter him. He managed to get the engine going and left Kauai about one a.m. Sunday morning.

It was five a.m. when he reached Ni'ihau, having made his way through fairly choppy seas. Once offshore, he threw an anchor over the side of the sampan, jumped overboard and swam ashore. Then he walked twenty miles to his parents' home. In the meantime, back on Kauai, the sampan's owner – Tamotsu Kimura of Waimea – reported its theft to the police.

When they heard Kimura's suspicions about who had stolen his sampan and where it might be, the police called the Coast Guard station at Nawiliwili. The cutter was dispatched to Port Allen where Kimura boarded it to go to Ni'ihau to identify his stolen craft. Late Sunday afternoon they spotted the sampan. Levi had not secured the anchor. The sampan had been washed ashore. Coast Guard Ensign Harris and owner Kimura had to swim 200 yards from the cutter to the beach where the wrecked sampan lay. They found the propellor shaft broken and several holes in the sampan's hull. It was in such condition that only the engine was salvageable.

The following day a Gay and Robinson sampan brought Kauai Police Captain Vidinha and Patrolman Chu to track and catch the thief, which they easily did. It was a short visit Levi Shintani enjoyed with his parents. Vidinha and Chu took him into custody and the Robinson sampan returned him to Kauai to face charges, and a return to jail.

In December of that eventful 1955, eight years after the 1947 Senate Committee's investigation, the territorial government claimed to have found documents that might reveal there were public lands on Ni'ihau. These were presumed to be potential sites for another school building, a public wharf, and perhaps an airport (or heliport) as the 1947 Report had recommended. According to Attorney General Edwin N. Sylva several records had been found revealing that the territory might well own 14.76 acres of land on Ni'ihau. The acreage included six school sites which had been designated in Royal Patent #42, dated September 30, 1882. In addition Grant #1615, dated January 20, 1855, proved government ownership of a school lot, a church lot and landings at Omalumalua and Kaimalino.

Attorney General Sylva wrote a letter to the co-owners of Ni'ihau, Alice Gay Robinson (now ninety) and her sons saying, in part, "This office will soon request the Surveyor of the Territory to accurately locate on the ground these sites and landings. Would you kindly advise me at your early convenience what arrangements can be made with you regarding the surveyor's trip and also, whether any claim is made by you to the government lands above mentioned."

The youngest of the Robinson brothers, Lester, when queried by telephone, told an *Advertiser* reporter that he had not yet seen the letter but he didn't think it would lead to any trouble. "We have always had pleasant dealings with the government," he is quoted as having commented.

Lester Robinson was correct. Not only did the letter not lead to any trouble, it did not lead to a surveyor's trip. However, the matter of that 14.76 acres was to surface over and over again. In 1967, when I first visited Ni'ihau, the Department of Education was actively seeking to determine whether the school and church yard at Puuwai might be government property.

Apparently this was not discussed in October 1957 when the Robinsons' island had another visit from the School Commissioners. With the group, on his fourth visit to Ni'ihau School was School Superintendent Clayton Chamberlain. School Commissioners Mrs. Marjorie Hind, Dr. Charles A. Goo, A. H. Case, Mrs. Shizue Yoshino, Deputy superintendent Richard Meyer and Mrs. Martha Martin, secretary to the Commissioners, enjoyed an unprecedented seven hour stay on Ni'ihau.

It was World Series time. The visitors were astonished to find the Ni'ihauans all listening to the games on their battery radios, and rooting for the Milwaukee Braves. Ni'ihau School elicited mixed reactions. One Commissioner was distressed to see the fifty-four pupils being taught in unlit classrooms. He obviously did not realize that the only lighting possible on Ni'ihau was from kerosene lamps – hardly practical on an overcast day in a school room. Another commissioner felt that although the teachers were inadequately trained, the children seemed happy. One hour was spent on the school visitation. Students did arithmetic problems on the blackboard, read aloud, and impressed everyone with the harmony of their group singing.

For the remaining six hours of their time on Ni'ihau, Aylmer Robinson took the visitors on a tour of the island, treating them to a box lunch from Kauai Inn on one of Ni'ihau's beaches. At that time, the commissioners were told, Aylmer visited Ni'ihau at least three times a week. On all his trips, and on the sampan bringing over these visitors, he brought along pigeons trained to fly to Makaweli "in case of disaster aboard the sampan, such as engine failure". He was now keeping trained pigeons on Ni'ihau so that messages could be flown to Makaweli in case of an emergency. With the shutdown of the Coast Guard Loran Station, there was no longer the emergency radio connection with the outside worldd that facility had provided.

"Every adult male on Ni'ihau is on the Robinson payroll," Robinson told School Commissioner Marjorie Hind who, as wife of a Kona rancher, well understood the problems Ni'ihau Ranch was facing with the long drought, the cactus blight, and the difficulty of marketing their beef and wool. Robinson said he was considering other areas of employment for Ni'ihauans, such as raising mullet in his fish ponds, and the development of a charcoal industry from the kiawe trees that now covered so much of Ni'ihau.

On all of these visits since 1947 – those of the School Commissioners, that of the tax appraisers, and that of the two policemen, the various newspapers of the territory had asked and been denied the privilege of sending along a reporter and photographer. As a result, the articles were somewhat negative in their tone as if the press was suspicious the Robinsons had something to hide. What was really going on at Ni'ihau? Had Jean Keale, the School Commissioners, and the tax officers told how it really was on what for the press was indeed the 'forbidden' island?

The second weekend in November, 1957, the *Star-Bulletin*'s chief photographer, Warren Roll, decided to break the Ni'ihau press barrier. He rented a small plane, ostensibly for 'flightseeing'. Whether there was really engine trouble or whether the pilot of the plane was making possible Roll's uninvited stay on Ni'ihau is not known. At any rate, that Saturday morning, the plane landed on the island – suffering a smashed landing gear and a splintered propellor in the process. The old World War II furrows still made landings almost impossible. Unlike the Japanese pilot in December 1941, this craft came down a considerable distance from the village.

The pilot remained with the plane. Warren Roll and his cameras headed off for what he thought was the direction of Puuwai. After walking for what he said later was 'several hours', he came to the village. The first house he saw was that of school teacher Hannah Niau. She and her family were sitting around a table in their yard enjoying Saturday lunch.

"Hello! Will you help me?" Roll asked. By now he was hot, thirsty, and exhausted.

The Niau's at once invited him into their yard, sat him down, and put before him their Ni'ihau pot luck: a laulau, a dish of pork, poi, bread, peanut butter and eleomargarine, cake, water, and a quart bottle of orange soda pop. The photographer was most grateful for the water, but he was too tired to do more than nibble at the feast set before him.

Soon a crowd had gathered in the Niau yard, all of them as curious about the visitor as he was about them. Roll noted that almost all the men were in aloha shirts, had wrist watches, and wore shoes. As soon as he felt rested, he went for a picture taking stroll around the village. Bicycles were on the front porch of most houses. There were, people told him, about 250 inhabitants in Puuwai, most of whom owned battery operated radios. They all had kerosene stoves and kerosene powered refrigerators. On inquiry, Roll learned that Sears Roebuck and Montgomery Ward mail order catalogues were Ni'ihau's shopping centers. One boy showed the photographer his transistor radio and told him he had been really disappointed that the transistor battery had not lasted one month. As yet, he had not been able to obtain another.

Roll had heard that tobacco was prohibited but during his walk around Puuwai he saw both men and women smoking a popular brand of cigarettes. He'd also heard that the Robinsons permitted nothing but church-going on Sundays. However, after spending Saturday night and part of Sunday there he observed "there was all sorts of visiting going on." A baby luau was in progress. Every Ni'ihauan was a guest, and they invited him to attend.

The friendly openess of these Ni'ihau people amazed him. They certainly did not look, talk, or sound as if they were oppressed or in any way deprived. No visitors? Talking with the residents of Puuwai, Roll learned that from time to time Kauai fishermen land on Ni'ihau. Several had made friends with some villagers. During the 1940's an occasional small plane had landed and made contact without the knowledge of the Robinsons. The last Ni'ihau myth blasted for Warren Roll was that of 'no cats on the island'. At the Niau's he was given a pet kitten to hold and during the weekend he saw a number of cats in Puuwai. No dogs however.

Honolulu in 1957 was beginning to become security conscious. On Ni'ihau Roll saw that no one ever closed their doors, much less locked them. Yards and dwellings were neat and clean. Everyone had a garden patch. The houses were not the 'run-down' shacks he had anticipated. Puuwai houses were generally in need of paint but they were well built and in excellent repair. The myth of the owners as ogres began to vanish as Roll listened to the Ni'ihau people tell him how, before

Aubrey Robinson died, he had included in his will a provision that no Hawaiian was ever to be taken off Ni'ihau unless he wished to leave the island. That stipulation had been followed. Ni'ihau familes had the security of knowing that every boy would automatically be on the Robinson payroll.

This promise was kept even though an increase in population had come at the same time as the decrease in Ni'ihau Ranch income. With the market for beef and wool down, the Robinsons were trying the new ventures Aylmer had described to the School Commissioners in October: commercial fishing and charcoal manufacture. In November 1957 the cowboys told the Honolulu photographer that there were 50 of them on the payroll. Each week, half of them spent fishing and the other half did the herding and ranch work. The groups alternated every week and some took turns making kiawe charcoal. Old Shintani was still the beekeeper, in charge of honey production.

On Sunday afternoon a small plane made several passes over Puuwai, dropping cigarettes, candy, and a message notifying Roll that his plane had been repaired and would take off at 5 that afternoon. How this had been accomplished the ensuing story in the *Star-Bulletin* does not make clear. At any rate, at this information, about two dozen Ni'ihau men and women piled into the back of the World War II surplus ranch truck and invited Roll to get in. They drove him to the place where he – and they – thought the small plane would land.

When it didn't they followed the plane to the previous day's alleged crash site. On the forty-five minute ride, in a field close to the northern tip of the island, Roll saw a model 420 John Deere tractor with a cultivator in the back of it. Here and there stray cattle were standing in the road. When this happened, everyone hooted and yelled until the cattle ambled out of the way.

The truck kicked up a monumental amount of dust. Everyone was covered with the red powdery stuff but the joyous shouting went on unabated. It was a memorable visit – both for Warren Roll and for the people of Ni'ihau. Roll returned to his paper with an exuberant, myth-shattering story. The *Star-Bulletin* of November 16, 1957 carried a two page spread of Roll's magnificent photos of Ni'ihau people and of the village. The accompanying article, written by reporter George West, was headlined, "Free Though Feudal. They're Happy on Niihau" with the sub head, "Iron Curtain Lifted for First Time. Much of What You Hear About the Island Isn't So".

Roll was lucky. He just missed Hurricane Nina which roared across Ni'ihau early in December 1957, damaging a big warehouse, moving four buildings at Kii Point off their foundations, and damaging three of the seven quonset huts abandoned by the Coast Guard. Most of the 100 kiawe trees uprooted were well away from the village but at the height of the storm one of the huge old kiawes in the churchyard came crashing down, narrowly missing the school house. The storm, destructive though it was, had one benefit for which Ni'ihauans were grateful. The heavy downpour that accompanied the hurricane filled the island's five reservoirs and left each household water tank overflowing.

In August 1959, together with all their fellow islanders, Ni'ihauans became full-fledged American citizens when Hawaii was finally given statehood. The change in local government was minimal – Ni'ihau was still part of the County of Kauai but Ni'ihau voters, like those everywhere in the fiftieth state, could now vote for their congressmen, their senator, the president and – at long last – for the Governor of Hawaii. Everywhere else in the state, the Democratic party had become the majority's choice. On Ni'ihau the voters remained Republicans.

Kenneth Norris, curator of Marineland of the Pacific, the oceanarium at Palos Verdes, California arrived in Honolulu in time to enjoy the statehood celebrations. His mission on behalf of the U.S. Fish and Wildlife Service and the State Board of Agriculture and Forestry was to distribute 4,000 threadfin shad to stock the island's reservoirs and streams. It was hoped that the tiny fish, three to six inches long, would replenish the supply of bait fish whose scarcity was hampering Hawaii's tuna fishing industry.

In return for his shad distribution, Norris was to be allowed to collect reef fish from Hawaii to take back to his oceanarium. Ni'ihau was one of the islands where Norris wanted to collect specimens from the rich offshore reefs. He readily received permission to do so from the Robinsons. On Saturday September 12th, 1959, traveling in their own chartered boat, Norris and his colleagues set out for Ni'ihau. All weekend they roamed the reefs along its shores and as they did, two Ni'ihau cowboys in the ranch truck followed their progress. The permission given to Norris and his colleagues had been only to explore the offshore reefs, not to land, but during the afternoon, the two cowboys waved to Norris and his divers to come ashore.

"They were very friendly," Norris later told *Star-Bulletin* reporter Ben Thompson. "One of them was listening to a transistor radio and he didn't know what an aquarium was or where California was. But you know what he was listening to on that radio? The Dow Jones stock averages!"

Norris was astonished to see that one of the Ni'ihau men "was a redheaded Hawaiian. He didn't speak any English."

In October 1959, three weeks after Norris' Ni'ihau experience, *The Sunday Advertiser* published a front page feature on the visit of Deal Crooker, assistant superintendent of Hawaii's Department of Public Instruction and another ardent fisherman. Crooker wrote the article himself, and also took the photographs accompanying the article. "Well, I have finally made it – a trip to the legendary island, Niihau!" was his lead sentence under the bold headline "Curtain Parts on Amazing Niihau".

Crooker portrayed Aylmer Robinson as "that amazing person who has dedicated his life to the island and its people. Imagine if you can a Harvard man who speaks Hawaiian which sounds like flowing music. Imagine a man whose scientific understanding of conservation principles has saved an island from waste and erosion and made it productive – yet an island which still uses carrier pigeons to get messages back and forth. Imagine if you can a man 71 years old, in the peak of physical condition, spry enough to jump from an LCM into a small lighter in a surging sea. His dedication and love of his island, Niihau, and its wonderful people shines through his every word. His fund of information and knowledge of the land and its people will keep anyone engrossed for hours listening to him."

Walton Gordon, superintendent of schools, was on the one day trip with Crooker who was loquacious about the fishing he did on the trip over and the pheasants he saw on the truck ride to the village. Yet Crooker devoted only one short paragraph of the long article to the purpose of their trip, a visit to inspect

Ni'ihau School. Neither he nor Gordon made any comment on the curriculum or quality of instruction. They say only "We found the boys and girls, approximately 50, evenly divided between the two groups. They were very well ordered, in fact they were almost too well ordered. This was, we presume, a natural result of their awe at having their annual inspection."

Two trucks took the visiting officials from the village where Crooker was delighted to see at each house "the usual signs of fishing activity – poles, throw-nets and covered screened racks for drying fish." He comments that, like Punahou's campus, that of Ni'ihau School is graced by night blooming cereus growing on a low stone wall. Lunch was enjoyed on a beach by the western sea. "As we started back there was a general feeling we had had the privilege of looking back 100 years or more into a way of life that is truly Hawaiian."

Crooker's lengthy feature in the *Advertiser* brought out the competitive spirit in the *Star-Bulletin* who assigned its nightclub reporter, Shideler Harpe, 32, to somehow find a way to get to Ni'ihau with a camera and write a story, not from a sentimental visitor's viewpoint such as Crooker's account had seemed but through the how-things-really-are orientation of an experienced reporter, such as Warren Roll had accomplished with his 1957 scoop.

Harpe had the boat he'd talked into taking him to Ni'ihau drop him off on the island at 2 a.m. on Thursday, October 22nd – less than two weeks after the official visit of Deal Crooker and Walton Gordon. Being used to dimly lit night clubs, the reporter was not dismayed to find only the stars lighting the coast of Ni'ihau. He walked along the dark shore for a while, and then – deciding to wait for daybreak to find his way to Puuwai – he lay down and went to sleep.

He was still sleeping at 6:30 a.m. when some Ni'ihau cowboys discovered him. The last thing that Shideler Harpe looked like was a night club reporter – or any kind of islander. He had a heavy black beard. He was dressed in t-shirt and dungarees. The beard and his dark horn rimmed glasses sparked the cowboys' suspicions. This must be a Soviet spy!

They investigated the contents of the large bundle wrapped in a camouflage net which Harpe had with him. Inside was a substantial amount of canned goods and vitamin pills, at least a week's supply of food. This confirmed the cowboys' suspicions and led them to believe he was fresh off a Soviet submarine. In 1941 they had had a Japanese war plane land on their island, the only hostile craft landed anywhere in Hawaii-nei. In the cold war atmosphere of 1959 it was perfectly logical to them that the Russians might land a spy on Ni'ihau.

From the spot where they found him, about 20 miles north of Puuwai, they took Harpe by truck 10 miles south to Kii Landing. There they kept him in their custody while they sent a message by pigeon to Aylmer Robinson. When the pigeon arrived at Makaweli, informing Robinson that a strange *haole* had been landed on Ni'ihau under suspicious circumstances, Robinson called the Kauai police. For the second time in his career, Police Captain Antone Vidinha prepared to go to Ni'ihau in the Robinson's sampan.

Harpe was kept at Kii Landing overnight. The cowboys put him in a shack there and then went on home to sleep in their own beds. About 8 a.m. Friday, Police Captain Vidinha arrived at Kii, accompanied by Aylmer and Lester Robinson. For two hours Vidinha questioned Harpe who finally admitted he had been assigned by the *Star-Bulletin* to slip ashore at Ni'ihau and get a story and pictures to outdo Deal Crooker's October 11 article.

It was a while before Harpe returned to Honolulu to tell his tale – not until November 1 did his account of his trip appear in the *Star-Bulletin*, although on October 25th the *Advertiser* carried the story of Harpe being captured as a spy. He did his best to make something more out of his misfired adventure, stating that "after nearly 100 years of tight-rein control the natives of Niihau are growing restless." He really had nothing new or different to say. He felt the younger people of Ni'ihau were begining "to think that the simple life on Niihau may not be the best of all possible lives, after all. A few didn't hesitate to say so, after I got to know them."

He is the first to quote the Ni'ihauans as saying they would like to have a two-way radio and if possible a helicopter between Makaweli and Ni'ihau. He also is the first to provide information to the outside world that Ni'ihau now had five trucks and two tractors, and that several of the cowboys had become expert in repairing and maintaining the vehicles.

His escapade had not resulted in any problems beyond his being taken back to Kauai on the Robinson sampan and detained there by Vidinha whom Harpe said had been courteous. At Makaweli he had been met by Sinclair Robinson, a police commissioner on Kauai. After more questioning at the Kauai Police Station, Harpe was released to the custofy of Joe Arakaki, the *Star-Bulletin's* Kauai reporter.

The resulting flurry of media attention to Ni'ihau may well have prompted politicians to realize that they had not achieved any of the goals they had set for Ni'ihau a dozen years ago. Maybe, announced House Speaker Elmer Cravalho, another legislative investigation of conditions on the island of Ni'ihau was necessary. He wondered if health, sanitation, and wage and hour standards were being met as was mandatory in the other islands of the state.

The public appetite for news about Ni'ihau was whetted by this announcement on November 2nd. On November 4th the *Star-Bulletin* featured three articles on Ni'ihau. One opened the old question as to whether or not Ni'ihau cowboys faced 100% rejection as draftees because of their language and illiteracy problems. The second disclosed that state officials were again looking for eight parcels of government lands on the island, which they now surmised might total as much as 17 acres. The third quoted the state's first governor, William F. Quinn as calling for an investigation of Ni'ihau if there should surface "anything contrary to the public health, safety or morals" of that island's residents.

The Pandora's box of all kinds of government inquiries was opened, and much to the Robinson's annoyance would remain open for the next twenty years. The final Ni'ihau news item of 1959, a landmark of progress for that island and a tremendous boon to its residents, received only minimal press coverage on November 11. Negative news seemed to warrant far more space in the Honolulu papers than such a positive item as the December mention that Kentron Hawaii, island agents for Motorola, were to install a three-way short wave radio link between Kauai, Ni'ihau, and the converted landing craft which

was now the Robinson's major transport to their private island.
A wind driven generator was to furnish power for the equipment on Ni'ihau.

   This was to make a big political difference on Kauai.
Traditionally Ni'ihau had been the last precinct to report its
election results. The new radio communication meant that voters
of Ni'ihau, Kauai County's smallest precinct, might now be the
first to report how many votes had been cast for whom. For the
first few years of statehood, it turned out to simply be a swifter
communication of the same solidly Republican vote from the
Robinson's island. One of those proudly casting his vote from
1960 on was Beekeeper Shintani who had become a naturalized
American citizen.

The Grant That
Made A Difference

IN JUNE 1961 a Ni'ihau cowboy, Livy Milimili Nakalawelohile-
hua Niheu, who had come to work on Kauai the previous
February, rode as King in Kauai's Kamehameha Day parade. In
a news interview, the 34 year old son of the late Miriam Niheu,
longtime principal of Ni'ihau School, stated that "People of
Ni'ihau have lots of freedom." To counteract the reporter's
impression that Ni'ihauans were severely restricted in making
trips away from their island, or inviting guests to visit them, Livy
Niheu told how as long ago as 1946 he had been making frequent
trips to Waimea where he met his future wife, Rebecca Kapahu
of Waimea. She visited Ni'ihau several times before the couple
were married in the church at Puuwai.

Other similar stories are told by former crewmen of the
Interisland Steamship Company. A number of Ni'ihau men
worked on these ships. They would bring their shipmates home
to Puuwai for a meal and a few hours *holoholo* whenever a ship
put in to pick up a cargo of cattle, wool, or some of the 15,000
gallons of honey that were exported annually before a caterpillar
attacked the island's kiawe blossoms.

The many Ni'ihauans who were adjusting to life in the outside world were never the subject of articles in the Honolulu papers which Gilbert Pahulehua, the new principal of Ni'ihau School, sometimes read to his neighbors. News items about Ni'ihau were mostly about the problem of whether there were or were not public lands on this private island.

In May 1961 the matter of public lands on Ni'ihau was exhumed by Legislator David McClung (later president of the Hawaii State Senate). He proposed that the State should now move to obtain access to the beaches of Ni'ihau, which special deputy attorney-general Jon Chinen held belonged to the State. McClung also mentioned pursuing the location of the school sites long claimed as public lands. McClung was perhaps not aware that since April 1961 the Robinson family had supposedly been negotiating through its attorney for a settlement of the government's claim to the school lots.

The old 'camel in the tent' psychology began working when McClung said he believed that in addition to claiming beaches and settling the location of the school lots the state should also consider condemnation of land on Ni'ihau for an emergency air strip to be used by the small fish-spotting planes flying out of Kauai to seek schools of tuna in the fishing grounds near Ni'ihau. On other islands people applauded these measures. There was general agreement with the implication of the 1961 headline in Kauai's newspaper, *The Garden Island:* "Legislators Chip Away at Curtain Around Niihau." What few realized was this was a curtaiin existing only for reporters and curiosity seekers.

Then, in the fall of 1961 the 'curtain' was abruptly lifted for three reporters. The State's first governor, William F. Quinn, received the Robinson's permission to bring the press on his official visit to Ni'ihau. At 8:00 A.M. on September 29th the governor and his entourage landed on Ni'ihau after a thirty-minute flight from Lihue. The three helicopters from Marine Helicopter Transport Squadron 161 were the first choppers ever to whirl up the dust of this island. The historic flight was commanded by Lt. Col. Elbert S. Price. Accompanying the Governor were his Press Secretary Roger Coryell, Quinn's management assistant George Miyasaka, Clinton Childs, assistant manager of Lihue Plantation, and reporters Jim

Heckman and Jack Teehan. They were the first of their profession to legitimately be on Ni'ihau since the 'Alcatraz' headline of 1946.

Through the clouds of red dust kicked up as the helicopters settled down at Lehua, the visitors saw their hosts for the day– Aylmer andd Lester Robinson– waiting to transport them to Puuwai. The governor and Clinton Childs rode with the Robinson brothers in a jeep with the windshield folded down. The others rode in a ranch truck driven by a younger brother of the hero of the Battle of Ni'ihau.

Advertiser Reporter Jack Teehan's first impression was that "A bit of the old American frontier still lives on the Island of Niihau." He claimed that "Any back-country Montana cowboy would feel right at home on the 43,190-acre Niihau Ranch operated by Aylmer F. Robinson." Teehan was amazed that only two requests were made of the Governor's party: no smoking in the open and no photographs taken of the old Robinson home at Kiekie. "The no smoking rule was a sensible one," said Teehan. "The country is desert dry." He also understood the Robinson's rationale for making the century old house off limits for a camera lens. It had a strong sentimental attachment for the family and over the years, since it was no longer a permanent residence, had come to look rather unkempt.

Contrary to Jack Teehan's expectations, "it was apparent that modern times have made an impact on Niihau." He described seeing one attractive young Puuwai resident stylishly dressed in tight slacks and a sweater while another girl was wearing what in the sixties was called a 'kookie' muu.

The Robinsons were candid about the changes on their island. Aylmer told the governor, and the three reporters, that there "isn't enough work for all the people here" but he felt obligated to keep all residents on the payroll. Cattle, because of the cactus blight, had diminished from a herd of over 3000 to fewer than 1600. The parasite on kiawe blossoms had dropped honey production from 15,000 gallons a year to as low as 500 gallons. Wool often had to be stored for as long as two years while awaiting a buyer. Robinson explained, "Niihau wool is full of burrs and the wool is stained a rust brown by the soil, making it hard to sell."

Teehan learned that "even the wild pig population is dwindling, perhaps as the result of a hog cholera epidemic." No guns are allowed on the island. Ni'ihauans, the reporters learned, catch pigs by hand. Fishing? Inroads made by commercial fishermen in the waters off Ni'ihau were substantial. "The bountiful catches of old are gone forever," lamented the Robinsons. Surfing, still a popular sport on the island was no longer done on hand-crafted boards. "Today's youngsters on Niihau want modern Waikiki surfboards."

When Governor Quinn asked about sharks harassing surfers on Ni'ihau he was told that "Niihau people regard sharks as their friends." Both Lester and Aylmer Robinson confirmed that there were plenty of sharks around the surfing beach near Puuwai village, but "there has never been an attack on a swimmer". Lester Robinson described the one incident in which Ni'ihauans had finally killed a shark – not one of the local sharks but a "grey nurse shark or tiger shark". For months this foreign shark had made surfing so difficult that Ni'ihauans stayed out of the water.

What the shark had been doing was coming up from underneath surfers and catapaulting them off their boards. The day came when Ni'ihauans had had enough. They went out and killed that shark. Only the friendly sharks were around now, the visitors were told.

That September 29th was a totally pleasant day, for the Ni'ihauans, the two Robinson brothers, the Governor, and his party. One reporter seemed to express the subdued reaction of all three when he wrote, "I had the feeling that I had just entered the privacy of someone's home, almost uninvited. All the hard-learned newsman's instincts failed. No deep probing questions were asked".

At the end of the afternoon, each visitor was presented with exquisite Ni'ihau shell leis. Almost every Ni'ihauan was there to see the Governor and his party. Absent were two teenagers studying at Kamehameha Schools. Gileada Koahilaulii, 15, and his cousin Abigail Koahilaulii, 17, were receiving a high school education which Aylmer Robinson's encouragement and financial aid had made possible. Gileada thought he might want to become an astronomer. Abigail wanted to become a teacher and return to Ni'ihau.

The thrill of visiting Ni'ihau by helicopter was, for the next quarter century, to be reserved for gubernatorial visits. When the new superintendent of schools, Burl Yarberry, came to Ni'ihau on October 28, 1962, it was on the Robinson's landing craft. Unlike previous school inspection visits, Yarberry was allowed to bring a member of the press. He chose a prominent Honolulu editor, A. E. P. Wall. Also along were Representative James Wakatsuki, Chairman of the House Education Committee, State Senator Larry Kuriyama, Chairman of the Senate Education Committee and Joe Cherry, Director of Elementary Education for the DOE.

Yarberry, a poet by avocation, described Ni'ihau School as bring situated "in a grove of trees with lots of flowers and the quiet hanging heavy in the air". He felt it was "almost like visiting a school in the New Hebrides" and concluded "we are not going to change the lives of these children very quickly. One of the problems, as many of you know, is that English is a second language there. I think it's going to be a long, patient process before these children are prepared to meet the mainstream of life." Wall's assessment was that "according to the calendar it is late October, 1962 but in many respects, on Ni'ihau, the time is 1862.'' It was the standard assessment for someone unfamiliar with the island and its history.

In 1962 modernization of Ni'ihau School was nearer than either Editor Wall or Superintendent Yarberry could have guessed. A 'poverty' grant from the Office of Economic Opportunity was about to result from a proposal submitted jointly by the Hawaii State Department of Education, Kamehameha Schools, and the Robinson family – a grant request was submitted in November 1962, only one month after Yarberry's discouraged visit. In early spring 1963, Tom Gill received notice from Washington, D.C. that the Ni'ihau project was to receive $51,623 – a surprising $2,123 more than the $49,500 of the November request. The money had been and was being well spent when I made my first visit to Ni'ihau in October, 1967.

The grant proposal had specified using some of the money to send Ni'ihau's three teachers to attend special workshops on Kauai and summer courses at the University of Hawaii in Honolulu. By the fall of 1967 this had long since been done.

In addition, curriculum specialists like Bernice Ching, a statewide expert in elementary education, and Hartwell Blake, of the Department of Education's vocational and adult education division came to conduct workshops on Ni'ihau. Most visible of all these improvements was the change in the school plant,. The Robinsons supplied materials and furnished labor to construct a fourth classroom, which was wired for lights powered by the portable electric generator purchased with OEO funds.

Contributions from the Department of Education budget to the new multi-purpose classroom (which was also designated Puuwai's community center) included a piano, a 16-mm motion picture projector, a 35-mm filmstrip and slide projector, an overhead projector, language master machines, and – although they were not sure Ni'ihauans could get adequate reception – a television receiver. The new room was also the school library, stocked with books that DOE specialists felt were closely related to the island's environment. Speech, music, health, physical education, arts and crafts had been offered at a Kamehameha Schools sponsored summer school attended by 26 Ni'ihau children. A late afternoon program for parents and those Puuwai residents interested explained what the children were accomplishing in these new areas.

Dr. George Kanna of Hanapepe and Dr. Manuel Kau of the State Health Department's Dental Health Division were brought to Ni'ihau to examine the childrens' teeth. Later, Mrs. Royce Fujimoto, president of the Kauai County Dental Society Auxiliary provided free tooth brush kits to Ni'ihau's fourth graders.

Most important of all the chages in Ni'ihau School was the OEO's making possible the frequent visits and occasional week-long stays on Ni'ihau of a program coordinator who was a fine educator, and a Hawaiian fluent in the language. This remarkable man was Gabriel I (pronounced Ee) of Kauai, who arranged the OEO funded visits of small groups of Ni'ihau students and their parents to Honolulu where they experienced such wonders as Sea Life Park, Bishop Museum, and the Honolulu Zoo.

Aylmer Robinson does not make specific mention of any of these changes in his seven page letter written on Ni'ihau,

May 26, 1963, to his boyhood teacher. Miss Florence Boyer, now in her nineties. She was then living in Lansing, Michigan and had written to him recently. In one of her letters, written to her brother Virgil's daughter, Miss Boyer described her 1894 tutoring of Aylmer and his brother Sinclair in modest terms, insisting "I didn't know more than a cow how to teach". She remembered that she and her brother, Rev. Virgil Boyer of the Waimea Foreign Church, "were entertained at all the Robinson houses."

To her niece Miss Boyer had confided, "I should love to hear from the Robinson boys. They were so dear." At her niece's urging, she had then written to Aylmer whose May 26, 1963 reply brings her up to date on the life of himself, his brothers, and the status of the family management of their properties. Most important of all it gives an intimate insight into Aylmer Robinson's reason for being proud of the conservation of a Hawaiian population on Ni'ihau.

Aylmer also fills in his old teacher on the details of his education. In this uncatalogued item in the Hawaii State Archives he writes, "Beginning in 1900 we got part of our schooling in California and part in private tutoring at home until entering college." He relates how he and his older brother Sinclair spent two years at the University of California at Berkeley, living with their widowed Aunt, Eliza Gay (whom they called Aunt Lila). They then went east for their last two years at Harvard. Selwyn and Lester did the same. They were good company for Eliza Gay, who had been married to a Californian and whose house would have been lonely without the long stays of her nephews. Aylmer tells Miss Boyer that this Aunt lived to be 90.

"My father (Aubrey Robinson) passed away in 1936. He had given us all a splendid groundwork both in business and in Christian responsibility and since his death the reins of responsibility has rested on my generation, although Mother remained the head of the family until her death in December, 1960 at the age of 95."

There was a new generation to introduce to Miss Boyer. "Russell, Sinclair's son, has a home near Sinclair and works on the plantation under his father." At 77, Sinclair held a record in the Hawaiian sugar industry – he had been manager of Gay and

Robinson plantation for more than half a century. Selwyn was manager of Makaweli Ranch, "which has developed largely under his care and (he) is also in charge of all the accounting and financial records of the partnership. His son Warren works under him on Makaweli Ranch."

As to his only sister, Eleanor, "she devoted much of her life to the care of mother and father. She never married." On Kauai, she and Aylmer, who is a bachelor, lived in the home where their parents lived. "Eleanor also has a town house in Honolulu where she spends some time seeing her friends there."

"Lester has many varied duties. He is manager of a new ranch we have been developing on the north side of Kauai – Koolau Ranch and also is in charge of the ditch system which supplies water for our sugar plantation and houses, Olokele Sugar Company, and for the irrigated pastures of our Makaweli Ranch, and is assistant manager here on Niihau. Both Lester's sons are now attending the University of California."

"My own work has been divided between two spheres. On Kauai I have been the business manager of our partnership dealing particularly with contracts and leases, legal problems, taxation and similar questions as they arise from time to time. These duties are exacting and take a great deal of time and close attention. My particular pleasure has been the management of Niihau with its cattle, sheep, horses and other ranching activities. It still remains as you saw it, a Hawaiian community which is something distinctive now since other races, Japanese, Filipinos, and others, have become the larger elements in the population of the state.

"Niihau is the last place where Hawaiian is spoken almost exclusively in the daily life of the place and where the jobs of importance are still filled by Hawaiians. The island life centers around its church and so far we have been able to keep out liquor and the island has maintained its crime-free record. Outside pressure is heavy to break in on this last Hawaiian community but so far that has been withstood."

There were certain kinds of outside pressure against which both the Robinsons and the press (at least one newspaper anyway) were united at that time. On October 5, 1965, two U.S. planes on a practise bombing mission, thinking they were over their target island, Kaula Rock, dropped eight 250-lb. bombs on Ni'ihau. Congresswoman Patsy Takemoto Mink expressed the indignation of everyone in Hawaii. The military's use of Kaula Rock (thirty-seven miles from Ni'ihau) for bombing practice must be stopped!

"As we recall," said an indignant editorial in the following day's edition of *The Garden Island*, "the Navy insisted upon keeping Kaula Rock because aircraft using that island as a target would be under radar surveillance from ALF Bonham as well as their ship." Editor Mike Fern pointed out that the AD-5 Skyraiders dropping their bombloads on Ni'ihau were nine minutes flying time off their target.

"Are we to believe," asked Fern, "that while the bombers were making their passes nobody noticed what was happening or was in position to warn off the pilots? It seems to us that something more than mere inadvertence was involved. It also seems a matter of sheer luck that no one was fishing where the pilots chose to loose their bombs."

In November 1966 it was not our own U.S. planes missing their mark on target practise, but the cold war fear of nuclear attack by enemy aircraft that brought State Civil Defense coordinator Maurice D. Myers to Ni'ihau. He was accompanied by civil defense experts and radiological experts from the State Department of Health. On their departure (after the usual brief one-day visit) they were assured by Aylmer Robinson that he would build a fallout trench near Puuwai. The October 1965 bombs dropped on the island had not even awakened any Ni'ihauan but no one was taking any chances on what might happen in an enemy nuclear attack. The supposition was that if our own pilots had missed, enemy bombers might do so too.

We were not shown the fallout trench – if indeed there was one – when, on October 5, 1967, six of us from the state's first elected Board of Education visited Ni'ihau. Ron Harker of Kauai, George Adachi, Myrtle Kaapu, John Connell and the Rev. Robert Loveless from Oahu, and myself (from the Big Island) were accompanied by three DOE staff members and by Gabriel I. Together with several Ni'ihauans returning from visits elsewhere, we shared the limited space on the Robinson's landing craft with three horses, a mule, three hundred sacks each containing thirty-five pounds of poi, assorted cardboard cartons and sacks of freight, a case of Tide washing detergent, and numerous fifty gallon barrels of diesel.

It was not a comfortable four and one half hours crossing the Kaulakahi Channel. All of us were relieved when the landing craft snubbed its bow on the beach where two trucks and seveal Ni'ihau cowboys waited for us at the water's edge. We jumped out across the lowered ramp onto the hot yellow-- white sand. Mrs. Kaapu and I were given the choice seats in one truck cab. We pitied the men riding in the open bed of the vehicle, eating dust as the driver, an older Hawaiian with several missing teeth and a generous smile jounced us at a careful ten mph over the rutted set of tire tracks that served as a road. The other driver followed at the same cautious speed.

I had then no idea that what I was seeing had been described innumerable times, and much more vividly, by one hundred and eighty-nine years of visitors. Never mind. To me it was all a reve- lation, a marvelous experience. I was on Ni'ihau! I was struck by the driver's shy, yet elated expression – one that seemed characteristic of every Ni'ihauan we met that day. The island landscape was much like that of the Kawaihae-Puako area so familiar to me on the Big Island. No wonder Ni'ihau Eddie had settled there.

'Me born Ni'ihau," the driver volunteered to us as we jounced past a few cattle, a flock of turkeys, a few sheep, and passed several small groves of coconut palms. There were several cattle gates to be opened and closed along the way. They were the pole and wire variety that, on the Big Island, we called a Por- tuguese gate. As he approached each one our driver ignored the brakes, slowed down, jumped out of the cab while the truck was still moving forward, but left the wheel turned so that as soon as the tires hit the rut at the edge of the road the truck rolled back into the grass and stopped.

It took forty-five hot dusty minutes to reach the outskirts of the village. The houses of Puuwai were set back from the road, each one with its own large yard fenced off by low loosestone walls. The homes were neatly painted, many of them with a horse tethered nearby. I was impressed. This was immeasurably better housing than that provided to workers on the Kohala plantation where I then lived.

Just as Burl Yarberry had pictured on his 1962 visit, ancient gnarled kiawe trees with twisted low branches shaded the freshly raked churchyard that was the heart of the village, and the campus of Ni'ihau school. Except for the background country noises of birds and insects, and our own loud strangers' voices talking to each other, there was not a sound as we followed Gabriel I through the entrance in the stone wall boundary.

To the left of the wooden church was the first of the older school buildings. Gilbert Pahulehua, the principal and teacher for the seventh and eighth grade class, stood in the doorway awaiting our inspection. His pupils were all at their desks, 'working'. They were big handsome teenage boys and girls. The boys were dressed in their best aloha shirts and trousers. The girls were wearing their newest brightest dresses. Every hair was combed neatly and glistened with pomade. Every back was held in uncomfortably rigid attention. Every face bent dutifully over a notebook. There were only occasional shy stray glances at us as we entered.

On the blackboard was a science lesson written in English in Mr. Pahulehua's small beautiful script. It was most impressive – all about convex and concave surfaces, telescope mirrors, and light refraction. No one seemed upset by the "fat and plane surfaces" or other errors being dutifully copied by each student.

For the hour and a half before lunch, and the hour after lunch we wandered in and out of the three classrooms 'visiting'. All this while the 7th and 8th graders sat at attention at their desks, copying the same lesson. Towards the end of our visit some gave way to loking us over, but still from a disciplined silent stance at their desks.

Mr. Pahulehua walked with a limp. An accidental fall from a horse had left him incapable of carrying on the work of a cowboy. He himself was a product of Ni'ihau School. So was Mrs. Niau, the teacher of the fourth, fifth and sixth grade class. Jean Keale, also a Ni'ihau graduate, had gone on to complete high school on Oahu and attend Honolulu Christian College. It was she who had been the first Ni'ihauan to write about life on her own island, while she was a student in Honolulu. Her girlhood ambition had been fulfilled. She now handled Ni'ihau's first three grades. An extremely capable teacher, she had also spent a summer teaching Hawaiian at the University of Hawaii' Manoa campus.

Gabriel I told me that Principal Pahulehua was also the lay preacher at Ni'ihau Church. It was clear that Gabriel I was loved by the people of Ni'ihau and that he understood and loved them. When he walked ashore on the beach, the cowboys shook his hand, embraced him, spoke swiftly in Hawaiian in obviously delighted greeting. At the school, when Gabriel I got out of the truck, there was the same rush to welcome him from the mothers and preschool age children who stood around outside the stone wall to watch us. Mr. I assured us that in Hawaiian, which is their natural language, these silent children and their teachers are extremely expressive, loquacious, and poetic.

In each of the three classrooms, and in the bright new building constructed for the OEO programs, the textbooks and library books looked too new, with few signs of being used. One of Gabriel I's problems continued to be convincing the teachers not to save these new materials for such special occasions as a visit by DOE officials or the Board. While we ate our box lunches in this new building, Gabriel I told us about the first motion picture ever shown on Ni'ihau. For some inexplicable reason known only to the DOE, they had sent him James Fenimore Cooper's "The Last of the Mohicans" to show on the new movie projector, powered with the new portable generator which the 'poverty' grant had made possible.

That night, he reminisced, the people of Puuwai had him show that movie three times over. For many on the island, it was the first movie they had ever seen. Their usual recreation is not that passive. When the fish are running, everyone in Puuwai goes fishing. When the tide is right, the people like to go out and pick opihi. For luau occasions such as weddings, first birthdays, christenings, and New Year's the men go hunting for wild pig and the Robinsons donate a carcass of beef. Fish, maybe some of the Ni'ihau turkeys, sweet potatoes and breadfruit are layered with the pork and beef in the imu, the earth oven which cooks the food in the trapped steam of the hot lava rocks.

Surfing, I was told, is one of the great communal sports of Ni'ihauans. They love both to body surf and to surf on boards. One of their beaches is said to afford the best surfing conditions in all Hawaii-nei. Our visit to Ni'ihau came at a time when everyone in Puuwai was geting ready for the big annual Ni'ihau surfing meet.

Every year, in October, all of the men are given a week's vacation by the Robinsons. All ranch work is suspended. All normal activity stops. For one solid week the people compete with each other at riding the big waves. They are both participants and spectators in an event that they plan and carry out as a community tradition. An *imu* is dug on the beach. There is feasting and singing and story telling every evening.

Was that week in October a school holiday on this island? I didn't ask, for I was beginning to understand that the clock and the school calendar are not movers and shapers of daily life on Ni'ihau. This insight arose after I asked one of the teachers "What time do you start school every morning?"

To her this was a loaded question. What did I expect her to say? She looked as vague and taken aback as if I had asked about life in outer space.

"Oh----" she answered. "I don't know. Depends." Then, quickly, because I am a *haole* and *haoles* are fussy about time she added, "Maybe eight-thirty?" She nodded as if hearing this in her own voice sounded quite all right. She was equally dismayed by my next question.

"You dismiss school at two o'clock?"

Again the vague, faintly alarmed pause and then the quick smile. "Oh yes," she confirmed. "Two o'clock."

Only the little children in Mrs. Keale's primary classroom were not awed into silence by our presence. With obvious glee her first, second and third graders displayed for us the recent acquisition of three plastic covered foam mats which Mrs. Keale referred to as 'our beds'.

Hers was the most colorful of the classrooms. There were protestant Christian mottoes and Bible verses done in crayon decorating the walls, together with a number of the children's crayon drawings. "I filled them in for them," smiled Mrs. Keale when we commented on the neatness of the work. One was of a fire truck in bright red, drawn by a small boy who had been given a toy fire truck when he was a patient at Honolulu Shriner's Hospital. Another drawing depicted *pueo,* the Hawaiian owl, as one child had seen the bird roosting in a tree one night when he and his father came back through the darkness on their way home from a fishing trip.

On the blackboard Mrs. Keale had written the names of each of her students. There was a predominance of similar surnames and long beautiful middle names – often five or six words long – all in Hawaiian and all, she told us, expressing some special trait or inheritance or hope for that child. As had been state law until the 1966 legislative session, each child had been also given a Christian name.

These little ones were bright eyed, eager, excited. They tumbled on the mats. They grinned at us over their proudly held readers. They all raised their hands, wanting a chance to answer questions or read from the day's story. It was a story that must have seemed unreal to them – about a squirrel in a woods near a midwest American farm.

Recess had been delayed for our visit. Yes, confirmed Mrs. Keale, the little ones were getting restless. She rang the bell and they ran outside with the same enthusiasm of school children for recess time anywhere. There were a number of shiny, new looking tricycles, two wheeled bikes and coaster wagons near the primary building. Mrs. Keale told us these belonged to individual children who had brought them to school. Like the good looking clothes the children wore, these were catalog ordered, from Ni'ihau's two most patronized businesses: Sears Rebuck and Montgomery Ward.

While the little children were playing, we visited Mrs. Niau's classroom where 4th, 5th and 6th graders sat at silent attention at their clean desks. No pencils. No papers. Only a textbook on Hawaii opened to page one of a chapter titled "Cowboys in Hawaii". This text did have the appearance of use – smudges, worn edges, dogeared pages, but it was only being looked at, not read this morning by the roomful of silent students. Their teacher, a middle aged Hawaiian woman, whispered greetings to each of us, showed us the table of crafts her students had made. It was a small display of shells and some clay work. I had to remind myself that these children's parents and grandparents were the artists who made the rare and beautiful Ni'ihau shell leis, and that their more distant ancestors were expert in the unique artistry of designing and weaving the famous *makaloa* mats.

There is little a visitor can do in a silent classroom where there is nothing but respectful attention. We looked a second time at the page of the first chapter of "Cowboys in Hawaii" open on every desk, and at the bent, disciplined heads, at the pathetic display of crafts, and returned to the primary classroom. As we appeared, Mrs. Keale thought it prudent to end the recess. This must have been a strange, strained school day that teachers and students yearned to end as soon as possible. When would we visitors leave? Soon?

This was unspoken, only my personal inference from anxious expressions and the tense atmosphere. Apologetically Jean Keale said, "I don't like to use Hawaiian with the children unless I have to." Then she stood at the door, calling "Come!" No child did. They seemed not to hear. She called one boy by name. His head turned to listen, and she told him in English to tell the other children to come in. He looked confused. She added what was probably the same request, only this time in rapid fire Hawaiian and at once, the children put their toys away and came running back inside. Until we left at eleven to have our lunch in the multi-purpose room, they were kept busy making orderly towers from large sectioned cardboard blocks.

Special signs had been prepared for our visit on each of the two outhouses. One was labeled, "Teachers" and the other "Girls." Myrtle and I, qualifying on both counts, could use either one. The men decided they were all 'teachers'. How antiquated – and then we realized on an island where water is so precious, a flush toilet is an arrogant waste of this scarce natural resource. To those of us coming to Ni'ihau School for the first time it was hard to comprehend Bill Savard's comment over lunch. "It's better than it was when I first visited here five years ago, immeasurably better!" he told us.

There was no sign of a lunch break for teachers or students. Somewhere I had read that on Ni'ihau, no one eats lunch but Gabriel I contradicted my misimpression. I was later to learn that times had changed since David Larsen's 1942 visit.

A number of women with younger children were still waiting around the stone wall near the churchyard. One young woman accosted me, speaking excellent English. "You folks seen enough? You ready to go?"

Another group of women, young ones and older ones together, stood some distance away. I walked over to them, reassured by the English of my first encounter. "How old is your baby?" I asked, admiring an infant held by a mother who looked like a teenager. She looked at me in alarm, turned, consulted in Hawaian with the others and after an exchange between them that took some time she said, "One month."

Out by the truck, I spoke to an older woman. "I'm from Kohala, a country place on the Big Island."

"Ah!" she smiled. "Kohala! My husband has a cousin there!"

I tried to extend the conversation from that, but she did not remember the cousin's name – or at least said she could not remember it.

"Suppose we teach the children of Ni'ihau in Hawaiian. Better?" I asked.

"No! No! English better!" she shook her head, aghast at my suggestion.

The atmosphere of waiting for us to leave was such that I felt uncomfortable. Then, as the truck was readied, and it was really time for us to depart, the tension vanished. All the children came out from their classrooms to say good-bye. More parents came from around the village. Old Mr. Shintani the beekeeper was brought to us to be introduced. He too spoke Hawaiian.

Mr. Pahulehua presented each Board member with an envelope containing a beautiful Ni'ihau shell lei. Mrs. Niau gave Myrtle Kaapu and me each a white multi-strand shell lei, delicate as a lei of pikake blossoms. She kissed us, embraced us, we exchanged the aloha of parting. Each of the younger children rushed to shake our hands. Even the silent older ones were now vivacious, exuberant, loud with their "Goodbye! Aloha!"

As we drove off through the village, people came out to wave to us from their houseyards. Knowing nothing then about the island's rich history, nothing yet about the owner's point of view as expressed in his letter to Florence Boyer by Aylmer Robinson, I left Puuwai with the strong feeling that somehow, something must be done to bring Ni'ihau out of what in 1967 I regarded as its over-protected, under-privileged condition.

Ni'ihau Is Nothing
Like The Nene

WHAT I FELT that October of 1967 was characteristic of the times. Equal opportunity for all was the slogan on which the Democratic Party was winning elections and changing the economic and social patterns of the state. How could Ni'ihau become part of all this? I never asked myself whether it had its own Hawaiian agenda.

Lester Robinson had not accompanied the School Board on its 1967 visit to his island but he was waiting at Makaweli on our return – a slender courteous man in khaki shirt and trousers. I regretted not having met Aylmer Robinson but evidently he was already not well. Six months later, on April 2, 1968, Aylmer died.

With interest I read the April 24, 1968 *Advertiser* account of his estate. Independent appraisers had valued Ni'ihau at $1,182,142.00, a figure challenged by Kauai's State Tax Collector and Assessor Edward Medeiros. "We have a low rate for pasture land and Niihau is all pasture. If we raised it any it would drive them out of business. That's very poor grazing land over there."

Ni'ihau had never been less profitable an operation than the past few years with recurrent severe droughts, the blight on the cactus, the difficulty of marketing wool, and the devastation of the kiawe blossoms from which the Ni'ihau honey is produced. For a long time the ranch had been on the red ink side of the ledger. Aylmer provided in his will for continuation of the subsidy he had been paying out of his personal income to maintain the payroll and cover other expenses of keeping the island "a Hawaiian community that is something distinctive now."

Aylmer's heirs were Lester Robinson and his sons Bruce and Keith. There was much speculation as to whether Ni'ihau might change. Just before Aylmer's death, rumours had circulated that foreign investors were trying to buy the island. One investor reportedly wanted to convert Ni'ihau into a gambling casino. Another supposedly intended to develop tourist facilities such as were being built along the coast lines of Kauai and Maui. Former Police Captain Antone Vidinha, now Mayor of Kauai, was enthused by such a prospect. Ni'ihau, he reminisced, has the most beautiful beaches in Hawaii-nei.

Eighteen months later, in October 1969, Lester Robinson died, leaving his interest in the island to his wife, Mrs. Helen Robinson and to his sons Bruce and Keith who had been assisting their father in Ni'ihau's management. The family shunted off recurring rumours and speculation as to what might happen in the near future by stating "too much of a mystery has been made of the Niihau operation. It is simply a ranching operation and it would be disruptive to permit visitors who would come out of curiosity." "Those interested in the past," proclaimed an editorial in the *Advertiser* "will be encouraged to know that Lester Robinson passed on to his sons Bruce and Keith his feelings for the island and its status as something removed from time."

In 1969 the elected leadership of the State of Hawaii did not share the view that any Hawaiian island should be "something removed from time" unless the government so decreed. Land use, the encouragement of resort development as an economic alternative to dependence on sugar and pineapple jobs were being pursued at the same time as the conservation of island beaches for public use and preservation of such endangered species as the Hawaiian nene.

In 1970 I too was infected with the contagious political virus of a liberal social policy that defined good government as one which by its legislation 'saved' both the nene and the Hawaiians of Ni'ihau. Inflated with the self-importance of having personally spent a few hours on the 'Forbidden Island' I talked of writing a New Yorker type profile about Ni'ihau. I was therefore delighted by Governor John A. Burns proposal for the state to acquire Ni'ihau either by purchase or condemnation, a key point in his 1970 message to the Hawaii State Legislature.

After quoting five lines from Robert Graves' poem "Rocky Acres", Burns remarked that "from the time the Hawaiian Islands were discovered, Hawaii has been regarded and envied as the prime example of natural beauty. In the mountain forests exotic birds flew among trees found only in Hawaii. The offshore sea life presented a marine biologist's dream. This primeval environment no longer exists. Man's intrusion has wrought irrevocable changes throughout the islands."

He led up to his controversial proposal by saying "There are, however, a few areas in the State where our biological and botanical riches are relatively undisturbed. These areas should be preserved and protected from further encroachment. One such area, still relatively unspoiled by the physical trappings of progress is Niihau. . .This administration submits Niihau presents an unparalleled opportunity to establish a controlled natural preserve while, at the same time, giving the residents of Niihau a chance of moving into the mainstream of contemporary island life, and I mean a real choice."

Governor Burns was a sincere, able and idealistic statesman who enlisted expert support for his decisions. He personally did not know much about Ni'ihau but he had sought the advice of naturalists like J. Linsley Gressitt of Bishop Museum and Dr. Charles Lamoureux, eminent botanist of the University of Hawaii. Burns based his idea of making Ni'ihau a kind of cultural and natural history state park on their assessment of the potential for restoring Ni'ihau's primeval environment. His recommendation to the combined House and Senate in February, 1970:

''I propose we immediately take steps to acquire the entire Island of Niihau. This should be done before any private offers for the purchase of Niihau are entertained by its present owners. The possible sale of Niihau for commercial development would result in a tragic loss of a priceless treasure – a complete island which could be restored to its primeval condition and maintained as a natural preserve for the enjoyment of all who cherish the old image of Hawaii."

How to do this? Burns was confident in his optimism. He disregarded the million dollar plus appraisal made in 1968, choosing to go with Kauai's State Tax Collector Edward Medeiros' tax appraisal. "Early acquisition would be well within our present means," said Governor Burns. "The Island's present assessed tax value at 100 per cent is, roughly, $300,000." He concluded his plea to the legislators by saying, "Too much of what is really native Hawaiian has already been irretrievably lost. Accordingly, I herewith submit for your early and favorable consideration this proposal for the public purchase of Niihau."

At the end of February the House Lands and Kauai Select Committees met in joint session on Kauai to hold public hearings on the state's purchase of Ni'ihau. The Robinsons had issued a statement saying the island was not for sale but if at any time in the future it should become so, the state would have the right of first refusal. No one seemed to care about this or mention the family's century-long preservation of Ni'ihau as the state's only truly Hawaiian community. At the hearing, the protests of Ni'ihauans and their spokesman that they wished things to be left as they were on the island were assumed by many outsiders to be their obedience to the owner's wishes.

When his proposal to acquire Ni'ihau did not pass in the 1970 session, Burns was ready to push it again. That fall he won his third term as Governor of Hawaii. About this time I interviewed him for the article that, in retrospect, I am glad I never wrote. John Burns was reputed to be taciturn, but when he was in a one-to-one situation, asked to talk about a subject dear to his heart, he could be loquacious. Until his secretary interrupted to tell him he was way behind in his schedule, he talked to me for over an hour about his hopes for the Robinson's island.

One thing that troubled him was the rights of the Ni'ihau workers. Gay and Robinson, he reminded, was the only unorganized, non-union plantation in the state. He was critical of the Robinson's practise of bringing Ni'ihau workers to Makaweli during harvesting season, when work on Ni'ihau was too slack to keep the men busy. More than anything else, Governor Burns worried about the difficulties that Ni'ihau people were reported to have when they tried to locate elsewhere.

He felt he had two alternatives once the state acquired the island. First, the state could lease the island back to the Robinsons on condition that they improve labor and living conditions and restore the original flora and fauna of the island. Or, he said, as a second alternative, "we can take it and restore it ourselves." He felt that the only modern improvement he would agree to would be a helicopter pad.

"We treat Kalaupapa much better than we do Niihau," he lamented. "I'd like to see Niihau a state park, see the whole island one big conservation area and quiet retreat. We can use the people of Niihau as park keepers, and we can give them a good English education and commensurate state services." One of his worries, in the current isolation (or what was assumed to be isolation) of Ni'ihau's people was the effects of inbreeding. Governor Burns had never heard of, and at that time I was not aware of, the frequency of intermarriage of Ni'ihauans with Hawaiians from other islands.

To Burns' dismay, the 1971 legislative session spent most of its time arguing about a new Honolulu stadium and how to be austere on budget without arousing any constituents. Burns stated publicly that he would again push the acquisition of Ni'ihau in the 1972 session. Word was that Bruce and Keith Robinson were sustaining losses of as much as fifty thousand dollars annually on Ni'ihau Ranch, but no confirmation of this came from them. Again no one asked the key question. Was private property no longer private in Hawaii-nei?

Whether or not the scrutiny of the State Department of Labor and Industries was unusually severe on the payroll procedures of Ni'ihau Ranch is something that may never be addressed. However, to the casual observer it would certainly sound like harassment when in June 1972 a charge of issuing late paychecks to some of their Ni'ihau employees was filed against the Robinsons in Kauai District Court. The state's suit alleged that the Robinsons had not issued some pay checks within the 7 day period required by law. Despite the Robinson's explanation that the paychecks in question were of an amount already forwarded in goods purchased by the recipients, they were told that according to law they should have paid the cowboys in question a token of one dollar per payday in cash. A fine of $4500 was levied against Ni'ihau Ranch.

The death of John A. Burns from cancer left his lieutenant-governor, George R. Ariyoshi, to finish out Burns' term of office. In 1974, Ariyoshi was elected to the first of his own three terms as Governor of Hawaii, a twelve year period during which he made no effort whatsoever to pursue the acquisition of Ni'ihau. Yet, as a state senator, in the 1970 legislative session, Ariyoshi had been one of the twelve senators voting for Burns' acquisition proposal.

1974 also inaugurated a new system for electing members of the State Board of Education. Two people were to represent all of the neighbor islands. So in 1977 when the Board members again visited Ni'ihau School, I went along as an elected member representing the Big Island, Maui, Molokai, Lanai, Kauai and the people of the island of Ni'ihau. I again experienced four and one half hours of discomfort crossing the Kaulakahi Channel by landing craft. Again I rode in the cab of one of the trucks but on this second trip, I found the ruts of 1967 had been bulldozed into a much improved dirt road to Puuwai.

With us in 1977 was Betty Nakagawa, the innovative School Lunch Supervisor from the Kauai District Office of the Department of Education. With the encouragement of Helen Robinson, Mrs. Nakagawa had introduced the school lunch program to Ni'ihau School. It was probably the most positive and revolutionary of the changes in the decade since my first visit. Ni'ihauans have been no exception to the high risk of most Hawaiians in the category of high blood pressure and heart problems. Betty Nakagawa, a skilled nutritionist, had gradually introduced new food items into the school lunches sent to Ni'ihau, hoping these would become family favorites and begin to reduce the high-fat, high-salt intake characteristic of that island's diet.

At lunch time, whenever something new appeared on their plates, the children would rush home to have their parents taste the food before they would eat it. Mrs. Nakagawa packaged the school lunches for Ni'ihau in weekly increments that were readily prepared each day at the school. Naturally, because of lack of refrigeration and only once a week transportation few fresh items could be included but nutrition packed foods like pumpkin bread soon became Ni'ihau favorites.

I looked at Ni'ihau with fresh eyes on this 1977 visit. No longr did I yearn to change everything I saw. No longer was I an advocate of state takeover. After spending several years researching and writing a book about Lanai, and writing the Hawaii book for Norton's bicentennial State and Nation series, I had a more in-depth idea concerning the flow of Hawaii's history and the importance of what, for want of a better word, I must call the state's Hawaiian-ness. No longer was I eager to retreat to a primeval state on Ni'ihau. I had seen the problem activists had imposed on Lanai, where they successfully defeated an ecologically and ekistically sound development plan that would have provided economic opportunity and a diversity of jobs for the two thousand residents of Lanai City. I wholeheartedly approved of the demands for Kahoolawe to be returned to the State and its use as a bombing target and artillery range cease. I was appalled that so many years after the bombs dropped by accident on Ni'ihau, the Navy was still using Kaula Rock as a target.

I completed my last term on the State Board of Education in 1978, moved briefly into a Democratic Party chairmanship on the Big Island and then returned to devoting full time to my profession, writing. Ni'ihau was still a subject on the 'back burner' of my long range writing plans. When I was finally urged by Jane Pultz of Press Pacifica to get busy and write this book, my files on Ni'ihau spilled over one entire section of bookshelves. What emerged from the clippings of 1981 on was that the change everyone had been clamoring for had been quietly happening on Ni'ihau.

"What the Robinsons need is a good public relations person," commented one of my old politican friends.

"Why should they? It's not that kind of a business, Ni'ihau Ranch," I answered. "Other ranches like Kahua and Ulupalakua don't. Why should Ni'ihau?"

But my friend was, like so many, still imbued with the myth that Ni'ihau was somehow a 'Mystery Island' simply because they knew they had no valid reason – other than curiosity – for going there.

I was lucky. I too had had that yearning to go there but circumstances of my being elected a School Board member had made that possible. Over the years, I had noted that those with scientific, business, or sound government reasons continued to be granted access and, in most cases, provided transportation to and around Ni'ihau by Managers Bruce and Keith Robinson.

Ni'ihau youngsters were no longer a rarity at Kamehameha Schools. Most completed their high school education on Kauai. When thirteen Ni'ihau boys and girls came to Honolulu to compete in the annual Makahiki Summer Fun sports competition, they were hosted at the Waikiki Marina Hotel by labor Leader Art Rutledge. Although they were the smallest group numerically, the Ni'ihau youngsters went home with more first and second place medals than any other group in the state. Their chaperone, Lu Kuerte, who was then living on Kauai, told a reporter that yes, Ni'ihau was a quiet, peaceful place and that she looked forward to being able to return to that island when a job opened up there for her husband.

In December, 1985, a headline in the *Advertiser* announced, "Niihau – Charcoal, sheep aid economic comeback". Jan Ten-Bruggencate, the *Advertiser's* Kauai bureau chief and a topflight reporter wrote from Ni'ihau that "This small island off the west coast of Kauai, long a financial drain for its owners, is making a slow economic resurgence." It was also, TenBruggencate found, having its natural resources– soil and water– conserved and where possible improved by the family's naturalist, Keith Robinson.

In 1984, after four years of negotiation the family had leased two acres on a western hill of Ni'ihau to the United States Navy for building an installation to extend the capability of the Pacific Missile Range Station at Barking Sands, Kauai. The Navy wanted the Ni'ihau installation to aid in satellite tracking and other

activities carried out with the sophisticated equipment constantly being upgraded at Barking Sands. Lease rental to the Navy
was agreed upon as a token few dollars a year. In return, for a
like amount, the Navy leased to the Robinsons a landing craft
capable of going 40 knots, a far faster vessel than the one they
had long been using.

Unlike the Coast Guard Loran station that had brought
outsiders to Ni'ihau, the Navy installation was to be unmanned.
Construction workers flew to Ni'ihau by helicopter every
morning, and returned to Kauai each night. When the installation was completed, Ni'ihau men were hired to fuel the gener-
ators and keep the grounds around the installation neat. By 1985,
according to TenBruggencate, there was an increasing amount
of work for Ni'ihauans. He was told by Bruce Robinson that
improvement from the "decades-long economic stagnation" had
been brought about by good land management techniques, the
switch from wool to establishing new markets for Ni'ihau sheep,
the revival of the island's honey production, and – most of all
– the demand of mainland and local markets for all the Ni'ihau
Sunset brand kiawe charcoal that the island could produce.

Charcoal making was extremely labor intensive. New brick
kilns had been built. The kiawe wood was cut with chain saws.
Fast-growing kiawe replenished the wood supply quickly. In
1985 more than 900 tons of charcoal, some 36,000 pounds weekly
had been manufactured, bagged, and shipped from Ni'ihau.

The key factor had been conservation of water. "Our goal
was not to let a single drop of fresh water from Niihau run into
the ocean," Bruce Robinson was quoted as saying. Since 1970
he and his brother had been working on this goal. Dams had
been constructed across natural drainage channels on the north
end of the island, creating two large reservoirs which retained
water throughout the summer dry season. This resulted in the
sheep population increasing from its pre-1970 level of 12,000 to
30,000 sheep on Ni'ihau in 1985.

Knowing that many of these would starve over the summer
when the grass shriveled and dried, the Robinsons found a
market for their animals at Gil-Trans International of Bakers-
field, California. Initial sale of 10,000 sheep was completed, with
the herculean task of transporting the animals by landing craft

loads to Kauai, and then trucking them to the pier where Matson freighters could receive them. A favorable shipping rate was negotiated. Formerly, since 1981, Ni'ihau Ranch had sold a few hundred sheep to Kahua Ranch on the Big Island and Ulupalakua Ranch on Maui, but the Gil-Trans market offered continuous, planned sale of as many Ni'ihau sheep as the Robinsons wished. The decision, matching the island's resources with the sheep population, was that just before each summer's dry spell they would sell Gil-Trans culls and eight month old lambs.

Over the years, fences and pens ahd fallen into disrepair because they were no longer needed. Ni'ihau cowboys now had a big job repairing and restoring these facilities for the vastly increased sheep population. In December, 1985 Bruce Robinson told TenBruggencate that within a few years the island could well be making a profit from its various operations.

That same month Governor George R. Ariyoshi, his wife Jean and his daughter Lynn visited Ni'ihau by helicopter at the invitation of the Robinsons. At Puuwai, the Governor, his wife and daughter planted two palm trees in front of the church as part of Jean Ariyoshi's ambitious "Million Trees of Aloha" program. Governor Ariyoshi, who completed his third and last term of office in 1986, said "I came away from Ni'ihau and its approximately 250 residents with an especially warm feeling for them, for the island, and for all of Hawaii."

Speaking to the people of Puuwai, he assured them that "Government stands ready to offer assistance, but only if and when such assistance is sought by you. It is not for us to impose change on you or your place. Rather, it is important that we strive to protect your right to your own choice of lifestyle." He said in his official statement of the visit that "I was touched by the very close and personal relationship between the Robinsons and the people of Niihau. Most of the communication between them was in Hawaiian, and its flavor and spirit, as with the people themselves, was also warm and gentle."

A year later, Mrs. Helen Robinson confirmed that the family was purchasing a new seven-seat twin engine Agusta 109, a helicopter which would have the several functions of serving as a medi-vac helicopter in medical emergencies on Ni'ihau, serving in ranch activities, and at long last, opening Ni'ihau to tourists. Tours of the family properties of Makaweli and optional landings on Ni'ihau might be possible as soon as permission was received for a heliport, a landing pad at Makaweli and one on Ni'ihau.

One might think that such an announcement would result in joy throughout Hawaii-nei. Instead, those who had been calling for Ni'ihau 'to enter the mainstream of island life' which, in 1987, is tourism and the sharing of the islands' beauty, its balmy climate, and its aloha with visitors from around the world, were vociferous in their protests. The Office of Hawaiian Affairs, a state entity which was a brain child of John Waihee at the Constitutional Convention in 1978 was loudest of all in its opposition. In 1987 John Waihee, Hawaii's newly elected governor, made no comment on the opening of 'pristine' Ni'ihau to tourists. From many of his fellow Hawaiians however there was much rhetoric about the need to preserve the 'pure Hawaiians' of Ni'ihau from a visitor contact that would presumably corrupt them.

No one mentioneed that in Hana, the effect of tourism has been to mellow visitors and new residents into being as Hawaiian as the Hawaiians they meet. Nothing is ever perfect in paradise, and no paradise is ever totally that, but tourism in the 1980's was offering economic well being and a new cosmopolitan injection of ideas for Hawaii. It seemed odd that the strongest opposition to Ni'ihau's being served by the helicopter that they had first said they wanted twenty-five years ago should be one of their own – Ni'ihauan Moe Keale, chairman of the policy-making board of the Office of Hawaiian Affairs.

That lingering misimpression of a 'pristine' or 'primeval' Ni'ihau which had somehow remained apart from time must have been jolted in the minds of those who read Jan TenBruggencate's March 1987 *Advertiser* account that the most littered, polluted beach in all Hawaii is on that island. A photograph of the plastic and metal trash lying in a two foot deep strew along the beach of Keanahaki Bay confirms what TenBruggencate says in his article – "the white sand beach at Keanahaki is barely visible under the plastic". He attributes this not so much to the casual use of many islanders consigning unwanted items to the sea as to the fact that "trash from across the shipping lanes of the north Pacific blows down here and can bump along the base of the island's eastern cliffs". The little hook of land called Kawaihoa that sticks out at the south end of Ni'ihau corrals this accumulation of ocean garbage – "the trash that humans relegate to the sea" and dumps it on Keanahaki's crescent of beach.

Perhaps this, perhaps the realization that everything cannot be as we wish it to remain, that nothing is frozen in time, and most of all that his fellow Ni'ihauans really wanted the helicopter and its visiting passengers, much affected Moe Keale. Late in March 1987, he announced that OHA was withdrawing its objections. They had been assured by the Robinsons that helicopters would not land at Puuwai and that visits to Ni'ihau would be limited to twenty minutes. On the television news, the feelings of this big Ni'ihauan became understandable, and one's sympathy went out to him as a fellow human being with nostalgia for the place he was born, with a yearning for the Hawaiian tradition to be carried on as he felt Ni'ihau's isolation had made possible. With tear-filled eyes Moe Keale spoke of the island that had been his birth place as the one place left in all Hawaii where a child hears only Hawaiian spoken, and speaks this proud and beautiful ancestral language, until he is old enough to go to school. Keale himself had left Ni'ihau to go to school on Kauai when he was six years old.

Three months later, in June 1987, tours to Ni'ihau began with Tom Mishler, a 41 year old veteran Vietnam flier, piloting the Robinson's helicopter. Tourists taking the flight to Ni'ihau land briefly only at the northern and southern points of the island. Neither the ordinary everyday life of Ni'ihauans or the routine of Ni'ihau Ranch is disturbed.

To those who saw Moe Keale's March 1987 telecast, to those who take the helicopter tour of Ni'ihau, and – I hope – to all those who read this biography of the island, it will be clear that Ni'ihau is not and never has been the 'Mystery' Island. To those with legitimate reasons for wanting to go there, it has not often been a 'forbidden' island. Its history shows it is certainly not a 'hermit' island. Nor is it, as owner Bruce Robinson described it in 1987, a 'desert island'.

This small, dry, lovely island lingers in the hearts of all who experience it. Despite more than two hundred years of foreign influence, it is still the state's most Hawaiian island. This is why I chose the title "Ni'ihau: The Last Hawaiian Island". I hope this book will allow readers who may never go there to know Ni'ihau's story, and will enhance for those who do visit the island the feeling that this is a very special Hawaiian place.

Geographical Appendix

IN THE *GEOLOGY of the State of Hawaii*, Harold T. Stearns gives his geologist's view of how Ni'ihau began some five or six million years ago as an outpouring of basalt flows from a shield volcano whose eruption center was on the ocean floor about two miles east of the present day coastline of Ni'ihau. Those successive basalt flows, and a strongly developed rift zone extending southwestward from the center, gradually built the island and its two nearby islets: Kaula and Lehua. Today, Ni'ihau rises some 13,000 feet above the ocean floor, with its highest point rising more than 1200 feet above sea level.

When the initial volcanic activity ceased, and Ni'ihau had emerged, there was a long period during which high cliffs were formed on the eastern and southeastern coasts, with lower cliffs or bluffs forming on all its other shores. Like the other major islands of the Hawaiian archipelago, which were formed later, Ni'ihau experienced a gradual submergence but, Stearns writes, "probably reached stability by the end of the Pliocene or during the early Pleistocene period."

Shifts in sea levels were common during the Pleistocene, when volcanic activity on Ni'ihau was renewed. Lava and tuff then built the submarine shelf above sea level but at this time the northern part of Ni'ihau's present coastal plain was still under water. Lehua Island, its near neighbor, had not yet erupt-ed. During one of the shifts in sea level, to a minus 60 foot stand, sand blew inland to form extensive calcareous dunes. A lava dome built the northern part of the coastal plain so that it now rose above sea level. During this same period, a submarine volcanic explosion formed Lehua Island.

Ash from this explosion fell over most of Ni'ihau and was blown into dunes on the northern plain. When the sea level rose some 85 feet, the seaward part of the dunes were submerged. Vegetation spread over those that remained above water and cementation occurred. It was then that playa lakes formed in depressions on the lowland. At one period during the Ice Age the ocean regressed to 300 feet below Ni'ihau's present sea level but during the melting of the glaciers that regression reversed. It was as glaciers melted around the Pacific and the ocean returned to its present level that Ni'ihau's modern beaches and dunes were formed.

Everything is always changing on this island as it is through-out the universe. Stearns points out that Ni'ihau is much altered in its physical character as an island since Cook's arrival and the subsequent visits of numerous other foreign ships. One of the new animals introduced to Ni'ihau were goats. According to Stearns, "Feral goats ate so much of the vegetation that much of the deep red soil on the uplands, formed during the million years or more since the cessation of volcanism there, was washed into the lowlands, filling up Hawaiian fish ponds and many of the playas." In recent years however, he reports that "extinction of the goats and the introduction of kiawe, haole koa, and other desert plants are slowly reclaiming the eroded areas of the island."

What this long geologic process of volcanic activity and shift-ing sea levels achieved is presented in a precise, objective, and detailed account of Ni'ihau's appearance and particularly its shoreline and the navigation hazards existing there, in the United States Coast and Geodetic Survey publication *Hawaiian Islands* (3rd edition, 1950). The Hawaiian edition of the United States Coast Pilot describes Ni'ihau as "the seventh in size of the islands" and "at the westerly end of the group." The island "is about 16 miles long in a northeast-southwest direction and varies in width from 3 to 5 miles." Near the middle of the island is a high tableland with low projecting cones or peaks, the highest of which, Paniau Peak, has an elevation of 1,281 feet." The northerly and easterly ends of Ni'ihau's interior tableland are precipitous, varying in height from 600 to 1000 feet. The southerly and westerly slopes of this tableland are quite gradual.

Having offered this general impression of Ni'ihau, the *Coast Pilot* advises mariners that Lehua Island, the small, rocky, crescent-shaped islet which in prehistoric times exploded into its present location only six-tenths of a mile off the north end of Ni'ihau, is marked by a light erected on a white framework tower on the highest point (700 feet above the water). The pilot adviser goes on to say that the north point of Ni'ihau, Puukole Point, is as low as a neighboring point which lies one mile to the east. Between these two points the land is low and grass-covered with a few low hills.

The easternmost point of Ni'ihau is Kaunuopou, against whose rocks the seas break in the best of weather. Seven-tenths of a mile to the west is Kii landing, a small bight which is not usable in Kona, or southerly weather. About one mile and a half south of this landing a reef extends half a mile offshore. Beyond this reef, and for three and a half miles on to Pueo Point, Ni'ihau's coastline is a series of cliffs, some as much as 1000 feet high. These diminish after Pueo Point, which the *Coast Pilot* describes as "a prominent brown precipitous bluff about 800 feet high."

Lower bluffs interspersed with small bights and miniscule sand or pebble beaches characterize the coastline for a distance of six miles to Cape Kawaihoa, where a series of bluffs no more than 15 feet high are interspersed with "stretches of sand beach, a few sand dunes, and scattered trees." The southern lowlands of Ni'ihau are broken by two low hills, one on Cape Kawaihoa, the southernmost point of Ni'ihau, and the other "a gently rounded hill 315 feet high, which is 4 miles north of the cape and 1.3 miles inland from the west coast." This hill is named Kawaewae. Beyond Cape Kawaihoa the coast is low and rocky, with occasional small sand beaches.

Four miles northwest of this cape was once the village of Kamalino. Between its site and Puulole Point there stretches one long, low continuous beach marked only by occasional piles of rocks. Five and a half miles from Cape Kawaihoa, and beyond the site of Kamalino, is the principal landing place on Ni'ihau-Nonopapa Landing. It is usable only from May to September, because of the northerly swells prevailing there during the winter months.

Kuamoku Rock, 1.6 miles north of Nonopapa Landing, marks the beginning of a treacherous stretch of reefs extending for some 3 miles. Four and a half miles northeast of this rock, which protrudes only four feet above the water, is Kaununui Point and beyond it lies Keawanui Bay, a "slight curve in the shoreline" with a sand and coral bottom and a sandy shore.

Nineteen miles southwest lies Kaula, a small, bare, rocky islet 550 feet high, inhabited only by sea birds and often called Bird Island. In ancient Hawaiian creation chants, Kaula and Ni'ihau's offshore islet Lehua are usually mentioned in conjunction with Ni'ihau.

Index